DATE DUE

JY 3 1 '01		

ALSO BY MARILYN YALOM

Blood Sisters:
The French Revolution in Women's Memory

Maternity, Mortality
and the Literature of Madness

Le Temps des Orages:
Aristocrates, Bourgeoises, et
Paysannes Racontent

A History of the Breast

A History

OF THE

Breast

Marilyn Yalom

Alfred A. Knopf 🐕 *NewYork 1997*

THIS IS A BORZOI BOOK
PUBLISHED BY
ALFRED A. KNOPF

http://www.randomhouse.com/

Library of Congress Cataloging-in-Publication Data
Yalom, Marilyn.
A history of the breast / by Marilyn Yalom.—1st ed.
p.   cm.
Includes bibliographical references and index.
ISBN 0-679-43459-3
1. Breast—Social aspects.   2. Breast—History.
3. Breast in art.   4. Breast in literature.   I. Title.
GT498.B74Y35   1997
391'.6—dc20   96-25558   CIP

Manufactured in the United States of America

Published February 10, 1997

Reprinted Twice

Fourth Printing, July 1997

For Irv
For Ever

And the breasts that gently rise
Like the hills of paradise.

MEDIEVAL STUDENT SONG, J. A. SYMONDS, trans.

When poets speak of death, they call it the place "without breasts."

RAMÓN GÓMEZ DE LA SERNA, 1917

Uncorseted, her friendly bust
Gives promise of pneumatic bliss. . . .

T. S. ELIOT, "Whispers of Immortality"

A man is asleep in the next room
We are his dreams
We have the heads and breasts of women
The bodies of birds of prey. . . .

ADRIENNE RICH, "Incipience"

Contents

Acknowledgments

Friends, colleagues, and virtual strangers have helped me write this book. Whenever I doubted its merits, the encouragement of many people reassured me that the breast was still of interest. To all of you who kept me going, my heartfelt thanks.

First of all, I wish to thank my colleagues at Stanford University for their specialized expertise: Professors Marc and Vida Bertrand, Judith Brown (now at Rice), Brigitte Cazelles, Joseph Frank, Van Harvey, Ralph Hester, Iris Litt, Marsh McCall, Diane Middlebrook, Ronald Rebholz, David Spiegel. I owe a major debt of gratitude to Laura Kupperman, graduate student in the art department, for her faithful and intelligent service as my research assistant. At the Stanford Institute for Research on Women and Gender, many of the scholars attended readings of individual chapters and gave me thoughtful feedback. I wish to thank, in particular, Edith Gelles, whose work on the history of breast cancer has informed my own; renee c. hoogland from the Catholic University of Nijmegen, who, during her residence at the institute, contributed considerably to my understanding of Dutch history; Sidra Stitch, who brought to my attention pertinent material in American art and popular culture; and Susan Bell, who read the entire manuscript in progress and was my most indefatigable critic.

Special thanks to Chana Bloch of Mills College and to Berkeley author Marcia Falk (each of whom has published a translation of the *Song of Songs*) for helping me with biblical and classical materials. Similarly, San Francisco psychoanalyst John Beebe and Palo Alto psychiatrist Carlos Greaves provided valuable input for the psychological chapter. San Francisco novelist Beth Gutcheon and writer Minerva Neiditz of the University of Connecticut offered useful stylistic advice. Susan Gussow of the Cooper Union in New York broadened my perspective on contemporary visual arts. As in most of my past projects, I was able to count on Mary Felstiner of San Francisco State University for her unerring advice.

In France, my good friends Philippe Martial and Bertrand Féger offered me the benefits of their professional knowledge and contacts at the Bibliothèque du Sénat and the Assistance Publique. I am also deeply grateful to the late Claude Paoletti and his wife, Catherine, for their generous support. Similarly, the writer Elisabeth Badinter was a valuable source of information and encouragement.

My husband, Irvin, and my son Benjamin were ongoing soulmates and demanding critics. My daughter, Eve, and son-in-law, Michael Carstens—both medical doctors—critiqued the medical chapter. Son Reid, a photographer, oversaw the illustrations and contributed a few choice photographs of his own. Son Victor, a practicing psychologist, and my psychologist-in-training daughter-in-law, Tracy La Rue (Reid's wife), offered useful criticism for the psychological chapter. Daughter-in-law Noriko Nara (Victor's wife) sat for the beautiful photo of herself nursing our grandson, Jason. All in all, *The Breast* was something of a family affair.

Last, but certainly not least, I wish to thank my editor at Knopf, Victoria Wilson, for her penetrating criticism; Bram Dijkstra of the University of California at San Diego for his careful reading of the manuscript at a crucial stage of development; and his wife, Sandra Dijkstra, my literary agent and dear friend, for placing the book with excellent publishing houses both at home and abroad.

A History of the Breast

Introduction:
CHANGING MEANINGS

I INTEND TO MAKE YOU THINK about women's breasts as you never have before. For most of us, and especially for men, breasts are sexual ornaments—the crown jewels of femininity. Yet this sexualized view of the breast is by no means universal. In a number of different cultures in Africa and the South Pacific, where women have gone about with their breasts uncovered since time immemorial, the breast has not taken on the predominantly erotic meaning it has in the West. Non-Western cultures have their own fetishes—small feet in China, the nape of the neck in Japan, the buttocks in Africa and the Caribbean. In each instance, the sexually charged body part—what the French poet Mallarmé refers to as "the veiled erotic"— owes much of its fascination to full or partial concealment.

The assumptions we Westerners take for granted about the breast prove especially arbitrary when we adopt a historical perspective, which is the aim of this book. Covering some twenty-five thousand years, it will focus on certain moments when a specific conception of the breast took hold of the Western imagination, and changed the way it was seen and represented. Think of these moments as a kind of cinematic montage, progressing and sometimes overlapping, but not as a continuous reel of breast history.

Underlying this progression is a basic question: Who owns the breast? Does it belong to the suckling child, whose life is dependent on a mother's milk or an effective substitute? Does it belong to the man or woman who fondles it? Does it belong to the artist who represents the female form, or the fashion arbiter who chooses small or large breasts according to the market's continual demand for a new style? Does it belong to the clothing industry which promotes the "training bra" for pubescent girls, the "support bra" for older women, and the Wonderbra for women wanting more noticeable cleav-

3

age? Does it belong to religious and moral judges who insist that breasts be chastely covered? Does it belong to the law, which can order the arrest of "topless" women? Does it belong to the doctor who decides how often breasts should be mammogrammed and when they should be biopsied or removed? Does it belong to the plastic surgeon who restructures it for purely cosmetic reasons? Does it belong to the pornographer who buys the rights to expose some women's breasts, often in settings demeaning and injurious to all women? Or does it belong to the woman for whom breasts are parts of her own body? These questions suggest some of the various efforts men and institutions have made throughout history to appropriate women's breasts.

As a defining part of the female body, the breast has been coded with both "good" and "bad" connotations since the beginning of recorded time. Eve, we remember from Genesis, was both the honored mother of the human race and the archetypal female temptress. Jews and Christians may proudly claim that she gave suck to their ancestors, but they also associate the apple of the Fall with Eve's applelike breasts—a connection made visible by innumerable works of art.

When the "good" breast model is in the ascendance, the accent falls on its power to nourish infants, or, allegorically, an entire religious or political community. This was the case five thousand years ago, when female idols were worshipped in many Western and Near Eastern civilizations. It was the case five hundred years ago in Italian paintings of the nursing Madonna, and two hundred years ago in bare-breasted images of Liberty, Equality, and the new French Republic.

When the "bad" vision dominates, the breast is an agent of enticement and even aggression. This was the position taken not only by the author of Genesis, but also by the Hebrew prophet Ezekiel, who represented the biblical cities of Jerusalem and Samaria as wanton harlots with sinful breasts. And it was true for Shakespeare when he created the monstrous figure of Lady Macbeth, to mention only the most memorable of his "bad-breasted" women. The vision of the "bad" breast often issues from a combination of sex and violence, as found in much contemporary cinema, TV, advertising, and pornography. It goes without saying that most representations of the breast— or any other subject, for that matter—have traditionally expressed a male point of view.

To discover what women in the past felt about their breasts has been an ongoing challenge. I have tried to find instances of women deciding how their breasts would be clothed or used. To what extent could they choose whether or not to breast-feed their children? When have they had some say about the medical treatment of their breasts? How have they used their breasts as commercial and political vehicles? Have their literary and artistic representations of the breast differed from men's? I have been especially attentive to the times when women made efforts to reclaim the ownership of their breasts—most notably now, in the late twentieth century.

The journey from Paleolithic goddesses to the women's liberation movement undertaken in this book is long and full of surprises. Along the way, we encounter prehistoric statues whose breasts were invested with magical powers. We also meet the bare-breasted snake priestesses of Minoan Crete and the multibreasted cult statues of Artemis, marking the last wave of pre-Christian worship inspired by women's mysteries. In the world of the Hebrew Bible, we find women validated primarily as mothers, and in the world of the New Testament, the Virgin Mary celebrated as the miraculous mother of the Christian God. In both Jewish and Christian traditions, breasts were honored as milk-producing vessels necessary for the survival of the Hebrew people and, later, the followers of Jesus. The example of the baby Jesus suckling at his mother's breast became a metaphor for the spiritual nurturance of all Christian souls.

The nursing Madonna, invented in fourteenth-century Italy, soon had to do battle with a new, predominantly sexual, image of the breast. In countless paintings and poems that proliferated in Italy, France, England, and Northern Europe during the fifteenth, sixteenth, and seventeenth centuries, the breast's erotic potential came to overshadow its maternal and sacred meanings.

These sacred and sexual aspects represent two different tugs at the breast. The mandate to nurse and the mandate to titillate are competing claims that continue to shape women's fate. Since the beginning of the Judeo-Christian era, churchmen and secular males, not to mention babies, have considered the breast their property, to be disposed of with or without women's consent.

In the seventeenth-century Dutch Republic, a new force entered the contest—that of civic responsibility. The lactating mother who provided for her child was seen as making a major contribution to the overall well-being of her household and community. A century later, maternal breast-feeding became part and parcel of the French Revolution. Following Rousseau, many French subjects were led to believe that a general social reform would result if mothers nursed their own babies, as opposed to the common practice of sending them out to wet nurses. Individually, a woman's obligation to breast-feed merged with the collective responsibility of the Nation to "nurse" its citizens—an idea translated into numerous pictures of the Republic as a woman with uncovered breasts. Thus breasts became "democratized" in the passage from absolute rule to representative government.

No study of the breast can be complete without attention to its medical history. Although twentieth-century medicine has increasingly focused on breast cancer, early medical literature, as far back as the Greeks and Romans, was equally concerned with the nursing mother. Detailed advice on changes in the breasts during pregnancy, diet and exercise, proper modes of suckling, the care of abscesses, and the process of weaning can be found in numerous medical treatises in many languages, especially since the eighteenth century. Such works tell us much about the ways in which the medical profession not only advanced the health care of their patients, but valorized women primarily as breeders and feeders.

While nineteenth-century physicians placed a moral connotation on breast-feeding, the new disciplines of psychology and psychoanalysis highlighted the breast's crucial place in the child's emotional life. By the turn of the century, Sigmund Freud was mounting psychoanalytic evidence to prove that sucking at the breast was not only the child's first activity, but also the starting point of one's entire sexual life. On a popular level, the breast according to Freud found its way into movies and fiction, cartoons, jokes, and T-shirts, and countless magazines. All these representations loudly confirm the irrepressible attraction of the breast for the adult male.

Since the nineteenth century, the demands on the breast have multiplied with the speed of everything else in an industrial and postindustrial age. Commercial interests have barraged women with advertisements for breast supporters, shapers, and enhancers of all kinds: corsets, bras, creams, lotions, silicone implants, weight-loss programs, and body-building machines. Although breasts have always been commercialized in some way, it has only been in the past hundred years that the full force of capitalism has seized upon the breast as a profit-related object. Breast undergarments have been used as far back as the Greeks and Romans, and corsets were indeed common from the late Middle Ages, at least for the wealthy, but factory-made corsets, introduced in the mid-nineteenth century, and bras, invented at the beginning of the twentieth century, made specialized underwear available to women of all classes. With mass production, "breast control" became mandatory for everyone.

Since undergarments are always fashioned to fit the prevailing body ideal, the history of breasts can be charted according to the times when they have been downplayed or emphasized. For example, compare the flattened "boyish" look of the 1920s with the sexy projectiles of the 1950s. Corsets and bras have alternately been designed to constrict and conceal the breasts or prop them up like apples or torpedoes.

It is significant that the women's liberation movement of the late 1960s began with the much-publicized act of bra-burning. However maligned outside feminist circles, "bra-burners" established a paradigm of resistance to external strictures. By burning bras, more figuratively than literally, women undermined the basic idea of control coming from outside oneself. Henceforth women could question the authority of such previously sacrosanct agencies as medicine and fashion. Women started to decide for themselves whether to wear bras, whether to go topless, whether to breast-feed, and even whether to have a mastectomy.

The question of body image is central to all of these considerations. Clearly it is difficult to feel good about one's breasts if they do not correspond to the body ideal of one's time and place. Numerous studies have documented the extent to which many women are tyrannized by arbitrary notions of beauty, which, in the second half of the twentieth century, have taken the form of skinny bodies with conspicuous breasts. American women spend untold millions for products and services designed to reduce the lower half of their bodies and increase the upper half. The most frequent cosmetic-surgery operations performed in the United States today are liposuction and breast enlargement. At the same time, weight-loss programs multiply with religious fervor among women of all ages, and anorexia and bulimia have attained near-epidemic proportions among younger women. Though we cannot blame these consumerist practices and pathological behaviors solely on the images promoted by advertisements, magazines, movies, and TV, it would be foolish to ignore the influence of the media in spreading a normative picture of what a desirable female is supposed to look like. One can argue that both women and men form their standards for appearance, more than ever before, on the basis of the commercial images that constantly assault us.

Feminists and other activists have attempted to liberate women from the arbitrary ideals of beauty promoted by the media. Yet they, too, have their own mandates. At one point it was politically correct not to wear a bra and to de-emphasize body contours. In the past quarter-century, breast-feeding has once again become fashionable after a generation of bottle-feeders. Today many women are actively fighting for greater control over the medical decisions that affect their lives, especially concerning breast cancer.

Women have been obliged to confront the powerful meanings breasts convey as life-givers and life-destroyers. On the one hand, breasts are associated with the transformation from girlhood to womanhood, sexual pleasure, and nursing. On the other, they are increasingly associated with cancer and death. For women, the opposition between the "good" breast and the "bad" breast does not pit the mother or saint against the tramp and the whore, as in many male-authored texts. Nor does it evoke the opposition between the child's perceptions of the "good" nurturing breast and the "bad" withholding breast that underlies certain psychoanalytic theories. For women, their breasts literally incarnate the existential tension between Eros and Thanatos—life and death—in a visible and palpable form.

A cultural history of the breast inevitably fits within the context of "the reign of the phallus" that has dominated Western civilization for the past twenty-five hundred years. Yet the breast has had its own simultaneous reign, one constructed from the fantasies of men, to be sure, but one that increasingly expresses the needs and desires of the women to whom breasts ultimately belong.

One

THE SACRED BREAST:
GODDESSES, PRIESTESSES,
BIBLICAL WOMEN, SAINTS,
AND MADONNAS

I N T H E B E G I N N I N G was the breast. For all but a fraction of human history, there was no substitute for a mother's milk. Indeed, until the end of the nineteenth century, when pasteurization made animal milk safe, a maternal breast meant life or death for every newborn babe. Small wonder that our prehistoric ancestors endowed their female idols with awesome bosoms. Small wonder that such idols appeared in places as far apart as Spain, Central Europe, and the Steppes of Russia long before the creation of agriculture. It takes no great stretch of the imagination to picture a distraught Stone Age mother begging one of those buxom idols for an ample supply of milk (fig. 1).

Such figurines, fashioned in bone, stone, and clay, were often notable not only for their prominent breasts, but also for the excessive size of their stomachs and buttocks. Their plump bodies may not conform to our present aesthetic standards, but to the inhabitants of a world where food sources were precarious at best, obesity was a blessing. It offered the best chance for survival and the promise of being able to nurse one's offspring, even during periods of famine.

Those prehistoric statuettes were, in all likelihood, fertility goddesses, mother goddesses, or nursing goddesses.

1. The Grimaldi Venus. 23,000 B.C.E.

They were "most definitely not wives of male gods," in the opinion of noted anthropologist Marija Gimbutas.[1] With their hands often placed on their bellies or their breasts, they seem to be saying that the womanly powers of procreation and lactation were worthy of veneration.

At certain ancient sites, breast fetishes have been found isolated from the rest of a female body. Outside the French cave sanctuary at Le Colombel, Pech Merle, for example, a stalactite from around 15,000 B.C.E., resembling a female breast down to the nipple, was circled with dots of red ocher.[2] Almost ten thousand years later, at Çatalhüyük in south-central Turkey, rows of clay breasts were plastered onto the walls of a holy shrine, with animal teeth, tusks, and beaks inserted where the nipples should be.[3] Neolithic antlers carved into pairs of breasts have been found in Switzer-land, and Iron Age vases embossed with four and six breasts, in Germany.[4] Though we believe such objects were used in religious cults,

2. Vase found in Lausitz, Eastern Europe.
Ca. 1300 B.C.E.

This multibreasted vessel may have been used in one of the many ancient cults that practiced goddess worship.

their exact meaning and use remain uncertain.
Our efforts to imagine the ceremonies that occurred in mammary shrines, the dances that may have taken place around a wreath of breasts, or the drinks served in breasted goblets are probably only good for Hollywood scenarios (fig. 2).

Usually breasts were sculpted onto a full female body, as in real life. In the Fertile Crescent, breasts were the defining feature of countless idols worshipped in homes and shrines much as modern-day Christians honor the crucifix or images of the Virgin Mary. Many of these figures support their breasts with their hands or arms in a characteristic "breast-offering" gesture. Such images remained present in the popular religions of the area that became Syria until the advent of Islam in the seventh century C.E., when goddesses were definitively replaced by the belief in a single God, Allah.

Similarly, in the lands that have become present-day Israel, almost all the clay idols from the biblical period are females, and many of them lift up their breasts for emphasis. This is particularly true of the pillar figures from the eighth to the sixth centuries B.C.E. known as "Astarte" figurines, after the Phoenician goddess of love and fertility. This *dea nutrix* (nourishing deity) has been described as a "kind of tree with breasts" that was tantamount to a "tangible prayer for fertility and nourishment."[5]

When the biblical Israelites came to Canaan and saw these graven images, they were determined to eliminate them so that Jahweh would be the one and only God. It proved a very difficult contest. Though the priests and prophets fulminated against Baal and the Canaanite goddesses, many Israelites probably worshipped them secretly.[6] After all, what did Jahweh—a male war god—know about bearing and nursing babies, as compared with the fertility goddesses Asherah, Astarte, and Anat?

In neighboring Egypt, the mother goddess took the form of the awesome Isis, associated with the milk-giving cow, the Tree of Life, and the throne of the pharaohs. In this last capacity, she was equated with the royal throne itself, "so that ascending the throne was to sit upon her lap, and to suckle from her breast was to receive the divine nourishment that would give the king the qualities of kingship."[7] Whenever Isis was shown nursing a pharaoh, it was a means of confirming him as her son and attesting to his divinity. Pharaohs were portrayed nursed by Isis either at their birth, their coronation, or their death—all moments requiring divine intervention for a smooth passage from one form of life to another.[8] No one doubted that milk drunk from Isis's breast would confer immortality.

Elsewhere Isis offers her breast to her own son Horus (fig. 3). In these poses, the great goddess was brought closer to the concerns of real people. An

3. Seated figure of the goddess Isis feeding the child Horus. Egypt. Late period.

The figure of the goddess Isis nursing her son Horus is considered the prototype for the Christian image of the nursing Madonna.

Egyptian mother could invoke Isis's protection for her own child by reciting one of several common spells, such as: "My arms are over this child—the arms of Isis are over him, as she puts her arms over her son Horus."[9]

Breasts were also important features of other, lesser, deities, like Nut, the sky or moon goddess (the hieroglyph *mena* means both "breast" and "moon").[10] But the strangest Egyptian breast configuration belongs to portraits of the male god of the Nile, Hapi (fig. 4). Breasts are attached to his torso as a sign of fertility, for he was responsible for the annual overflowing of the Nile, which watered parched lands and irrigated crops. This was a rare but not unique appropriation of female breasts by masculine deities, as we shall see in the sections on Greek, Hebrew, and Christian religions.

When the human form was portrayed in the ancient world, breasts were usually the distinguishing feature of the female. They varied according to size and shape, and even to the number displayed, but they were almost always clearly in evidence. Consider, for example, the image of the breast in the two major civilizations that arose and flourished during the Bronze Age (3200–1100 B.C.E.) on the pre-Greek islands of Crete and the Cyclades.

In the Cyclades, which form a circle around the isle of Delos, female idols ranging from several inches to life-sized were carved from luminous white marble. Many of these highly stylized figures had discrete, round, uncovered breasts; a pair of arms folded across the chest; a pair of legs; and sometimes a triangle to represent the pubis (fig. 5). They were likely to have been used in the practice of a cult, which was "life-affirming and life-supporting," and connected to the rites of passage surrounding birth and death.[11] These elegantly abstract idols, stunning in their simplicity, speak of a lost world, where gender difference was summed up by two circles and a triangle, and women's mysteries were still considered sacred.

The other great pre-Greek Mediterranean civilization—that of Crete—was to leave behind more naturalistic representations of women with swelling breasts. On vases, sarcophagi, and especially on the walls of the immense palace of Knossos, women parade in procession carrying their offerings to sacrifices presided over by priestesses. Other women laugh or dance or simply chat, all with their breasts exposed and their limbs covered by bell-like skirts.

Did these frescoes represent real women in their contemporary clothing or an idealized version? Did Cretan women go about exposing their breasts or did they, like most women in Western and Near Eastern cultures, keep them covered? It is impossible to answer these questions with certainty, since

4. (Above) Relief of Nile god Hapi from the throne of King Ay. Ca. 1342 B.C.E. Egypt (XVIIIth dynasty).

The female breasts on the chest of the male river god Hapi symbolize his ability to overflow the banks of the Nile with the water needed for crops.

5. (Left) Cycladic female statue. Ca. 2500–2300 B.C.E.

High, small, stylized breasts are characteristic of the mysterious female statues found on the Cycladic islands.

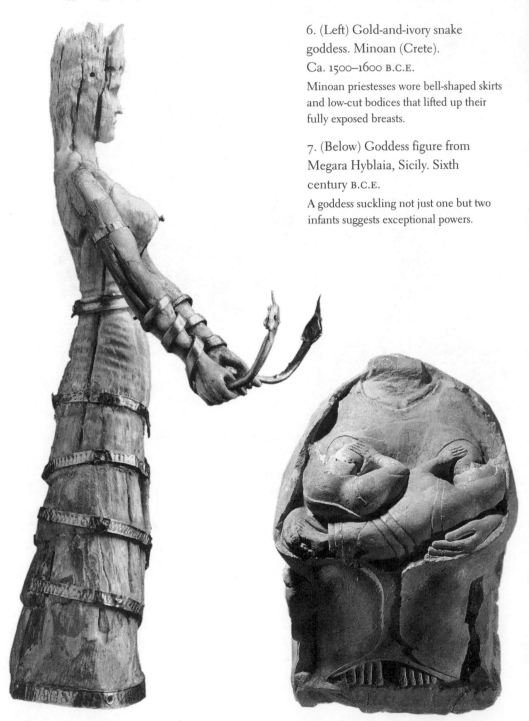

6. (Left) Gold-and-ivory snake goddess. Minoan (Crete). Ca. 1500–1600 B.C.E.

Minoan priestesses wore bell-shaped skirts and low-cut bodices that lifted up their fully exposed breasts.

7. (Below) Goddess figure from Megara Hyblaia, Sicily. Sixth century B.C.E.

A goddess suckling not just one but two infants suggests exceptional powers.

the visual arts do not necessarily mirror society. One interpreter suggests that women uncovered their breasts only during acts of religious worship; another considers open bodices the "normal clothing" of Minoan women.[12] What we can safely say from the preponderance of feminine figures with their naked chests, expressive faces, and exquisite clothing is that women commanded power and prestige in Cretan culture.

The famous images of the snake goddesses or priestesses dating from around 1600 B.C.E. reveal the authority Minoan women exercised in religious life. These figures are notable for their large, globular breasts jutting out from bodices with an almost aggressive dynamism (fig. 6). Fierce-looking snakes extend from the priestess's hands or are coiled around her outstretched arms. Snakes were thought of as communicators with the powers below the earth, and were also, in later, classical Greek times, associated with Asclepius, the god of healing, as can be found on the doctor's caduceus. But the Cretan statues with their prominent breasts and snakes may also be saying: "Take care not to offend this priestess. She can just as easily dispense poison as milk!"

On the pre-Greek mainland at this time, the Mycenaean people shared a similar respect for the breasts of their priestesses and goddesses. A Mycenaean seal from around 1500 B.C.E. shows three women dressed like Minoan priestesses, with one of them—presumably the goddess—seated beside a fruit tree and offering her right breast in a food-giving gesture.[13] We know very little about the lives of ordinary women during this period, but when the Mycenaeans evolved into the ancient Greeks, they must have looked something like the people we find in the Homeric epics. For one thing, mothers—even queens—were still nursing their own babies in Homeric times, without the help of the wet nurses who became popular a few centuries later.

Sacred representations of mothers with babies at the breast began to appear in archaic Greek society and were probably related to "Kourotrophos" cults (fig. 7). "Kourotrophos" refers to the mother or nursing principle manifested through suckling. Statuettes of nursing mothers were placed in tombs and sanctuaries, probably as offerings to one of the various Kourotrophos goddesses—for example, Gaia, Hera, Aphrodite, Demeter, Persephone, and even the virgin goddesses Artemis and Athena. Other offerings included edible items, such as honey, oil, and cakes, some of which were made in the form of breasts. For the most part, the rites practiced by the Kourotrophos cults took place in simple shrines or in the open air, and were lacking in the grandeur reserved for the Olympian gods. Nonetheless, these popular cults continued to thrive until the dawn of Christianity.[14]

The most astonishing examples of the veneration of the breast in ancient times are the famous polymastic statues of Artemis of Ephesus. In Ephesus, a thriving Greek city on the coast of what is today modern Turkey, two life-sized cult figures of the goddess Artemis were found among the ruins of the city hall (fig. 8). These multibreasted statues have traditionally been seen as symbols of mammary abundance, though certain interpreters now maintain that the globes hanging around the torso are really rows of eggs or even bull testicles, the latter reminiscent of the ancient rite of nailing the testicles of sacrificed bulls to wooden cult statues.[15]

According to another interpretation, the original Ephesian Artemis was adorned with clusters of large dates—symbols of fertility—which later came to be mistaken for multiple breasts.[16] Perhaps they were first inspired by the physical anomaly that does indeed provide some women with "supernumerary" breasts or nipples along the mammary ridge; this anomalous anatomical condition recalls our genetic links to other mammals, with their multiple teats and udders. But whatever the origins of the statues, the "many-breasted" Artemis of Ephesus came to symbolize the idea of a miraculous milk supply, responding to a timeless human fantasy. Artists from later centuries leave no doubt as to what they thought the globes represented: they often show a child at one of the breasts, or milk streams flowing from several breasts into the mouths of children.

The fantasy of the multibreasted woman (which did not disappear with the ancient Greeks) springs from an enduring association between the female body, Nature, and nurture. With their breasts represented like udders or fruit on a tree, women have traditionally been conflated with the animal and plant kingdoms and isolated from the "thinking" or "spiritual" realm reserved for men. Because women have breasts and the potential to provide milk for their young, females have been seen as closer to Nature than their male counterparts—indeed, as the very personification of Nature—and assigned major responsibility for all the food that humans ingest on a daily basis.

The prominence of the breast in early Greek religions would gradually be supplanted by what Eva Keuls has dubbed the "reign of the phallus."[17] Younger Hellenic deities would eventually overshadow the ancient goddesses, though the latter managed to survive in reduced circumstances. Zeus took over Mount Olympus from the oldest Greek deity, Gaia Olympia, the Deep-Breasted One, and became the undisputed chief of the Olympian Pantheon, with his consort, Hera, in a distinctly secondary position. A curious wood carving from the seventh century B.C.E. shows Zeus holding out Hera's

8. Statue of the *"Beautiful Artemis."*
Ephesus. Second century C.E.

The famous Artemis of Ephesus is covered
with carvings of bees, bulls, lions, flowers,
grapes, and acorns, with more than twenty
pendulous globes—presumably breasts—
appended to her torso.

breast in the way goddesses usually offered it themselves, without spousal assistance.[18] Offering the breast was, among other things, a sign of the capacity
to grant favors.

As the great goddesses who had inspired Paleolithic, Neolithic, and
Bronze Age civilizations became "Olympianized," they fragmented into less
powerful deities, each with her own more specific and more limited attributes. Their breasts also underwent significant transformations in keeping
with their individual identities. Athena, the virgin goddess of wisdom, was always fully covered with heavy draperies. Her chest was hidden under a
breastplate adorned with snakes; her head was crowned with a helmet, and

she carried a spear. These were the identifying attributes of the one female deity accorded the "manly" attributes of reason, war, and handicraft.

On the other hand, from the fourth century B.C.E. onward, Aphrodite (Venus), the goddess of love, was regularly represented in some state of undress, with her breasts clearly outlined or exposed. Her breasts were molded to the erotic ideal of firm, slightly muscular bosoms, referred to as "applelike" in classical texts. This was the ideal associated with the legendary Helen of Troy, who, upon her return from the Trojan Wars, bared the "apples of her bosom" to her husband, Menelaus, causing him to lay aside his sword and forgive her (Aristophanes, *Lysistrata*, 411 B.C.E.). In the Hellenistic period, Aphrodite became something akin to a pin-up figure, an object of male desire as well as awesome worship. It is hard to say for certain whether the change in Aphrodite's image reflected changes in the status of real women, but the analogy with more modern times leads us to wonder what kind of power sex goddesses, in stone or in flesh, really have. Think of Marilyn Monroe as the classic modern example.

Statues and statuettes of Aphrodite proliferated throughout the ancient world, and replicas of these works can still be found in numerous Mediterranean gift shops. One of the most popular is the *Venus Pudicitia* or the *Modest Venus*, so named because she holds one hand in front of her breasts while the other covers the genital area (fig. 9). Whereas male figures were portrayed completely nude in upright positions, the female nude usually appeared in art "with drapery near at hand and with

9. *Aphrodite, Eros, and the Dolphin*. Fourth century B.C.E.

The *Modest Venus*'s self-protective gestures would never have been considered appropriate for a Greek male.

a forward-bending, self-protective posture."[19] These gestures of modesty or shyness were considered appropriate for all women except outright prostitutes.

In fifth-century B.C.E. Athens, women were carefully controlled by a patriarchal system, which assigned them indoor duties, excluded them from political life, and imposed head-to-foot coverage of their bodies. In the house they wore the long, shirtlike "chitons" or tunics, and outdoors cloaks for warmth with veils covering their heads. Only in Sparta were females granted somewhat greater freedom of dress. There girls wore a short tunic that ended above the knee and was slit on the side to expose the thigh.

For the most part, Greek girls were segregated from boys, and when married, often to men twenty years their senior, they were expected to stay indoors. Young women simply exchanged confinement in their fathers' homes for confinement in their husbands' homes.[20] Whereas men spent much of their time in the agora, which served as the public forum and the marketplace, or in the gymnasium, where they exercised in the nude, or in brothels, where both female and male prostitutes plied their trade, or at banquets given in the homes of other men, it was not considered seemly for women of the citizen class, especially in Athens, to appear in public, or even in the presence of the men brought into their homes.

The drawings found on antique vases show citizen-wives seated sagely with their oil flasks and wool baskets and an occasional lyre or child. They are always sensibly covered from neck to toe, sometimes with veils draped over their heads as well. Their breasts are scarcely suggested and never exposed, except for the rare image showing a nursing mother or wet nurse. On the subject of wet nurses, we know from the evidence of written contracts, grave stelae, epitaphs, and statues that they were very common in classical Greek society and that good wet nurses were highly regarded.[21]

There was, however, another class of women valued for their erotic, rather than their maternal and domestic, capacities. These were the hetairai—courtesans—whose job was to provide sex and entertainment, including intellectual companionship, for Greek males. Hetairai are usually shown on vase paintings either fully nude, nude to the waist, or in draperies that reveal the female rotundities.

An interesting breast story is associated with the fourth-century B.C.E. courtesan known as Phryne. Phryne had been accused by one of her lovers of the crime of blasphemy, then a capital offense. During her trial, when her defender, the orator Hypereides, "was making no progress in his pleas, and it became apparent that the judges meant to condemn her, he caused her to be brought where all could see her; tearing off her undervests he laid bare her bosom. . . ." The sight of her lovely breasts and the lawyer's overwrought pleas aroused such compassion in the hearts of the judges that "they refrained from putting her to death."[22] After she had been acquitted, a decree was passed stipulating that no accused person on trial be allowed to show his or her private parts, for fear of making a similar impression on the judges.

Most hetairai, as well as common prostitutes and some wet nurses, were slaves, and all women, even citizen-wives, were heavily fettered by societal constraints. Yet we should not see them exclusively as victims: like most gender-segregated people, they found ways to conduct their own affairs, and sometimes in clear defiance of men's ideas about how they should behave.

Classicist John J. Winkler looked to the festivals of Demeter and Aphrodite as events that allowed ancient Greek women the opportunity to express "The Laughter of the Oppressed."[23] The festivities honoring Adonis, Aphrodite's ill-fated young lover, took place on Athenian rooftops in late July. Here informal women's groups danced and chanted and carried on for at least one night every year and probably more, in full view of those who might wish to spy upon them from afar.

Aristophanes's *Lysistrata* gives us an ironic picture of the male version of these happenings: A pompous legislator was expounding in the Assembly, "while his wife, a teensy bit drunk on the roof, / exclaimed 'Beat your breasts for Adonis!' "[24] The female version of this festival, as the celebrated lyric poetess Sappho (c. 610–c. 580 B.C.E.) had formulated it much earlier, has a very different, empathetic, tone: "Gentle Adonis is dying, Cytherea, what should we do? beat your breasts, maidens, and rend your chitons."[25]

The "breast culture" that had flourished for millennia around the altars of ancient Greece continued to find expression in all-woman groups on the rooftops, or indoors and "underground." It would be transmitted orally from generation to generation in the form of myths that recalled women's mysteries at the very time when these mysteries were no longer publicly honored. In the Greek society which celebrated male genitalia, the power of female breasts existed mainly in lingering legends that continued to credit breasts with supernatural powers.

A mythological explanation for the creation of the Milky Way, for example, was linked to Hera's breasts in the following tale. It was believed that mortals could become immortal if they were suckled at the breast of the queen of the goddesses. So, when Zeus wanted his son Hercules—whose mother was the mortal Alcmena—to have immortality, he had him placed quietly at Hera's breast while she was sleeping. But Hercules sucked so vigorously that she was awakened and realized he was not her own child. Indignant, she drew the breast away with such force that the milk spurted into the heavens and created the Milky Way. Hercules, who had drunk Hera's milk,

10. Jacopo Tintoretto. *The Origin of the Milky Way.* Late sixteenth century.
Tintoretto portrays the Milky Way being created from a jet of milk that issued from the breasts of the goddess Hera, according to an ancient Greek legend.

thus became immortal and one of the gods. During the Renaissance, both Tintoretto (1518–94) and Rubens (1577–1640) turned this myth into stunning paintings (fig. 10).

And let us not forget the myth of the Amazons, a legendary people reputedly from the Cappadocia region in Asia Minor. Believed to be descended from the god of war, Ares, and to have worshipped the goddess of the hunt, Artemis, Amazons lived in an all-woman society governed by a queen. Once a year, the Amazons slept with foreign men in order to perpetuate the race. All male offspring born from this annual rendezvous were either sent away, or crippled and turned into slaves; all female children were nursed and raised as warriors.

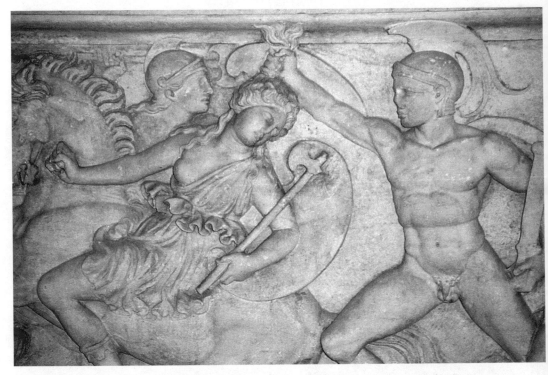

11. Amazon sarcophagus, *Combat Between the Greeks and the Amazons*. Hellenistic (Salonika). Second century C.E.

Amazons were usually depicted in Greek art with the "good breast" exposed and the mutilated one covered by clothing.

Whether the Amazons did or did not have a historical reality is impossible to prove.[26] By the time they first appeared in Homeric literature, in the eighth century B.C.E., they had already been defined by centuries of oral legend. In *The Iliad*, Homer grants to Penthesilea, the queen of the Amazons, the heroic virtues of men, though she is nonetheless defeated at the hands of Achilles. Within classical Greek literature of the fifth century B.C.E., Amazons are invariably presented as the reversal of what women should be: they refuse to marry or have sons, and, like men, they go to war. Fiercely independent, they not only are detached from men, but bear them active enmity.

The Amazons' special place in a history of the breast derives from the legend that they cut off their right breast so as to have greater ease in drawing the bow. A common etymological interpretation of their name is to root it in the two Greek words *a* (without) and *mazos* (breast). A late-fifth-century B.C.E. medical treatise known as *Airs, Waters, Places* attributes the missing right breast to removal by cauterization in infancy so that all the strength would go into the right shoulder and arm. But we have no more reason to believe that interpretation than any of the many fanciful speculations propagated in our own time.

When depicted in art battling their traditional Greek enemies, Amazons were often shown with one breast bare and the other hidden under draperies (fig. 11). In the Greek imagination, Amazons represented the destructive forces unleashed when women abandoned their role as the nurturers of men and appropriated virile attributes instead. Keuls sees in the Amazon story the "archetype of the battle of the sexes" and one of the charter myths of classical Attic society. She points to the eight hundred portrayals of Amazons in Greek art as "the most prominent expression of men's gynophobia, or fear of women." Wherever a fifth-century Athenian turned his gaze, "he was likely to encounter the effigy of one of his mythological ancestors, stabbing or clubbing an Amazon to death," sometimes striking her in the breast near the nipple.[27] Like husbands who batter their pregnant wives, reserving their most violent blows for the swollen belly which contains the fetus, so too Greeks battered their legendary antagonists at the breast because it represented both female potency and vulnerability.

This myth takes on added psychological meaning when we consider it successively from both male and female perspectives. From the male perspective, it can be seen as an expression of the fear of vengeance slumbering in the psyche of those who are in positions of dominance. Men fear not only that the nurturing breast will be taken away from them, but that its very absence denotes aggression. Amazons are seen as monsters, viragos, unnatural women who have misappropriated the masculine warrior role. The missing breast creates a terrifying asymmetry: one breast is retained to nurture female offspring, the other is removed so as to facilitate violence against men.

For women, however, Amazons represent what the psychiatrist Carl Jung called a "shadow self" in reference to those socially unacceptable behaviors which we usually manage to keep underground. Here the shadow self emerges to claim its place in the sun. By a willful act of breast removal, women become transformed into powerful creatures commanding fear and respect. The removal of the breast and the acquisition of "masculine" traits suggests the mythic Amazon's desire to be bisexual, both a nurturing female and an aggressive male, with the nurturance directed exclusively to other women and the aggression directed exclusively toward men. This is indeed an unpalatable vision for men to swallow, the culmination of their worst gynophobic nightmares. Throughout Western history, whenever women threaten to transgress traditional gender roles, the specter of the Amazon can be called forth, either to vilify the new transgression or to shore up the courage of women who turn their backs on conventional feminine behavior.

The myth of the Amazons entered into recorded history at a time when fertility goddesses were being replaced by phallic gods. Perhaps the Amazon figure contains remnants of those earlier female deities, now maimed and modified to suit the reign of the phallus. One breast—the "good" breast—continues to hold the sacred meanings associated with maternity and nurturance, while the "bad" breast, the mutilated one, has suffered grotesque desacralization. The Amazon figure has persisted in the Western imagination to represent the dual meanings breasts convey. As powerful life-giving organs, women's breasts are regarded with awe. At the same time, they are highly vulnerable to destruction, not only from natural forces but also from the hands of men who fear female power. Women sense in the Amazon a mirror image of the sacred and antisacred powers invested in their breasts. They carry them with caution in memory of the Amazons' fate, which, symbolically and sometimes quite literally, could be their own.

WHEN THE CENTER of the classical world shifted from Athens to Rome, Greek gods and goddesses were honored under the Latin names of Jupiter, Mars, Juno, Venus, Diana, and Minerva, rather than Zeus, Ares, Hera, Aphrodite, Artemis, and Athena. And with the change in names came more fundamental changes. The imported Hellenistic deities had to vie with the indigenous traditions of the early Romans, descendants of the legendary Romulus and Remus, who were the twin sons of the mortal Rhea and the war god Mars. At their birth, Romulus and Remus were thrown into the Tiber and then recuperated by a she-wolf, who suckled and fed them. The idea of an animal miraculously nursing a human—indeed, two humans—thus became associated with the founding of Rome itself. Nursed on the milk of a predatory animal, the founders of Rome ostensibly imbibed the wolf's martial qualities, which later served them well as kings. To this day, Rome is represented by the image of a she-wolf suckling Romulus and Remus with her multiple teats.

Another Roman legend—this one of later date—brings the suckling breast down from the realm of gods and goddesses, or mythical animals and warrior-kings, to the level of human alimentation. But it, too, entails a novel shift in nursing partners, one that now reflects the Roman concern with familial and civic duty. The story, traditionally referred to as "Roman Charity," tells of a woman who gave her lactating breast to an imprisoned parent. Derived from the first-century C.E. Roman historian Valerius Maximus, it was repeated by Pliny the Elder (23–79) in the following version:

> Of filial affection there have, it is true, been unlimited instances all over the world, but one at Rome with which the whole of the rest could not compare. A plebeian woman of low position who had just given birth to a child, had permission to visit her mother who had been shut up in prison as a punishment, and was always searched in advance by the doorkeeper to prevent her carrying in any food. She was detected giving her mother sustenance from her own breasts. In consequence of this marvel the daughter's pious affection was rewarded by the mother's release and both were awarded maintenance for life; and the place where it occurred was consecrated to the Goddess concerned, a temple dedicated to Filial Affection. . . .[28]

This reversal of roles, with the mother nursing a parent rather than a child, was commemorated by a special temple dedicated to the goddess of filial piety. Centuries later, during the classically oriented Renaissance, this theme was linked to the Christian virtue of Charity, and dramatically depicted in various works of art.[29] Significantly, in all of these works that I have seen, the parent has undergone a sex change: the mother has become a father, thus introducing a cross-gender, incestual note into the story (fig. 12).

By the time Pliny was making his contribution to the legend of Roman Charity, maternal breast-feeding was definitely on the decline in affluent Roman households. Pliny looked back nostalgically to the days when Roman children had presumably imbibed civic virtues along with their mother's milk, instead of being relegated to wet nurses. Both he and Tacitus (56–120) counseled the women of imperial Rome to look to the past, when "each man's child . . . was reared not in the room of a nursemaid who had been

12. Jean Goujon. *Filial
Charity.* Mid-sixteenth
century.

The original Roman story of
Filial Charity tells of a
daughter nursing her mother
in prison. The Renaissance
interpretation of this story
changed the parent to a father,
thus introducing a
heterosexual incestual note.

bought but in the bosom and embrace of his mother."[30] It appears that this
counsel passed over the heads of latter-day Roman matriarchs, who were
quite content to hand over their children to servants and nursemaids. All that
remained of the earlier breast-feeding ethos were the legends of a nursing
she-wolf, a pious daughter, and Roman mothers sanctified long after they had
ceased to suckle their young.

WHEN WE CONSIDER the Hebrew world that predated and coexisted
with the world of the ancient Greeks and Romans, we must rely almost entirely on literary sources—on the Bible rather than on statuary—since the
Law of Jahweh explicitly forbade the creation of graven images. The first

chapters of Genesis tell us that Adam and Eve were both naked in the Garden of Eden "but they had no feeling of shame towards one another" (Genesis 2:25). It was only after they had broken God's ban against eating the fruit of the tree of knowledge that their eyes "were opened and they discovered that they were naked" (Genesis 3:7). At this point they stitched fig leaves together and fashioned loincloths for themselves. There is no specific mention of a breast covering for Eve.

In the Hebrew Bible, women were valued primarily as vessels of creation. Once the patriarch Abraham was designated as the father of the Israelite people, the overriding obligation for women was to procreate. Certainly some biblical women were admired for their beauty, loyalty, or levelheadedness, or even for their courage, but, on the whole, parenthood constituted their major worth. As in many Orthodox Jewish (and Muslim) households today, a woman became complete only when she gave birth to a male offspring.

The Judaic concern with procreation expressed itself in the oft-repeated blessing "Be fruitful and multiply," a blessing and a command for both women and men. Hebrew scholar David Biale sees similarities between the blessings of the breasts and the womb found in Genesis and the fertility cults of the Israelites' Canaanite neighbors. He suspects the influence of Canaanite goddesses, such as Asherah and Anat, "whose iconography featured prominent breasts. . . . These goddesses are referred to in one Canaanite text as 'the wet nurses of the gods.' Another speaks of 'the divine breasts, the breasts of Asherah and Raham.' "[31]

The sacred breast found in early Judaism is directly connected to God Himself. El Shaddai, the name of God that is always associated with the fertility blessings, meant something like the "God (El) with breasts" or the "God who suckles."[32] Even if this language was to be understood only metaphorically, it is obviously a masculine appropriation of a fundamentally female attribute. God could be seen as both male and female, transcending the narrow confines of human gender.

Fertility, then, was as central to early Judaism as it was to pagan religions, and the breast, like the womb, was openly celebrated. Sarah, the wife of Abraham and mother of the Hebrew people, laughed with joy at the birth of Isaac in her old age and exclaimed: "Whoever would have told Abraham that Sarah would suckle children?" (Genesis 21:7). Hannah, the mother of the future judge Samuel, refused to go on pilgrimage to make the yearly sacrifice until after her son had been weaned—that is, for a period of two to three years (I Samuel 1:21–22). Later, the Talmud would formulate a breast-feeding mandate for all Jewish women: "A baby nurses for twenty-four months. . . . The nursing period should not be cut down for the baby may die of thirst."[33] In an emergency, wet nurses could be substituted for the biological mother, or some form of animal milk, mainly sheep, goat, and cow.

A biblical husband was enjoined to take pleasure in his wife's breasts: "Rejoice with the wife of thy youth. . . . Let her breasts satisfy thee at all times." Conversely, he was warned not to "embrace the bosom of a stranger" (Proverbs 5:19–20). He who followed this counsel could look forward to the blessings of legitimate progeny, the reward for monogamous sexuality.

The arid breast, like the barren womb, was seen as a curse. The God of Israel held sway over both eventualities, determining whether one deserved the "fruitful womb" or the "womb that miscarries and dry breasts" (Hosea 9:11, 14). The curse of dry or shriveled breasts, hurled at those who defied the will of God, became particularly vehement on the tongues of the prophets.

The sixth-century B.C.E. prophet Ezekiel associated breasts with the sins committed by Jerusalem and Samaria. In the parable of the two harlots who symbolized those cities, he attacked their breasts with a vengeance unusual even for a prophet of doom. Jerusalem and Samaria were represented as lascivious sisters, who "played the whore in Egypt, played the whore while they were still girls; for there they let their breasts be fondled and their virgin bosoms pressed" (Ezekiel 23:3). They also "played the whore" with Assyrians and Babylonians, and would ultimately be destroyed by their former heathen lovers.

Speaking in the name of the Lord, Ezekiel warns Jerusalem that she will be severely punished, like her sister, Samaria. "You shall drink from your sister's cup . . . full of mockery and scorn . . . a cup of ruin and desolation . . . and you shall drink it to the dregs. Then you will chew it in pieces and tear out your breasts" (Ezekiel 23:32–34). It is a brutal picture of divine revenge, so oral and sadistic that one almost feels pity for the biblical commentators obliged to defend it. Suffice it to say that Ezekiel's prophecy proved true within his lifetime: the Babylonians under Nebuchadnezzar destroyed the kingdom of Israel and carried the Hebrew people off into captivity.

A very different attitude toward breasts is found in *The Song of Songs*. Traditionally attributed to King Solomon, *The Song of Songs* is a collection of love poems possibly written by more than one author over an extended period of time. Marcia Falk, one of the recent translators of the *Song*, believes that women contributed significantly to the oral composition of this work. She points out that "females speak over half the lines in the Song—an exceptionally large proportion for a biblical text—and, even more remarkably, they speak out of their own experiences and imaginations, in words that do not seem filtered through the lens of patriarchal consciousness."[34]

Contrary to the relative lack of interest in erotic love in the Bible, these lyrics convey a frankly sensual interest in the body and a hearty approval of physical desire. Here breasts appear naturally at key moments in the narrative. The woman calls out to her lover:

> Oh, if you were my brother
> Nursed at my mother's breast,
> I'd kiss you in the streets
> And never suffer scorn.

A sibling identifies a younger sister by the developmental stage of her breasts:

> We have a young sister
> Whose breasts are but flowers.

Female bodily delights are enumerated in a poetic inventory that became the model for untold imitations throughout the centuries to come:

> How fine
> you are, my love,
> your eyes like doves'
> behind your veil
>
> Your hair—
> as black as goats
> winding down the slopes
> . . .
> Your breasts—
> twin fawns
> in fields of flowers

Or again:

> There you stand like a palm,
> Your breasts clusters of dates.

> Shall I climb that palm
> And take hold of the boughs?
>
> Your breasts will be tender
> As clusters of grapes,
>
> Your breath will be sweet
> As the fragrance of quince,
>
> And your mouth will awaken
> All sleeping desire
>
> Like wine that entices
> The lips of new lovers.

It is a poetry unlike any other in the Bible. Female breasts compared to towers, fawns, clusters of dates and grapes, become the sensual symbols of reciprocal pleasure. They take on the feel and taste and fragrance of creaturely love. Certainly other religions, such as that of the Babylonians or the Greeks, had a place for carnal love in their stories of gods and mortals. But because the Israelites specifically rejected the vision of an incarnate God and denounced lovemaking outside the bonds of marriage, *The Song of Songs* stands out like a dream of sexual pleasure in the midst of didactic scripture.

Later apologists for the *Song,* both Jewish and Christian, interpreted it as a metaphor for the relationship of God to the people of Israel, or for the relation between Christ and the faithful. But these interpretations belie the reality of the text; indeed, in the apt words of *Song* translators Ariel Bloch and Chana Bloch, "This kind of exegesis requires considerable ingenuity and linguistic acrobatics, and some of its more extravagant 'findings' now seem very curious," such as the interpretation of the woman's breasts as representing the brothers Moses and Aaron, or the Old and the New Testaments![35] Attempts to justify the *Song* as the expression of a sacred marriage between God and the Jews have today given way to more secular interpretations: our own age has no problem reading it as lyrical love poetry concerning mortal men and women.

Although it is dangerous to interpret biblical texts as though they chronicled history, we can safely draw some conclusions about Hebrew women. Like their Greek counterparts who were neither slaves nor prostitutes, biblical women were honed to chastity under their fathers' roofs and to monogamy in their husbands' homes. A wife was obliged to keep her body hidden from all but her husband's eyes; her head, too, was probably covered from the time she put on the wedding veil.[36] Aside from a few exceptional figures, like the mighty prophetess Deborah or the heroic Judith, biblical women seem surprisingly close to their sisters in the modern Western world. Dutiful daughters, obedient if sometimes outspoken wives, and worried mothers, they inclined to the dictates of the men in charge of their lives. Their breasts belonged to their husbands and children by divine decree.

WHEN WE TURN to the New Testament, and especially to the Gospels of Matthew and Luke, the two major female figures are the two Marys—Mary Magdalene and the Virgin Mary. In the centuries to come, the Virgin Mary proved to be the more popular figure. Once again it was the image of the mother that was validated, a mother with a body like that of all women, yet set apart in mystical specialness. On the one hand, she carried a baby in her womb and gave birth like all other females of the species. On the other, she was distinguished from ordinary women by the special circumstances surrounding the conception of her son: she was not impregnated by the man to whom she was betrothed, but by the Holy Spirit. In this way she provided her body for the son of God, without acquiring the taint that female flesh and the sexual act began to acquire among the early Christian fathers. Other women could not hope to attain Mary's unique status, but they, too, could at least be sexually pure.

Although it can be argued that the New Testament itself does not deprecate the flesh, early Christian theology saw the body primarily as an adversary to be defeated. Flesh, and particularly female flesh, was seen as a threat to spiritual perfection because it deflected attention away from God and lured human beings into sinful practices like fornication and adultery. From Saint Jerome's battle cry of "Conquer the flesh" in the fourth century to Saint Teresa's efforts to "gain dominion over the body" in the sixteenth, Christianity taught its adherents to minimize (if not to mortify) corporality.

In this vein, the story was told of a fourth-century virgin, later canonized as Saint Macrine, who discovered that she had a tumor of the breast. Refusing, out of virginal modesty, to let a doctor touch her breast or operate upon it, she asked only that her mother trace the sign of the cross on the near-gangrenous organ. The Benedictine monks who recorded this story concluded that God looked with favor on her refusal to be touched by a male hand other than His own; He Himself cured the breast, leaving behind only a little scar.[37]

For the most part, the church's negative view of corporality translated into early-medieval art that made little distinction between male and female bodies. With rare exceptions, the heavenly figures adorning church façades revealed none of the protuberances associated with adult bodies. The women's chests were often as flat as the men's.

In the instances when women's breasts were shown nude, there were usually negative connotations involved. Naked women and naked men were shoved into the mouths of Hell above the portals of Romanesque and Gothic churches, whereas saved souls dressed in tunics covering their asexual forms were ushered into Paradise. Male devils sometimes sported large and pendulous breasts to symbolize their corrupt nature, as in the murals painted in the French church of Sainte-Cécile d'Albi. Whereas breasts had been one of the dominant features of the sacred in the ancient world, Christian art suggested that the absence of breasts was a surer sign of sanctity.

Symbolic images of the cardinal vices often depicted women with their breasts uncovered and sometimes mutilated as a form of punishment. Lust, in particular, one of the supreme Deadly Sins, was commonly attributed to women and punished through the bodily organs by which the sinner had offended—namely, her breasts and genitalia. In an early-medieval mural painting at the Church of Tavant in France, Lust is portrayed as a woman piercing her own breast with a spear (fig. 13). A late-medieval Last Judgment scene executed at Saint-Alban's in Cologne by the Brussels painter Colyn de Coter shows Lust in the form of a woman in Hell with a toad on her breast and flames rising up from her pubis.

Conversely, martyred saints were also depicted enduring physical suffering, though they were made to look ennobled by the process. There was often a distinct relationship between the specific harm endured and the powers attributed to that particular martyr. For example, the legendary virgin Saint Agatha suffered martyrdom during the third century in Sicily at the hands of the pagan governor, who had her breasts cut off because she refused to accede to his sexual demands or to sacrifice to the Roman gods (fig. 14). Canonized by the Catholic church and popularized through religious stories and images, Saint Agatha became the patron saint of nursing mothers and nursemaids, who prayed to her for healthy breasts and a good supply of milk. In the Sicilian province of Catania, as in certain parts of Bavaria, her feast day on

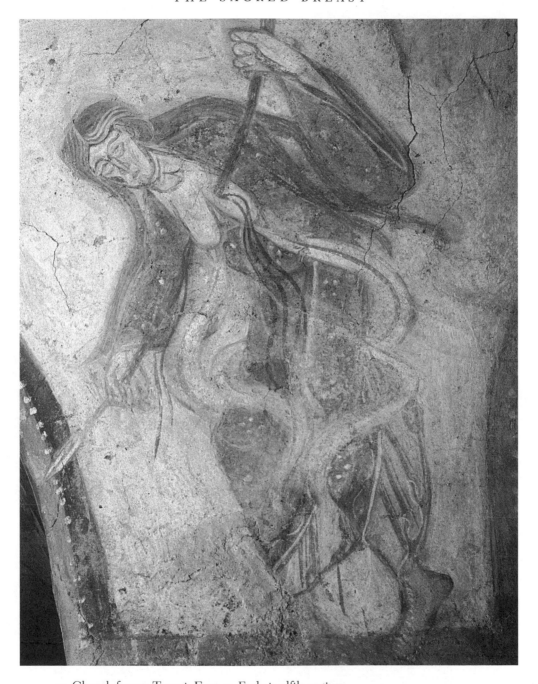

13. Church fresco. Tavant, France. Early twelfth century.

A woman representing Lust agonizes from the wounds of a long spear piercing her left breast, while two snakes reach up from her feet to bite both breasts.

14. (Left)
*Martyrdom of
Saint Agatha.*
Attributed to
Pieter Aertsen.
Sixteenth century.
Saint Agatha was an
early Christian
martyr whose breasts
were mutilated by
Roman soldiers.

15. (Right)
Francisco de
Zurbarán.
Saint Agatha.
Seventeenth
century.
Later Renaissance
and Baroque
paintings of Saint
Agatha show her
carrying her breasts
on a tray, as if she
were serving a pair of
puddings or
pomegranates.

February 5 was celebrated with a special bread, blessed in the bakery and given to people with diseases of the breast.

Some of the most striking paintings of Saint Agatha show her carrying her two breasts on a tray (fig. 15). Reflecting on the Spanish painter Zurbarán's seventeenth-century version of this scene, the twentieth-century French poet Paul Valéry wrote ecstatically of "the joy of torture" and "the sweet breasts made in the image of the earth."[38] For all the beauty of Valéry's words, it is unlikely that any of his female contemporaries would have had a comparable reaction.

Similarly, the third-century virgin martyr Santa Reparata had her breasts mutilated by red-hot branding irons at the hands of Roman soldiers. By the fifth century, she had become the patron saint of Florence, with a church erected in her honor that later became a part of the present cathedral. A vivid fifteenth-century painting of her martyrdom can be found today in the Museo del Duomo. Pictorial narratives of female martyrdom, whatever their didactic intent, afforded some artists the opportunity to vent their sadistic impulses on women's breasts.

One curious exception in medieval iconography shows the baring of the breast as a sign of supplication. In essence, it was the same gesture used by the bold Greek courtesan Phryne at her trial, but in the Christian context there was considerably more humility. No less a personage than the Virgin Mary is shown baring her breasts in a Last Judgment scene painted on the church wall at North Cove, Suffolk, in England.[39] She offers this supreme gesture in an attempt to intercede for a group of sinners destined for Hell. Looking every inch a fourteenth-century queen with her bejeweled crown, and with her elegant breasts squeezed together by a narrow bodice, Mary raises her arms to implore Christ for mercy. Even Christ, one presumes, was subject to second thoughts at the sight of his mother's breasts.

But pictorial representations do not tell the whole story. If we look at literature from this period, we find other networks of meaning surrounding the breast, many connected to the institution of motherhood. Within medieval society, the breast had a singular importance: it was the sign of attachment between mother and child, the link from one generation to the next, with all that implied in terms of rank, wealth, and moral responsibilities. In one influential thirteenth-century treatise authored by Bartholomew the Englishman, the mother was actually defined as the one "who puts forth her breast to feed the child."[40] (In a thoroughly different context, it is interesting to note that the Chinese character for "mother" is made up of two stylized square breasts.)

Even when the mother herself did not nurse her own child, which was already the case among some members of the upper classes, the nursing breast was understood to be the mother's responsibility. Breast milk that came directly from the mother, or from the wet nurse who suckled in her place, was the visual equivalent of the family bloodline, around which feudal society was organized. One owed to one's legitimate progeny, and especially to one's male heir, the best milk possible in view of his role as the inheritor of the paternal name.

A good account of infant care at the upper levels of society can be found in the *Lai Milon*, written by the late-twelfth-century poet Marie de France. In it, an infant taken on a long journey is fed seven times every twenty-four hours by its wet nurse, who also removes the baby's swaddling clothes, bathes it, and puts on fresh swaddling at each stop. Of course, most infants did not receive such fine care. Peasant babies were lucky if their mothers had the wherewithal to breast-feed and change them between other duties, with supplemental feedings provided by cow's milk. In *L'Oustillement le Vilain*, a witty record of all the provisions necessary for a male peasant contemplating marriage, he is advised: ". . . let him find a cow with milk which he can use without delay to nurse the child when it is needed. For if the child is not appeased, it will cry all night and prevent others from sleeping. . . ."[41] Cow's milk for the lowly, wet nurses for the well-born—life's inequalities began with the first drop of milk.

One medievalist has concluded from a study of French stories written between 1150 and 1300 that the mother who either nursed her child herself or confided it to a wet nurse in the best interest of the child was considered the "good" mother, whereas the mother who gave her child to a nurse to get rid of it and enjoy a freer life was explicitly condemned.[42] Wet nurses were commonly brought into the infant's residence—sometimes two or more for one child—and not sent to their own homes with the baby, as they would be in later centuries. Chosen with care, preferably from good families, they were generally well treated and shared in the family's emotional life. People were not unaware of the close psychological bonds that often developed between an infant and the woman who nursed it, be it the mother or the wet nurse.[43]

In some tales, we find the upper-class mother breast-feeding her child herself, for fear that a nurse's milk would not be good enough. The mother in *Tristan de Nanteuil*, for example, would not permit "the child to drink milk other than her own. She wanted to nurse it and nourished it tenderly."[44] Later in this same work, the mother, Clarinde, shows an even more extravagant form of devotion to her child. In flight with her baby in a little boat, "She gives him her breast, the child opens his mouth, but he has suckled and withdrawn so much for two days that the milk could no longer come out." At this point, as Clarinde openly despairs for her baby's life, her prayers to God and the Virgin Mary accomplish a miracle: her milk begins to flow so abundantly that it almost fills up the boat.

Narratives like this one, fabricated from a weave of realistic and miraculous threads, offered models of devoted mothers who had themselves internalized the lessons of the Virgin Mary. Milk was seen as both a material and a spiritual form of nourishment. To give the breast to one's baby was decidedly more than a simple matter of alimentation: the mother transmitted with her milk a whole religio-ethical belief system.

16. ABC tablet.
Bartolomeo da Bologna di Bartoli. *Panegyric of Bruzio Visconti*. Italian.
Fourteenth century.

The mother in this miniature holds a switch in one hand and her breast in the other. The child can expect one or the other—punishment or reward—depending on how well he has learned his ABC tablet.

In this connection, it is interesting to consider a drawing found in a fourteenth-century Italian manuscript (fig. 16). It shows a mother nursing a child who is carrying an alphabet tablet. He is clearly of an age to learn his letters, probably around three. Learning to read was something of an "oral" affair for the child, for he imbibed the ABCs with the expectation of a tasty reward, be it the mother's milk or some other delicacy, such as honey.[45] The breast, then, was the sweetener for learning, the gateway to knowledge, with the mother called upon to nourish her child both physically and mentally.

This maternal model, closely linked to the ideal of the Madonna, had to do battle with the spreading influence of courtly love, which had no place for lactation. Twelfth-century French narratives, such as *Garin le Loherain* and *Ogier le Danois*, were already singing the praises of little breasts (*"les mamelettes"*), always firm, always white, and often compared to two apples. The author of *Aucassin et Nicolette* preferred even tinier contours, for his heroine had blond hair, laughing eyes, small lips, fine teeth, and "firm breasts that lifted up her gown as if they were two round nuts."[46]

La Clef d'Amors, a manual of courtesy based on Ovid's *Art of Love*, gave this immodest advice: "If you have a beautiful chest and a beautiful neck, do not cover them up, but your dress should be low-cut so that everyone can gaze upon and gape after them."[47] The fourteenth-century poet Eustache Deschamps favored the wide-open neckline and tight dress with slits on the side, "through which the breasts and the throat could be more visible." For droopy breasts, there was the remedy of sewing into the top of one's dress "two pouches into which the breasts are squeezed so that the nipples are thrust upwards."[48]

This and other sources evoke the great changes in clothing that were taking place in the late Middle Ages. Previously men and women had worn very similar attire—ankle-length tunics that did not emphasize sexual difference. But by the early fourteenth century in most of Europe, men had abandoned their long tunics for shorter apparel, extending only to mid-thigh and exposing the legs. Though women continued to wear ankle-length garments, they lowered their necklines and molded their clothes so as to accentuate the bust.

Many saw the new revealing fashions as direct invitations to sexual misconduct. The Chevalier de La Tour Landry, in his book written for the education of his daughters (1371–72), admonished his readers not to show their throats or breasts or any other part of the body. He mocked the new style that took material from the front and back of the dress and added it to the frivolous train, where it was certainly not needed for coverage or warmth. In con-

trast to the hussies who flaunted their bodies in such attire, La Tour Landry
cited examples of virtuous women known for their modesty, meekness, obedience, patience, forgiveness, and charity—traits he related to the supreme
model of the Virgin Mary.

Above all, a woman should be subservient to her husband, even if the
husband found it occasionally necessary to beat his spouse into subservience.
The good wife should bring to her husband "the sweetness of the milk, which
signifieth the sweetness that should be in true marriage."[49] For La Tour
Landry, the breast took on its rightful meaning in marriage, and especially in
relation to the husband; it was not to appear wantonly for the sake of fashion
or a prospective lover.

In Italy, a comparable concern with the sexualized breast incited Dante
(1265–1321) to decry the show of cleavage fashionable among Florentine
women. In *The Divine Comedy*, he foresaw the time when the church
would publish from the pulpit a decree against those "brazen jades of
Florentines / Flaunting unveiled the bosom and the paps" ("*a le sfacciate
donne fiorentine / l'andar mostrando con le poppe il petto*").[50] It was in this
Italian atmosphere of transition between the ascetic ideals of the Middle
Ages and the earthbound humanism of the Renaissance that an extraordinary
artistic happening took place.

In the early fourteenth century, on the canvases of painters working in
the area of Tuscany, the Virgin Mary was shown offering her bare breast to
the infant Jesus. It is true that isolated images of the nursing Virgin, *Maria
lactans*, can be found in Christian art as early as the second century. But the
early-Renaissance proliferation of nursing Madonnas was a unique phenomenon that took hold of the Western imagination for centuries to come.

The *Madonna-del-latte* paintings and sculptures made by numerous
fourteenth-century artists all share certain common features (fig. 17). The
Virgin exposes one small round breast, while the other is hidden under her
cloak; the infant Jesus suckles at the exposed breast; yet the breast itself seems
unrealistically attached to the Virgin's body, almost like a small piece of
fruit—a lemon, apple, or pomegranate—that had accidentally dropped onto
the canvas.

We, in the twentieth century, familiar with the nursing Madonna from
innumerable Italian, French, German, Dutch, and Flemish paintings, cannot imagine the novelty of this image when it first appeared. We must try to
put ourselves in the skins of those late-medieval Italians, most of whom could
not read, when they saw for the first time the Virgin suckling a baby as would

17. Ambrogio Lorenzetti. Madonna del Latte. Italian. Fourteenth century.

The first nursing-Madonna paintings showed a tiny, unrealistic breast stuck onto the body like an extraneous decoration.

any other common woman. Did they react with shock, indignation, horror, or pleasure? Remember that, up till that moment, the Virgin had been incarnated in far less human figures—as the regal Byzantine empress radiating golden splendor, or as the ethereal Queen of the Heavens surrounded by saints and angels, or as the fleshless Virgin drawing back modestly from the angel of the annunciation. When she had been depicted as a mother, the infant held in her hands was often a miniature man posed stiffly in front of her. Sometimes he looked into her face, or held a religious symbol, but never before had he been seen as a greedy suckling.

The breast, it is true, did not seem to belong to the rest of the body. In this way the artist conveyed the ambiguous nature of the mother of Christ: she was, and she was not, a woman like other women. She did indeed have a functional breast (at least one) capable of producing milk, and she did indeed use it to nurse her child, but everything else suggested that she was "alone of all her sex."[51]

Why did this particular image of the Virgin appear and become popular during the early fourteenth century in Italy? Perhaps it was related to the chronic malnutrition and anxiety over food supply that wracked Florentine society at the time when paintings of the nursing Virgin began to proliferate.[52] The image of a plump Jesus suckling at the breast of the Madonna would have been comforting to a population that, in the early fourteenth century, had experienced severe nutritional crises caused by crop failures and, later, by successive waves of plague.

Perhaps it was related to the expanding practice of sending Florentine children away to wet nurses in the country. From around 1300 onward, infants from the urban middle class were usually delivered into the hands of a *bàlia* or wet nurse immediately following baptism.[53] When the mother would or could not nurse her own child, or was not permitted to do so by her husband, the *bàlia* was considered a necessity. Contractual arrangements, usually made by the father, stipulated that the *bàlia* nurse the baby until weaning, usually at two years, but in practice it was fairly common for an infant to be nursed successively by two or three wet nurses. The carnival songs of country girls offering their services present this jolly form of self-promotion:

> Here we come, *bàlie* from the Casentino,
> each one looking for a baby,
>
> . . .
>
> We're fine in our way of life,
> prompt and skillful in our trade,
> always when the baby cries
> we feel our milk returning.

And in another song:

> With lots of good fine milk
> our breasts are full.

To avoid all suspicion,
let the doctor see it. . . .

Since it was generally believed that children inherited the physical and mental characteristics of their milk source, parents were advised to choose a wet nurse very carefully, in the hope of finding one who would not transmit undesirable qualities. Certainly there was no lack of churchmen and moralists reminding the public that wet nurses were of base condition and had dirty habits, among these the popular preacher San Bernardino of Siena. In practice, there was probably a considerable gap between the wet nurses' self-congratulatory songs and the dubious care they provided.

All of this leads to the question raised by several interpreters of fourteenth-century Florentine life: How can we understand the fascination with the mother-child relation that is the single most important motif in Florentine art during the first century of the Renaissance? What relation do paintings of a nursing Madonna and a chubby child bear to reality? As one historian asks, "Could these religious pictures represent a secular fantasy of maternal intimacy which the artists themselves probably never knew?"[54]

Given the evidence from present studies on maternal separation during the first two years of life, there is much to be said for this psychohistorical interpretation. It is possible that those urban middle-class children who later became the painters and sculptors of the early Renaissance were marked with a longing for a maternal intimacy that may have been denied them as babes. They may indeed have latched onto *Maria lactans* as a substitute mother, elevating nursing to a sacred level because they and their generation had missed it in real life. Mary may well have represented the "dream mom . . . the consummate breast, ever full and flowing, which we all wish we once had."[55]

Oddly enough, it was not through images of the Virgin Mary that the idea of the nursing mother had first entered Christian theology. As early as the twelfth century, the analogy of the church to a mother nourishing the faithful with the milk of religion had already been established. Giovanni Pisano's marble pulpit in the Cathedral of Pisa, completed in 1310, depicts the church as a queenly lady nursing two miniature Christians at her breasts. Carolyn Bynum, who called attention to this image in *Holy Feast and Holy Fast*, documents the widespread use of nursing images in religious art and literature, including the explicit parallel between the blood flowing from Christ's chest wounds and the milk from Mary's breasts.[56]

Catherine of Siena (1347–80)—an Italian saint famous for the extremity of her religious practices as well as her unflagging service to the needy—left two bodies of writing peppered with images of the breast, her *Dialogue with God* and 382 letters. In *The Dialogue*, she endowed God, Christ, the Holy Spirit, the Holy Church, and Charity with succoring breasts, as in this vision of perfect bliss: "So the soul rests on the breast of Christ crucified who is my love, and so drinks in the milk of virtue. . . . how delightfully glorious *is* this state in which the soul enjoys such union at charity's breast that her mouth is never away from the breast nor the breast without milk."[57] Though Catherine was a nonmother who had sworn herself to virginity at the age of seven, she clearly modeled this scene on the satiated contentment of a suckling infant.

Catherine's English contemporary Julian of Norwich (1342–after 1416) envisioned Christ as a mother who fed the faithful through the blood flowing from his wounds. The analogy to a nursing mother was spelled out with Middle English explicitness: "The moder may ley hyr chylde tenderly to hyr brest, but oure tender mother Jhesu, he may homely lede vs in to his blessyd brest by his swet opyn syde."[58] As late as the sixteenth century, God was still conceptualized as a nursing mother. Saint Teresa, for example, wrote in her *Way of Perfection:* "The soul is like an infant still at its mother's breast. . . . It is the Lord's pleasure that, without exercising its thought, the soul . . . should merely drink the milk which His Majesty puts into its mouth and enjoy its sweetness."[59] This mystical language, with its vision of reciprocity between the divine breast and the human soul, communicates a state of rapture that, even for modern skeptics, may stir up unconscious memories of infantile bliss.

Throughout the Middle Ages, breast milk—and other fluids, such as the blood of Christ or the Virgin Mary's tears—carried mystical connotations. Milk and blood were understood to be essentially the same substance, the former concocted from the latter to nourish the young. Many popular stories and paintings played upon the nonverbal appeal of these two fluids, sometimes bringing them together for miraculous effect: for example, Saint Catherine of Alexandria, when beheaded, reputedly spurted milk instead of blood from her neck.[60]

Next to the blood of Christ, Mary's milk was the most holy and most miraculous of fluids, its wonders retold in numerous poems, stories, and songs. A late-medieval English narrative describes Mary "with a full pap," laying her baby "in her barme [bosom]," and "as she was taught of the Holi Gost, she weshe [washed] him all aboute with her sweet milke."[61] Here Mary is depicted as a simple country lass given to the affectionate ministrations of a first-time mother; yet we are not to forget that her swelling paps and sweet milk were supernaturally produced by a higher power.

This duality between flesh and spirit is spelled out more completely in the following Christmas carol, written in alternating lines of French and Latin. "The infant takes the breast / And feeds on milk / It's the milk of a virgin / And therefore incorruptible. / The thing is certainly new / For a virgin to be a mother. / And for a child to be born / Without carnal sin."[62] Only the milk of a virgin, untainted by sins of the flesh, could be considered capable of producing miracles.

Innumerable vials of Mary's milk were placed as relics in churches, where they reputedly cured a wide assortment of maladies, including blindness and cancer. The sixteenth-century Protestant reformer Calvin, observing the samples of Mary's milk throughout Europe, sardonically remarked in his *Inventory of Relics* that "there is no town, however small, no monastery or nunnery, however insignificant, which does not possess it, some in less, and others in greater quantities. . . . Had the breasts of the most Holy Virgin yielded a more copious supply than is given by a cow, or had she continued to nurse during her whole lifetime, she scarcely could have furnished the quantity which is exhibited." In the same cynical tone, he went on to ask "how that milk . . . was collected, so as to be preserved until our time."[63]

Simpler folk had no doubt that the milk came from their beloved Virgin. They were comforted by the relics and statues of Mary and the protective saints, some of which were specifically earmarked for pregnant women and nursing mothers. Notre-Dame-de-Tréguron in Brittany (Gouërec), for example, houses a statue of the Virgin Mary with uncovered breasts, the right one held in her hand as an offering. Nubile young women would bring her gifts of baby hats and miniature wax body parts, along with their prayers for a good milk supply. These practices continued in rural France among the peasant population right up to the twentieth century.[64]

One of the most curious medieval stories concerns Veronica Giuliana, who took a lamb to bed with her and nursed it in memory of the lamb of God. For this extreme act of piety she was beatified in the fifteenth century by Pope Pius II. A choir stall in the Spanish Cathedral of León, inspired by her story, shows a young woman giving her breast to a small animal that looks like a unicorn.[65] She represents the theological virtue of Charity, which was more commonly represented as a mother nursing a human child or even two children (fig. 19).

18. *The Lactation
of Saint Bernard.*
Flemish. Ca. 1480.
In a vision, Saint
Bernard received a
stream of milk
directly from the
Virgin's breast.

Whenever men appeared in breast stories, they were usually on the re-
ceiving, rather than the giving end. The twelfth-century Saint Bernard re-
counts how the Virgin Mary appeared before him while he was kneeling in
prayer and that she pressed from her breast a stream of milk, which fell onto
his lips. From the thirteenth century onward, numerous paintings were devoted to this theme, all careful to avoid any suggestion of sensual enjoyment,
and to convey only the idea of spiritual nourishment (fig. 18). A most unusual representation of this theme is found in the Museo Colonial in La Paz,
Bolivia, showing Mary nursing a friar—presumably Saint Bernard—at one

19. Tino da Camaino.
Charity. Florence.
Fourteenth century.

Charity is represented in
the form of a robust
Italian woman nursing
two babies through the
slits in her dress

breast, and the baby Jesus at the other. This is the only painting I have seen
of Mary simultaneously breast-feeding both a baby and an adult.

Aside from this and a few other variations on the theme of *Maria lactans*,
it was usually her son who received the benefits of her breast. Whatever the
historical reasons for the appearance of the nursing Madonna in early-
fourteenth-century Italy—the shortage of food supply, the increased practice
of wet nursing, the introduction of form-fitting clothes, the new focus on
earthly experience, and the greater naturalism of early-Renaissance art—
there is something timeless about the vision of a mother nursing her child.

Seen from the long view of human history, the nursing Madonna is merely one in a lengthy procession of feminine deities extending back to Paleolithic goddesses. Like her ancient sisters, she symbolizes female nurturance on a supernatural scale. The breast is her defining feature, because it produces the food essential to the preservation of newborn life. The lactating breasts of the Virgin Mary and the great goddesses were nothing less than sacred symbols of all that was benign in the universe.

Yet, in another respect, Mary is different from prehistoric mother goddesses. Her breast had value only because it nourished the future Christ. Her significance always depended on a male more powerful than herself. Without Jesus, Mary would have no history. But without Mary, Christianity would have lacked a deeply moving feminine presence. Mary's breast offered to the faithful that one symbol of femininity with which all Christians, both male and female, could identify, since they had all suckled at some motherly bosom.

Throughout the early history of man- and womankind, the milk-bearing function of the breast was bathed in a sacred aura. Though we do not know the specific meaning of certain feminine deities—for example, of those small-breasted idols on the Cycladic islands—most ancient goddesses were maternal figures whose bodies promised fecundity and nurturance. It was the mature female form with her milk-producing breasts that was generally honored in pre-Christian times.

The Virgin Mary brings that earlier tradition into the modern world. From the fourteenth through the sixteenth centuries, the nursing Madonna was the prototype of female divinity. Pressing her breast with two fingers so as to facilitate the flow of milk, smiling serenely at the baby held in her arms, she infused holiness into a common maternal act. Though she always had to compete with more secular breast cults, the *Virgo lactans* made of breast-feeding a sacred occupation.

Two

THE EROTIC BREAST:
"ORBS OF HEAVENLY FRAME"[1]

A CENTURY AFTER the appearance of the nursing Madonna in Italy, the mistress of the king of France—Agnès Sorel—was also painted with one breast uncovered (fig. 20). Her breast was no miniature appendage stuck onto a shrouded form, as found in fourteenth-century Madonna paintings, but a voluptuous globe bursting out of the bodice. Placed in the center of the canvas, the naked breast—which hits the onlooker in the eye—does not seem to concern its owner, pensively gazing inward, or the child seated in front of her, who stares blandly into the distance. This work, known as *The Virgin of Melun*, may well have shocked its earliest viewers, accustomed as they were to images of the divine mother solemnly nursing the infant Jesus. They found in her place a courtly lady, whose bare breast was served up like a piece of fruit for the delectation of an observer outside the picture, and certainly not for the baby seated placidly within the frame.

Dutch historian Johan Huizinga, commenting on the association of religious and amatory sentiments in this painting, says it has "a flavour of blasphemous boldness . . . unsurpassed by any artist of the Renaissance."[1] Anne Hollander isolates it as the moment when the single bare breast became "an erotic signal in art" and a reference to pure pleasure.[2] Stripped of its relation to the sacred, the breast became the uncontested playground for male desire.

The story of Agnès Sorel was both the harbinger of a new era in French history, and the sign of a new social construction of the breast. As the first official mistress of a French king, Agnès was rewarded with castles, jewels, and other luxuries previously unknown to royal favorites. She received the considerable sum of three hundred pounds a year, wore the most costly clothes in the kingdom, and had a retinue larger than the queen's. Queen Marie

4 9

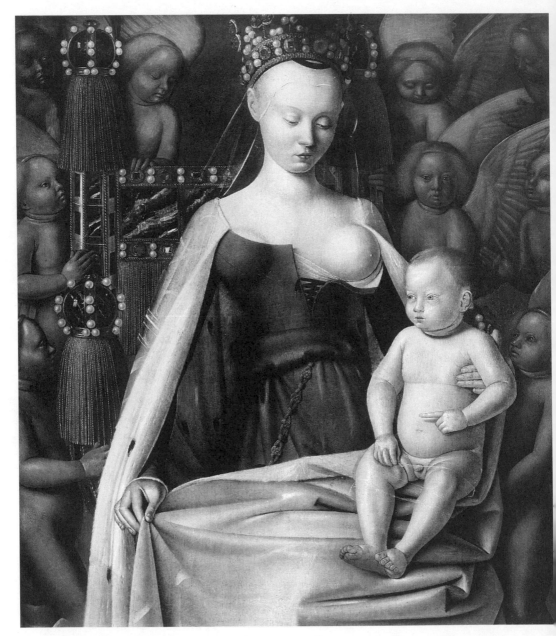

20. Jean Fouquet. *Madonna and Child*, known as *The Virgin of Melun*. Second half of the fifteenth century.

This portrait of Charles VII's mistress, Agnès Sorel, painted under the guise of the Madonna, marks a transition between the sacred breast of the Middle Ages and the erotic breast of the Renaissance.

d'Anjou, who was to bear fourteen children and lose many of them early in their lives, suffered the presence of Agnès without public protest. Others, however, showed her open hostility. The king's son, the future Louis XI, may even have run after her with a knife. Agnès's extravagant dresses with their long trains and generous display of bosom were the source of widespread criticism, but the king paid no heed. He would, in time, even recognize her three daughters as his own. And who was this king who made his extramarital passion so public? None other than the doleful Charles VII (1403–61), who owed his coronation at Reims to the military victories of Joan of Arc, and who later abandoned her to the English.

Charles VII was over forty when he first saw Agnès Sorel in the winter of 1444. Half his age, remarkably pretty, she quickly captivated the unprepossessing king, who bestowed upon her a castle near his own, and with it the title *dame de beauté*, by which she was subsequently known. With all these excessive luxuries, she has nonetheless come down in French history as a positive figure because she encouraged Charles VII to abandon his natural apathy in matters of kingship and to reconquer from the English the province of Normandy. Charles, it appears, needed to be aroused into military action by women. Fifteen years earlier it had been the saintly Joan of Arc; now it was the turn of a more earthly creature. Agnès became the first of the royal mistresses to reap full benefits from sexual favors.

But her reign was short. Six years after her initial meeting with Charles VII, she fell sick and died within a few days. She left behind the legacy of her single-breasted beauty in two well-known portraits that marked a transition from the ideal of the sacred breast associated with motherhood to that of the eroticized breast denoting sexual pleasure. Increasingly, in art and literature, the breast would belong less to the baby, or to the church, and more to men of worldly power who treated it solely as a stimulus to desire.

We do not know for certain whether Agnès Sorel ever appeared in public bare to the waist or with one breast fully uncovered, as was rumored during her lifetime. She certainly wore the very low-cut dresses that had already become fashionable at court. Isabeau de Bavière, Charles VII's headstrong mother, is credited with introducing this style. In 1405, Isabeau was publicly censured by the bold priest Jacques Legrand for the bad example she was setting. He thundered from the pulpit: "O mad queen! Lower the horns of your *hennins* [saddlelike headdresses] and cover up your provocative flesh."[3] But despite such pronouncements, the new décolletage quickly became an option for women of all classes.

From the time that breasts began to be featured in late-medieval fashion, moralists rose up in every country to protest their exposure. Spokesmen for the Christian church referred to the laced openings of women's bodices as "the gates of hell." The Czech religious reformer John Hus (1369–1450) vehemently condemned the wearing of low-cut dresses and the artificial props that made breasts look like two projecting "horns." The chancellor of the University of Paris, Jean Gerson (1363–1429), lambasted the sight of women's "open bosom and uncovered breasts" squeezed upward between rigid corsets and tight sleeves.[4]

Faced with these criticisms, coquettish women found ways of keeping the low-cut fashion alive through the use of a transparent piece of material placed across the bust. Michel Menot, one of the most virulent orators of the fifteenth century, explicitly denounced this stratagem as a wicked enticement that only pretended to cover the breasts. Women purveying their flesh in this manner were compared to fishmongers displaying their wares, and also to lepers, who should go about with small noisemakers to alert passers-by of their dangerous presence.

Another French priest, Olivier Maillard, assured breast-revealing women that they would be strung up in Hell by their "shameless udders," a punishment obviously chosen to fit the crime.[5] The bishop Jean Jouven des Ursins, lamenting the dissolute practices of Charles VII's court, zeroed in on the openings of bodices "through which one sees women's breasts, nipples and flesh," concrete symbols in his mind of the general atmosphere of "whoredom and ribaldry and all the other sins."[6]

In England, Charles VII's younger English counterpart, the pious Henry VI (1421–71), was affronted by the bare bosoms he saw around him, and firmly discouraged their display at his court. English moralizers joined the chorus of outrage, condemning women for showing their breasts, and chiding men as well as women for their ostentatious apparel — most notably, their sumptuous sleeves, piked shoes, and the exuberant codpiece, which was in fashion for almost two hundred years (circa 1408 to 1575).[7] During this period, numerous sumptuary laws regulating clothing were passed in most of the kingdoms of Europe, both to distinguish between the classes and to discourage sexually provocative attire. Despite these repeated efforts, visible breasts continued to affront zealots and to delight the frankly earthbound.

Look at the many bathing scenes, from various social settings, that show men taking obvious pleasure in women's breasts (figs. 21 and 22). Listen to the words of the realistic poet François Villon (1431–after 1463) as he places on

21. (Left) *Bathing Couple.* German woodcut. Fifteenth century.

A man and a woman are together in a wooden tub, his hand placed under one of her breasts.

22. (Below) *Le Roman de la Violette.* French manuscript. Fifteenth century.

Another bathing scene portrays a man staring with delight through a peephole at the naked breasts of a woman in a tub. The illuminated manuscript reads: "How the false old woman betrayed her mistress and how she made a hole in the wall of the room so the Count de Forest could see the mark that the beautiful Eurydant had on her right breast."

the tongue of an elderly prostitute wistful words of lament for her former physical charms:

> Those sweet little shoulders,
> Those long arms and nimble hands,
> Little breasts and fleshly hips.[8]

Note that the standard of beauty was very different from that of our own era, when "little breasts" and "fleshly hips" are hardly the rage.

The rating system for breasts established in the Middle Ages remained essentially the same throughout the Renaissance: they should be small, white, round like apples, hard, firm, and wide apart.[9] In Italy, young men commonly memorized the female body parts from verse written by Petrarch (1304–74) or wrote their own anatomical love poems. A particularly Italian twist on breasts set them to motion in imaginative metaphors of fluctuation, undulation, rising and falling, as in Ariosto's oft-imitated scenario of two apple breasts that "move to and fro like a wave."[10]

The Italian writer Agnolo Firenzuola—author of the *Dialogue on the Beauty of Women*, first published in 1548—imagined "fresh and leaping breasts, moving upward as if unwilling to remain forever oppressed and re-strained by clothing, demonstrating their desire to leave their prison."[11] Such breasts are treated as little temptresses, with a "beauty of such charm that our eye will dwell on them even against our will."[12] Elsewhere, the author pro-fesses irritation at women who go out of their way to conceal their breasts; he tells one of the women in the dialogue that if she does not withdraw the veil she has placed over her bosom, he will not continue his speech. That woman, and others in the book, were real people disguised behind fictitious names. Firenzuola's *Dialogue* was only one (albeit the most famous) of many sixteenth-century Italian works devoted to the subject of female beauty, which found enthusiastic audiences at all the courts of Italy.

At the worldly papal court of Leo X (1513–21), Augustinus Niphus com-posed *De Pulchro et Amore* (*On Beauty and Love*) with the celebrated Jeanne d'Aragon in mind. In it, he mentally undressed Jeanne and described all the parts of her body, including, of course, her breasts, imagined as medium-sized and perfumed like fruit. A nineteenth-century French commentator on this treatise paused at this point to remind his reader that a certain kind of peach still carried the name "breast of Venus."[13] But Niphus had a different kind of fruit in mind, and one that departed from the conventional apple-bosom. Jeanne d'Aragon's breasts were compared to pears turned upside down, with their bases presenting ravishing curves that rounded to narrow cones at their tips.

Whether in Rome at the seat of the papacy, or in the notoriously venal city of Venice, or at any number of regional Italian courts, breasts were celebrated as a part of the new sexual freedom that marked the Renaissance. Women of all classes became bolder in revealing their bodies, and prostitutes, in particular, went about with their breasts more or less uncovered. Women in the sex trade were divided into two major categories: the common prostitute and the "honest courtesan" (*cortigiana onesta*), the latter offering not only sexual services but also, like the Japanese geisha, conversation and entertainment. Honest courtesans were trained in song and dance, letter writing and painting, and were able to earn "honest" money from sources other than sexual acts per se. The most successful Venetian courtesans were legendary creatures, rivaling patrician ladies in their beauty, clothing, and social graces, and at least one of them — Veronica Franco — became famous as a writer.

Veronica Franco's rise from prostitution to literature would have been remarkable in any time and place.[14] One had to be an especially clever courtesan to succeed in the literary arena, where simple prostitutes could never venture and only a few noblewomen had made their mark. By dint of Franco's innate verbal gifts, her determined efforts at self-education, and the astute use of male patronage, she was able to participate significantly in the intellectual life of her day. She published a volume of verse and a volume of letters, and held her own against the many satirical male writers who envied her success.

Typical of their vicious attacks was this ad-hominem remark made by her chief enemy, Maffio Venier: her breasts hung so low that she could paddle a gondola with them. Venier's insult could not have applied to the young Franco, judging from the pictures of her in her prime (fig. 23). But whatever the natural level of her breasts, she may indeed have resorted to the cleverly constructed supports resembling balconies that Venetian women commonly wore inside their bodices to push up their bosoms.[15]

Courtesans like Franco had every reason to fear the time when their breasts would begin to sag. That spelled the end of their commercial value. Given the Renaissance fixation on youthful flesh and its horror at vital decline, artists would often juxtapose the charms of eighteen with the ravages of eighty (figs. 24 and 25). The contrast between the high-perched breasts of youth and the hanging dugs of old age became emblematic of the rise and fall of the courtesan over her life span.

23. Veronica Franco. Portrait by an anonymous artist found in an album of 105 watercolors of Italian costumes and scenes from daily life. Venice. 1575.

The courtesan-writer Veronica Franco is portrayed with the perfectly round, small, high breasts that were the Renaissance ideal.

During their active period, courtesans were more than tolerated by the Venetian city-state, since they provided a substantial source of revenue in taxes and fines. In fact, in an attempt to provide a sexual outlet for unmarried men and to counter the widespread "vice" of sodomy among homosexual men, it granted courtesans numerous concessions. For example, they were allowed to stand naked from the waist up on the Ponte delle Tette (Bridge of Breasts) to display their wares and lure passers-by. The Ponte delle Tette is in the neighborhood of the Castelleto, a key zone for prostitution. In fact, according to historian Guido Ruggiero, legislation was passed around 1500 ordering prostitutes to return to the Castelleto from other parts of the city and requiring them to uncover their breasts. The reason for this was that some prostitutes had been dressing as men in order to attract a gay clientele.[16]

To make their breasts even more visible, some courtesans painted them with the same bright cosmetics they put on their faces. In their homes, they were seen at their windows displaying their bosoms and making amorous signs to entice customers inside. Uncovered breasts were generally associated with prostitutes, as were the yellow veils they were required to wear in public,

24. and 25. *Youth* and *Old Age*.
Colored wax medallions.
Italian. Seventeenth century.

These wax reliefs are elegies to the
fate of the female breast. The first
portrays a woman of eighteen; the
second shows her at eighty.

26. Venetian courtesan. Sixteenth century.
The cross in the cleavage buttressed by bare breasts drew vehement
criticism from outraged Italian and French priests.

and the absence of pearls, forbidden them by law. Yet, despite attempts to
control their dress and jewelry, well-paid courtesans continued to flaunt their
lavish attire and the crosses that dangled provocatively on golden chains in
their cleavage (fig. 26).

It was during the Renaissance that the nude bust emerged in art, corresponding to "a new sense of feminine beauty, whereby the breasts were
somehow part of the face."[17] Many of these portraits, exposing one or both
breasts, were of well-known courtesans, which did not prevent them from
being hung alongside those of kings and popes. Elevated from mere prostitution to the allegorical realm of a "Flora" or a "Venus," courtesans now
claimed some of the honor due to the goddesses of old.[18] Often an uncov-

ered breast was made to look as if it had slipped out accidentally from the courtesan's clothing in the wake of events that had taken her by surprise. This was an art convention that would be used over and over again for erotic effects in the centuries to come.

In the plastic arts of this period, the notion of feminine beauty presented Greek and Roman statuary as the ideal human form. A woman's body should be long, her head small, her breasts round and high. Venuses and Dianas, painted and sculpted, reclining and standing, glorified the firm-breasted, long-legged female figure. Jean Cousin's (1490–1560?) *Eva Prima Pandora* offers a stunning example of this eroticized ideal, and one that also reveals the not-so-hidden underside of Renaissance attitudes toward seduc-

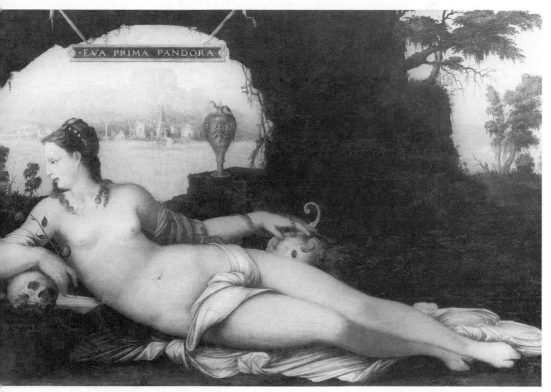

27. Jean Cousin. *Eva Prima Pandora*. French. Sixteenth century.

Eve, "the first Pandora," with her disproportionately long torso and legs and her compact breasts, seems at ease in her fluid nakedness. With her head posed to the side, she averts the gaze of the viewer, presumably male, who is invited to contemplate her fully exposed flesh.

tively beautiful women (fig. 27). Here, as in most Western erotic art, the female nude is presented as a passive figure, a "sex object" corresponding to *his* rather than *her* desire. Yet, despite the passivity of the female body, there are disturbing accents lurking nearby. Eve's right arm rests on a skull, and her left arm reaches out to touch a mysterious vessel. Above her head, the clearly written sign "Eva Prima Pandora" establishes an analogy between Eve and Pandora. The former was considered responsible for the first act of disobedience against God's commandments; the latter, according to Greek mythology, gave her husband the fatal box from which both good and evil flew into the world. Eve and Pandora are presented as dangerous twin sisters whose sexual beauty masks a sinister truth. Such paintings perpetuated the Judeo-Christian notion that women in general, like Eve, were diabolical temptresses.

While elite women's bodies were idealized in art and sumptuously decked out at court, less fortunate bodies were being burned at the stake. The Renaissance, with its brilliant high culture, was also the time when witchcraft was arduously pursued by both Catholics and Protestants, and most of the witches condemned to death—estimated between 60,000 and 150,000 over two or three centuries—were women. (About 20 percent of those accused of witchcraft and 15 percent of those actually condemned were men.)

One aspect of the witch-hunt that touches upon our subject was the search for "unnatural" marks or protuberances on the body, said to be signs of the witch's profession. In England and Scotland, this mark was often thought to be an extra teat from which an imp or a devil, known as a "familiar," presumably sucked the witch's blood as a form of nourishment.[19] It was common to appoint a man to search the suspect's body for the "witch's teat." He was supposed to know a true witch if she showed no feeling when he pricked the presumed teat with a pin, and many an innocent woman, terrified into numbness by this procedure, was then led to execution.[20]

Trial records often included the depositions of witch prickers: on one occasion, they found a teat "the bigness of the little finger, and the length of halfe a finger," which looked as though it had recently been sucked, and on another, three teats in a woman's privy parts, the likes of which the informants had never seen before.[21] Often the teat was found in the witch's pudenda, a site that suggests a displaced form of eroticism in the very notion of the "witch's teat."

Even when sex was not explicitly among the charges, it was always assumed that the witch had consorted with the devil and was involved in some kind of perverse sexual practice. In the case of Anne Boleyn, Henry VIII's ill-fated wife accused of adultery, the rumor arose that she possessed a third breast; this claim, which was subsequently recorded in books of medical anomalies, may have been only a further attempt to darken her name with the stigma of witchcraft. The "witch's teat" may have been merely a mole or a wart, a freckle or a blemish, or even a supernumerary nipple, which occurs in approximately one out of two hundred women; but for susceptible minds, it was an aberrant breast in the service of the devil.

Witches' breasts—real or imagined—were often subject to humiliating and excruciating treatment. They were commonly exposed at public whippings and mutilated in some of the more brutal cases. The case of Anna Pappenheimer, member of an outcast family of gravediggers and latrine cleaners in Bavaria around 1600, presents one of the most shocking examples. Tortured into confessing sexual relations with the devil and then condemned as a witch, she and three members of her family were burned at the stake. But before that final ordeal, Anna's breasts were cut off and forced into her mouth and then into the mouths of her two grown sons. This was "a hideous parody of her role as mother and nurse."[22]

Although even children were occasionally executed as witches, most witches were mature women, and many were conspicuously old. Pictures of witches show them with hanging dugs, symbolizing advanced age and loss of fertility—evils in and of themselves, not to mention the witches' reputed propensity for casting spells that took away fertility or sexual potency. With no babes at their breasts, witches were seen as envious of the offspring of younger women and frequently indicted for bewitching children. Age was certainly a factor in determining who was or was not a witch, along with gender and class. In the tart words of historian Margaret King, the European witch-hunt was "tantamount to a war waged by men . . . upon women" who were, for the most part, "poor, uneducated, sharp-tongued, and old."[23] Such was the flip side of the high-culture homage to female erotic beauty.

In France, the breast cult reached a verbal paroxysm between the 1530s and 1550s, launched by Clément Marot's famous poem "Le Beau Tétin" ("The Beautiful Breast"). Composed in the winter of 1535–36, "The Beautiful Breast" was largely responsible for the vogue of a certain kind of poetry, called the "blazon," that celebrated every part of the female body: eyes, eyebrows, nose, ears, tongue, hair, chest, stomach, navel, buttocks, hand, thigh, knee, foot, and especially the breast. Marot playfully described the perfect breast in the following manner:

> A little ball of ivory
> In the middle of which sits
> A strawberry or a cherry.
>
> . . .
>
> When one sees you, many men feel
> The desire within their hands
> To touch you and to hold you.
> But one must satisfy oneself
> With being near you — for my life!
> Or another desire will come.
>
> . . .
>
> For every reason, happy is he
> Who will fill you with milk,
> Turning the virgin's breast into
> The breast of a beautiful, complete woman.[24]

While focusing on the breast, the poem never raises questions about the feelings of the person behind the breast. It tells us only about the effect produced by the sight of the breast on the male viewer. A beautiful breast is not only a stimulus to his desire, but also a source of masculine pride, since it is his seed that impregnates the female and transforms her into a milk-bearing creature; such a breast allows the poet to spend himself in verbal ecstasy, and to act out a power fantasy of triggering the milk-production process. But whatever masculinist motives we may find in the poem, it is hard not to love it simply for its grace and wit.

The blazon presented the pretty side of Renaissance eroticism. Yet, as in Cousin's *Eva Prima Pandora*, there was also a misogynist underside, which sprang to the foreground in the practice of the antiblazon. Antiblazons dissected female anatomy with a violence akin to mutilation. Their aim was to satirize the courtier-poet's sweet-mouthed words and to uglify as crudely as possible every piece of the womanly body. In his "Antiblazon to the Breast," Marot turned the breast into an object of loathing.

Breast, that is nothing but skin,
Flaccid breast, flaglike breast

. . .

Breast with a big, ugly black tip
Like that of a funnel,

. . .

Breast that's good for nursing
Lucifer's children in Hell.

. . .

Go away, big ugly stinking breast,
When you sweat, you could provide
Sufficient musk and perfume
To kill off a hundred thousand.[25]

Whereas the blazon honored the female body, the antiblazon tapped into men's more negative feelings about women's essential "otherness." Men projected onto women's bodies not only their erotic longings, but also their fears of old age, decay, and death. The antiblazon gave men an opportunity to express, through women's breasts, thighs, knees, feet, stomach, heart, and genitals, their own unconscious anxieties concerning mortality. Far better to dismember and deride the female body than to examine the anatomy of one's own ugliness and decomposition.

As in the case of Marot, gallant praise and vicious satire could spring from the pen or paintbrush of the same person. The German writer and physician Cornelius Agrippa (1486–1535), known for his high-minded philosophical treatises and enlightened views on witchcraft (which earned him excommunication), composed both types. In his encomium to the female sex (*De Praecellentia Feminei Sexus*), he listed women's perfections from head to toe and included his personal preference for a full chest with equally balanced breasts. Judging from their prescriptive literature and art, Germans were not as committed to small breasts as the French and Italians. In a later work (*De Vanitate Scientiarum*), Agrippa devoted an especially savage chapter to women's physical imperfections.

All of these works of art and literature, laudatory or satirical, were exclusively male creations. When we look at the few women poets whose works have survived from this period, we find a very different sensibility, albeit a similar obsession with erotic love. Pernette du Guillet and Louise Labé, two women writing in Lyons at the time of the great vogue for blazon poetry, presented distinctly feminine aesthetics of desire. For du Guillet, the highest form of love was Platonic, a longing for beauty mediated through the beloved. As the student and muse of the neo-Platonist Maurice Scève—whose popularity was due, in part, to his clever blazons on "The Throat" and "The Sigh"—she wrote of her struggle to liberate her mind and soul from the hold of the body. The body had prevented her from seeing clearly and acting judiciously (Épigramme XI). She expressed astonishment at its overpowering force: "The body ravished, the soul is much amazed" (Épigramme XII). She wished to be cured of the misfortune of loving, as if it were some dread disease (Chanson III).

Yet du Guillet was occasionally conscious of the power that she, too, had in the dialogue of love. In one poem, she imagined herself nude in a stream with her lover nearby (Élégie II). With her body set in place like a trap, she would lure him to the site by playing on her lute. She would allow him to approach, but if he wanted to touch her, she would throw water into his eyes and force him to listen to her song. In this way, she became something more than the passive object of his gaze—indeed, his verbal equal on their common road to spiritual perfection.[26]

The other famous Lyonnais woman poet, Louise Labé (1524–65), had no trouble naming corporeal desire. In her poetry, the voice of the body is frank, even violent: "I live, I die. I'm burning and I'm drowning."[27] Bemoaning the silence of her former lover, she longs to be gathered up at his breast (Sonnet XIII) or to hold him once again at her own "tender breast" (Sonnet 9).

> Since the first moment when cruel Love
> Poisoned my bosom with his fire
> I have burned from his divine fury,
> No respite for my heart for even a day.[28]

Breast, bosom, heart, are all victimized by Love—poisoned, inflamed, tortured. There is no relief from the pain localized in the chest and intensified by its very association with past pleasures. Such is the inner reality of the breast experienced by this particular woman. Even if we take into account the literary conventions that commanded poets—both male and female—to suffer and moan in behalf of the beloved, Labé's breast imagery differs significantly from the marmoreal conceits elaborated by Renaissance men.

The most celebrated French poet of this period, Pierre de Ronsard (1524–85), was clearly a breast man. In the long cycle of love poems dedicated to Cassandre, he refers over and over to her "beautiful breast," "virginal buds," "lawns of milk," "generous throat," "overly chaste breast," "hill of milk," "alabaster throat," "ivory breast," and so forth. He tells us that if he could only "grope around her breasts," he would consider his obscure fate more fortunate than that of kings. Occasionally, his hand will not take orders from his brain: ". . . sometimes my hand, in spite of myself, / Transgresses the laws of chaste love / And searches at your breast that which inflames me."[29] Yet even the pleasure of touching her bosom is not enough, since it leads to an admittedly greater need, which the beloved is not willing to satisfy:

28. Ronsard and Cassandre. Frontispiece for *Les Amours*, 1552.
Ronsard, crowned and draped like a Roman poet, stares across the page at the image of his muse, Cassandre. Such were the conventions of the time that Ronsard, a tonsured cleric, could proclaim his erotic torments for the beautiful Cassandre and have her nude breasts displayed at the head of his book.

I wish to God that I had never touched
My loved one's breast with so much mad desire.

. . .

Who would have thought that cruel destiny
Would have enclosed beneath that beauteous breast
So great a fire, to make of me its prey?[30]

It can be argued that Ronsard inherited many of his breast metaphors from earlier French and Italian poets. More than once, in the tradition of Petrarch, he contemplates the joys of being transformed into a flea with the opportunity of biting the loved one's bosom. Elsewhere, in the mode of Ariosto, he imagines the female chest as an earthly paradise where "twin flows of milk" come and go like the ocean tide (Sonnet CLXXXVII).

Yet the object of Ronsard's imagery was more than a poetic fiction; Cassandre was a real person, the daughter of a Florentine banker in the service of the king of France, and her sensual reality worked wonders on the amorous imagination of the young Ronsard. Unable to offer her marriage because of his position as a religious cleric, he spent the period between 1546 and 1552 writing his first series of love poems, collected under the title *Les Amours*. Two medallions graced its frontispiece, one of Ronsard, the poet, crowned with a laurel leaf, and the other of a bare-breasted Cassandre (fig. 28). Though it is unlikely that Cassandre herself posed in the nude for this image, it is supposedly a portrait of her at the age of twenty, when she was still very much alive.

While Ronsard suffered his fitful love for Cassandre, many other French poets and painters at the court of Henri II (1519–59) found their midcentury muse in the person of Henri's mistress, Diane de Poitiers (1499–1566). Her story, even more than that of Agnès Sorel a century earlier, offers a conflation of sex, art, and politics raised to a quasi-mythological level. Diane de Poitiers was treated in her lifetime, and for several generations thereafter, as the flesh-and-blood embodiment of the goddess Diana. It was her face, her breasts, her legs that became the model for Diana in countless paintings, drawings, engravings, statues, bronzes, and enamels.[31]

Metamorphosed into the goddess of the hunt, she was painted and sculpted with bow and arrow in hand, or a deer at her side (fig. 29). In discussing the plethora of works reputedly based on her face and figure, her biographer Philippe Erlanger claims that she established an idealized type with her high forehead, thin nose and lips, and "high, proud chest," though only a

29. *Diane de Poitiers.* School of Fontainebleau. Sixteenth century.

Diane de Poitiers, the mistress of Henri II, was the most honored Frenchwoman of her day.
Here she is pictured leaning over a deer, her reclining nude body stretched out against a
pastoral backdrop and her tiny conical breasts framed between languid arms and coils of hair.

handful of such works can be considered truly faithful representations.[32]
Henri II's open attachment to his mistress—a woman twenty years his senior—was the inspiration for so much art and literature, not to mention contemporary gossip and posthumous nonsense, that it is still difficult to separate
the historical facts of their liaison from the legend they created.

It is useful to know that Diane was, by all accounts, a remarkably beautiful,
highly intelligent woman with great style and taste. Married at fifteen to the
Grand Seneschal Louis de Brézé, a man forty years older, she became an or-
nament at the court of François I (reigned 1515–47), without adopting its sexual

license. There was nothing in her irreproachable conduct that would predict her later career as a king's mistress, unless one remembers that her husband was the grandson of . . . Charles VII and Agnès Sorel! The model of power wielded through sex can be seen as a part of Diane de Poitiers's marital inheritance.

After her husband's death, the young widow of thirty-one was at the height of her legendary beauty when she reputedly captivated the young prince Henri on the verge of adolescence. Diane was to become the great, undisputed love of Henri's manhood, despite his marriage to Catherine de Médicis, who bore him ten children in thirteen years, and despite a few royal excursions into other beds. Henri openly assumed the pose of a chivalrous lover toward the widow of the Grand Seneschal, carrying her colors—black and white—into jousts and tourneys, and patronizing the poets and artists who immortalized her charms. Diane acquired through the king's favor a number of prestigious titles, a colossal income, and several outstanding prop-erties—among them Chenonceaux, which she transformed into what many today consider the most elegant château in France. Her fame, riches, and in-fluence reached an unprecedented level.

Diane de Poitiers's store of charms included many attributes more signif-icant than her bosom, but as we have seen, her small breasts were consistent with the contemporary ideal. There is little doubt that Henri II found them seductive. A letter describing the king's manner of behaving in semiprivate with his mistress shows him "touching her breasts now and then and looking at her attentively like a man surprised by his feelings."[33]

Henri II's personal goblet was modeled on the shape of her breast, a prac-tice which the chronicler Brantôme traces back (through Pliny) to Helen of Troy. The Greek tradition invoked Helen's breast as the original source for the first wine cup. In his characteristically irreverent, not to say licentious, manner, Brantôme makes fun of the women whose "great ugly breasts" would make less attractive goblets: "We should be bound to give the gold-smith a big supply of gold, and then all our expense would but end in laugh-ter and mockery."[34] In his description of the female parts, Brantôme offers an antiblazon in prose: breasts, legs, even women's pubic hair and labia are de-scribed in their most repulsive forms. To cite but one example: there are women "the nipples of whose breasts are for all the world like a rotten pear."[35] The tradition of misogynistic insult was alive and well in Brantôme's late-Renaissance hands.

To keep from having "great ugly breasts," Frenchwomen had recourse to a panoply of practices. In the late fifteenth century, Eleanor, the favorite of

Charles VIII (1470–98), enhanced the beauty of her bosom with the use of poppy water, an infusion made of ivy, rose oil, and camphor.[36] Diane de Poitiers was said to have employed certain washes compounded of gold and rainwater or sow's milk.[37] Certainly there was no lack of imagination in the production of lotions, balms, ointments, powders, pastes, and creams concocted in apothecaries and sold by traveling vendors.

If we are to believe some of the many beauty manuals that were published in the sixteenth and seventeenth centuries, skin formulas contained anything from crushed pearls and lard to pigeon droppings and toad's eyes. Certain products were considered especially effective for keeping the breasts small and firm. Jean Liebault, author of *Three Books for the Embellishment of the Human Body* (*Trois Livres pour l'Embellissement du Corps Humain*, 1582), counseled the following treatment: "She who has small and solid breasts will keep them in this manner if she crushes cumin seeds with water into a form of pulp, and applies it to her breasts, then binds them tightly with a band dipped in water and vinegar. . . . After three days, she should take everything off, and in their place put back a crushed lily bulb mixed with vinegar, tightly bound with a band, and leave it there for three more days."[38]

This upper-class obsession with appearance was related to the new cult of the bath and boudoir. Oval bathtubs first appeared in France during the reign of François I, replacing the public baths and round tubs of the previous century, at least for a select elite. We should not, however, harbor any illusions about cleanliness. Immersing oneself fully in water was considered dangerous, because it was believed to open the pores to noxious substances; cleansing took place through the frequent change of linens and white chemises, which acted like sponges to lift off the dirt.[39] Perfumes were probably more common than soap.

What mattered was the illusion of cleanliness and the glowing effect that could be produced through cosmetics. A new genre of painting shows women in the intimacy of the boudoir, with the bathtub visible in an adjoining room, and the objects of their toilette prominently displayed: mirrors with erotic motifs, perfumes and beauty ointments, strings of pearls and jeweled rings. The female subject was usually depicted grooming herself in full or partial nudity, with her breasts uncovered or visible through a transparent gauze.[40]

To preserve their breasts from stretching and disfiguration, many affluent Renaissance mothers decided not to nurse their children. Both French and Italian upper-class women had been using wet nurses since the late Middle

Ages, when they were usually brought into the baby's home. But increasingly during the Renaissance—except in the case of very wealthy families—it became common practice to send babies to the country for a period of eighteen to twenty-four months. Whether this constituted a form of neglect is difficult to determine, since we do not know how often the child was visited, if at all. For poorer women, paid wet nursing was not an option: throughout Europe, most adult women were probably nursing one or more babies most of the time, their own and those in their care.[41] Given the contraceptive effect of lactation, such widespread breast-feeding may have provided a form of population control among the masses in preindustrial Europe.

Conversely, breast-feeding was not encouraged in upper-class families, where children represented yet another form of wealth. Sons were desired as heirs to family titles, fortune, and properties; daughters were valued for the alliances they would eventually make through marriage. Moreover, in an age when child mortality was very high—it was not uncommon for a family to lose half its children—wealthy women were expected to bear as many children as possible to ensure the survival of an heir.

Husbands often favored the use of a wet nurse, since it was believed that couples should refrain from sexual intercourse while the mother was nursing. It was widely thought that a mother's milk was a form of vaginal blood, transformed from blood to milk as it passed from the womb to the breasts. The agitation of intercourse would have the consequences of corrupting the milk supply, curdling the milk, and might even kill off any fetuses that managed to be conceived. As for the aesthetics of breast-feeding, many husbands did not like the appearance of their wives with a child at the breast. Nursing, a praiseworthy occupation for ancient goddesses and the Virgin Mary, was not considered attractive when practiced by highborn ladies. Many upper-class women, subservient to the eroticized ideal of a youthful bosom, were thus obliged to entrust their babies to wet nurses.

The practice of sending babies away to rural wet nurses was roundly condemned by medical doctors, humanists, priests, preachers, and other moralists throughout Europe. A body of literature sprang up during the Renaissance declaring that it was a mother's duty to breast-feed and that the use of a wet nurse was a risky substitute for the biological mother. Thomas Phaer, whose *Boke of Children* (1545) was the first original treatise in English on childhood diseases, advised women that "it is agreeing to nature so is it also necessary & comly for the own mother to nource the own child."[42] Some moral arbiters went so far as to call the refusal to breast-feed a sin, especially in countries like Germany and England, where Protestant reformers were calling for a more stringent morality.

Others, like the French doctor Ambroise Paré (1509–90), hoped to encourage breast-feeding by describing the physical and emotional pleasures a mother could derive from it. Indeed, in keeping with the Renaissance validation of the erotic, Paré described nursing as a sexually pleasurable act for both mother and child, as in the following passage: "There is a sympathetic connection between breasts and the womb; as the breast is tickled, the womb is aroused and feels a pleasurable titillation, since that little tip of the breast is very sensitive because of the nerves that end there." These enjoyable sensations were interpreted as an inducement "for the female to offer and exhibit her breasts more willingly to the child, who tickles them sweetly with its tongue and mouth, from which the woman derives a great delectation, especially when her milk is abundant."[43]

Paré's medical language is not so very far removed from that of the poets, and the content is surprisingly close to the thinking of twentieth-century Freudians, who emphasize the erotic aspect of breast-feeding, especially for the child. Women themselves who have known the sexual pleasures of breast-feeding have been more reluctant to speak about those sensations until very recent times.

Caught between the doctors who ordered them to breast-feed and their husbands who ordered them to do otherwise, many upper-class mothers in Renaissance France declined to nurse their young. In a century when the erotic potential of the breast began to obscure its maternal function, many ladies were simply not willing to devote themselves fully to their babies, at the expense of their relations with their husbands, not to mention their lovers.

There were two kinds of breasts in Renaissance society: compact "upper-class" breasts intended for male delight, and full, lactating "lower-class" breasts belonging to the women who nursed their own children and those of their affluent employers. A portrait of Gabrielle d'Estrées, the favorite of Henri IV (reigned 1572–1610), vividly represents this hierarchy (fig. 30). Gabrielle was the last of the royal mistresses whose nudity added to the Renaissance gallery of high-culture "pin-ups."

Like Diane de Poitiers, Gabrielle d'Estrées was renowned for her beauty and for the hold she had on the king. Similarly, she, too, acquired colossal wealth and wielded great political power. But there the comparison ends. Diane, twenty years older than Henri II, was elevated in the popular imagination to the ranks of a demigoddess. Gabrielle, twenty years younger than

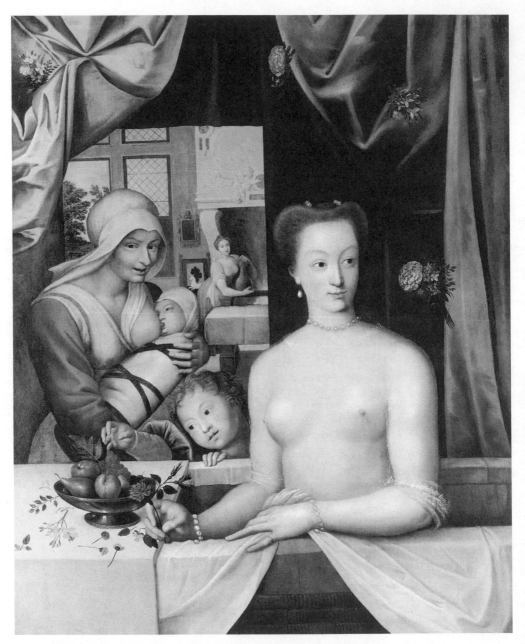

30. Gabrielle d'Estrées at her bath. Early seventeenth century.
Gabrielle d'Estrées, the mistress of Henri IV, displays her "unused" breasts.
In the background, a wet nurse offers a large, globular breast to a babe
in swaddling clothes, one of the three children born to Gabrielle from
her liaison with Henri IV.

Henri IV, was hated by the populace, which considered her little more than a high-class whore. Indeed, the word *putain* (whore) was so often applied to Gabrielle that it became a code word for her in popular songs and poems.[44]

Certainly differences in character accounted, in part, for the different treatment accorded these two women. Diane had lived "virtuously" for more than thirty years before she devoted herself exclusively to the king. Gabrielle, on the contrary, had had at least two lovers before Henri IV set eyes on her in her seventeenth year. Despite her initial repugnance at this "old" suitor of thirty-seven, she was persuaded by influential relatives to submit to his advances. It was to be a venal liaison that made her fabulously rich at a time when most French people were suffering from the devastation caused by the religious wars between Protestants and Catholics. One more reason—and not the least—for her to be so hated. Well might she give the king the children he had not had from his marriage to Marguerite de Valois, from whom he was officially separated. And well might Gabrielle name her sons César and Alexandre, in the hope that they might someday succeed their father.

Just at the moment when it seemed possible that Henri IV, imitating the English King Henry VIII, would follow his heart's desire and set his mistress on the throne, she died in childbirth at the age of twenty-six. Her death was widely viewed as an act of divine punishment intended to free the king from her adulterous grip. The king was devastated. He was seen sobbing with his children and wearing black at court, although it was not the custom for French kings to wear the signs of mourning even for their wives. But within months Henri IV took as his new mistress the fifteen-year-old Henriette d'Entragues.

The advent of a new favorite so soon after Gabrielle's death has caused certain art critics to reinterpret the famous painting that shows Gabrielle d'Estrées nude to the waist with one of her sisters pinching her nipple (fig. 31). According to this new interpretation, the blonde figure on the right is indeed Gabrielle d'Estrées, but the brown-haired woman on the left is none other than Henriette d'Entragues.[45] She tweaks Gabrielle's nipple as a symbolic gesture of succession to the royal bed. The new mistress appropriates the nipple of desire from her predecessor, as if it were an erotic badge. But the ring held in Gabrielle's left hand will go to another. Eighteen months after Gabrielle's unexpected demise, in the autumn of 1600, the king married Marie de Médicis, thus signaling an end to the century during which so many artists had been obsessed with the female breast.

One can say that Renaissance France and Italy made of the female nude, and especially of her breasts, the centerfold of high-culture eroticism. Paint-

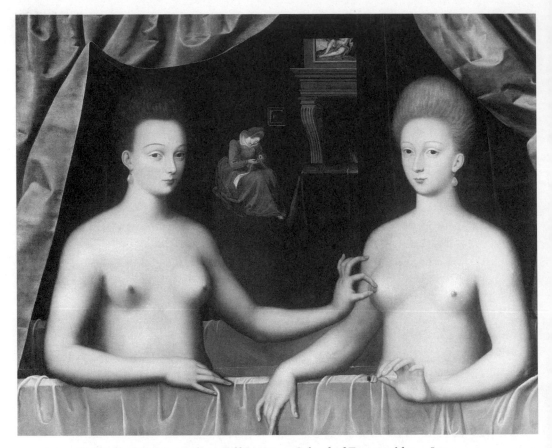

31. Gabrielle d'Estrées and one of her sisters. School of Fontainebleau. Late sixteenth century.

The striking feature of this painting is the dark-haired woman's hand on the blonde woman's breast. But is the woman tweaking Gabrielle d'Estrées's nipple her sister Julienne or Henriette d'Entragues, the woman who succeeded Gabrielle as Henri IV's mistress?

ings of nude women—alone or in company, in nature or in boudoirs—were stimulants to male lubricity. Often, as in the different versions of Titian's *Venus with Cupid and Organist,* a man stares unambiguously at the private parts of an unclothed woman, as if she were on display for purchase.[46] When men and women were portrayed amorously together, she was frequently in some state of undress and he fully clothed, often with his hand on her breast. The meaning of the breast in Renaissance high culture was unequivocally erotic.

While 90 percent of European women functioned as milk bearers, the other 10 percent pampered their breasts and reserved them for their mates. It goes without saying that the mates were usually male, though there were some women, then as always, who preferred lovemaking with members of their own sex. Lesbian love was by no means unknown to medieval and Renaissance communities, even if its reality was hidden away in convents, castles, and cottages as far from the sight of prying neighbors and punitive priests as possible. A rare poem written by a nun to her female lover gives us a unique glimpse of lesbian lovemaking in premodern Europe: "When I recall the kisses you gave me, And how with tender words you caressed my little breasts, I want to die Because I cannot see you. . . . Know that I can bear your absence no longer. Farewell. Remember me."[47] This is the kind of frank physicality, with its specific reference to the pleasures of the breast, that we have not found in other female-authored writing.

Officially, sex between women was a sin "against nature"; in practice, however, such acts between women were rarely punished in and of themselves, and much less so than homosexuality between men.[48] Historian Judith Brown, who unearthed the story of an Italian lesbian nun tried by ecclesiastical authorities for her "immodest acts," found only a handful of similar proceedings in all of Renaissance Europe, alongside the hundreds if not thousands of prosecuted cases of male homosexuality.[49] Surely part of the shock value produced by the portrait of Gabrielle d'Estrées and her bathing companion, whatever the artist's symbolic intent, derived from the fact that two women were shown in an act officially reserved for men or babies. In a culture that glorified the juxtaposition of breast and baby and sanctioned the male hand on the female chest, the portrayal of a woman touching another woman's breast was, at the least, subversive.

Many of the breasts in sixteenth-century art look remarkably similar, as if one slim model had posed for all the paintings in France, and her broad-chested sister for all the ones in Italy. Few women, except for wet nurses, peasants, and witches, are portrayed with very large or pendulous breasts. It is as if ideal breasts were weightless and beyond the laws of gravity. Real women, with normal breasts shaped like pears, melons, or eggplants, might have felt the discomfort experienced by corpulent women today as they confront the cult of thinness.

But for most Renaissance women—that is to say, the vast majority, who lived outside the boundaries of elite society—their breasts had more practical meanings: they had to be covered from the cold and from hostile or rapacious eyes; they had to be ready to serve the needs of their babies, and the needs of other babies suckled out of economic necessity; they had to be treated for abscesses and tumors with remedies that often contained more superstition than medicine; and then, if they were lucky, they might derive pleasure from a lover's caress.

THE EROTIZATION OF THE BREAST in Renaissance France and Italy was linked to the output of poets, painters, and sculptors under the patronage of kings, dukes, princes, and their royal favorites. Across the Channel, in Elizabethan England (1558–1603), there is an absence of nude bodies in the plastic arts, but no lack of breast words on the lips of the poets. The visual display of flesh that had thrived among the Catholic elite was more suspect in Protestant circles, and especially among the Puritans, who tried to counter the frank carnality that had been enjoyed by Elizabeth's father, Henry VIII. From the first years of the reign of Elizabeth I, they pressed for austere modes of dress and chaste sexual behavior. Yet moderate, rather than zealous, Protestantism would triumph under Elizabeth—the most beloved of monarchs, despite her initial handicap as the female offspring of Henry VIII's ill-fated marriage to Anne Boleyn.

When Elizabeth ascended the throne in 1558 at the age of twenty-five, she was red-blonde, tall, thin, and bony. Disinclined to make of her court a showcase for feminine beauty other than her own, she surrounded herself largely with men; the requisite ladies-in-waiting were largely a decorative backdrop for their resplendent queen. During her childhood and youth, Elizabeth had been schooled in personal adversity, including the loss of her mother on the executioner's block and her own experience of imprisonment. She had also learned a crucial lesson from the widespread glory of Diane de Poitiers. The new English monarch would avoid at all costs the tripartite rule Diane had shared with Henri II and Catherine de Médicis, or any other form of divided rule. There was to be only one star in the English firmament, shining as queen, king, and mistress all in one.

To that effect, she projected an androgynous image. Too much femininity would undermine her authority, too much masculinity would make her appear monstrous. She knew how to make the most of both feminine and masculine attributes, as in her oft-quoted 1588 speech to her troops at Tilbury after the defeat of the Spanish Armada, when she proclaimed: "I know I have the body of a weak and feeble woman, but I have the heart and stomach of a

32. Elizabeth I. The "Darnley" Portrait. Unknown artist. Ca. 1575.
Elizabeth I, in her early forties, wears the constricting apparel of her court—the flattened
bodice, inflated sleeves, and starched ruff around her neck.

king." Her womanly weakness was emphasized so as to make her manly strength all the more remarkable. She set the model for that line of "iron ladies," most recently incarnated in Margaret Thatcher, whose role is to keep both "feminine" weakness and "masculine" unruliness in check.[50]

During most of Elizabeth's reign, the body of the "weak and feeble woman" was generally hidden under heavy, elaborate clothing that crushed her chest and left only her hands and face uncovered. This is how she appears in most of her portraits, the purpose of which was to present an image of regal magnificence (fig. 32). In the few paintings that expose her neck and upper bosom, those parts are flattened out so as to suggest a stiff and formal icon, rather than a flesh-and-blood woman. Her breasts would remain, to the end of her life, those of the "virgin queen," married only to her people.

Elizabeth's dresses were cut according to the armorlike style that had been imported from Spain earlier in the century: the upper half of the body was encased in a stiff, boned bodice, which compressed the bust and descended to the waist. The bodice was referred to as a "body" or "pair of bodys," because it was made in two parts, the back and front tied together at the sides. Separate sleeves could be tied to the bodice, and, for the sake of modesty or warmth, a semitransparent gauze scarf or a piece of linen known as a "partlet" could fill in the neckline.[51]

Women of the popular classes wore stiffened bodices laced up the front, as one still sees in the traditional national dress of many European countries, but in upper-class families, the more substantial "body," reinforced with whalebone and wood or metal busks, became mandatory even for girls as young as two and a half or three years. Such garments were so tight and inflexible that they not only flattened women's breasts into boardlike surfaces, but occasionally caused inverted nipples, fractured ribs, and even fatalities.[52]

The crushing of breasts at the highest social levels did not prevent courtier-poets from fantasizing about them. Never were more breast words available, everyday words like "paps," "milk-paps," "teats," and "nipples," as well as the euphemistic "bosom," "bed," and "fountain." "Dugs" had not yet acquired the derogatory connotations that it began to carry in the following century, as evident from Henry VIII's letter to Anne Boleyn expressing his ardent desire to kiss her "pretty dugs."[53] Fruit and floral expressions such as "buds," "strawberries," "apples," and "cherrylets" were especially favored, alongside cosmic and geographical terms like "orbs," "globes," "worlds," and "hemispheres," which reflected the burgeoning interest in astronomy and overseas discovery. Thomas Lodge's *Rosalynde* (1590) may well offer the best mammary two-liner of the period: "Her paps are centres of delight / Her breasts are orbs of heavenly frame."

Breasts were generally presented as objects of beauty and male desire. Their sight entrances, their touch inflames, or, better put by John Lyly, "To feel her breast, her breast doth blow the fire" ("A Counterlove," 1593). They usually appear in literature following a conventional sequence of sight, arousal (his rather than hers), and, occasionally, possession. Yet all three stages were problematic for the Elizabethan, because they collided with philosophic and religious beliefs that judged sensual experience as vastly inferior to the realm of the spirit.

As in France and Italy, blazon writing offered English poets a showcase for the display of female body parts. The English word "blazon" not only derived from the French *blason* (a heraldic shield), but also from the English word "to blaze" (to proclaim as with a trumpet). All of this heraldry and trumpeting made for a kind of poetic publicity: if one could not paint the naked breasts of one's beloved, there was at least the option of verbal display.

Enumerating the glories of one's mistress allowed the poet to assert his property rights and, by sharing them with a male listener, to experience a form of male-to-male bonding. As Freud noted centuries later, the female is often the apex of a triangular relationship, with two males connected to each other through her person. Thus the male poet (or painter) attracts the male reader (or spectator) through the medium of the blazon (or portrait) that honors (or dishonors) the feminine body. Robert Greene's *Menaphon* (1589) provides a fairly standard example:

> Her locks are plighted like the fleece of wool
> . . .
> Her lips are roses over-wash'd with dew
> . . .
> Her paps are like fair apples in the prime,
> As round as orient pearls, as soft as down.

Here breasts call out to three of the five senses—sight, taste, and touch—in a long list of well-worn analogies.

Edmund Spenser (1552–99), equating female parts with different flowers, created an anatomical English garden in his sonnet 64:

> Her lips did smell like unto Gillyflowers;
>> Her ruddy cheekes like unto Roses red;
>> Her snowy broews like budded Bellamours;
>> Her lovely eyes like Pinks but newly spread;
> Her goodly bosom like a Strawberry bed;
>> Her neck like to a bunch of Columbines;
>> Her breast like lilies, ere their leaves be shed;
> Her nipples like young-blossomed Jessamines.

Elsewhere he carried his similes from the garden to the kitchen. His "Epithalamion"—a poem celebrating marriage—presented the bride in frankly oral terms, with the breasts offering the *pièce de résistance* in a menu of edible delights:

> Her cheeks like apples which the sun hath rudded,
> Her lips like cherries charming men to bite,
> Her breasts like to a bowl of cream uncrudded,
> Her paps like lilies budded.

Shakespeare, who composed his share of blazons, also knew how to make fun of them. His Sonnet 130 turns the convention around to the advantage of his own beloved:

> My mistress' eyes are nothing like the sun;
> Coral is far more red than her lips' red;
> If snow be white, why then her breasts are dun;
>
> . . .
>
>> And yet, by heaven, I think my love as rare
>> As any she belied with false compare.

The neo-Platonic tradition that Shakespeare and his fellow Elizabethans had inherited required that the beloved be both beautiful and virtuous, her virtue consisting primarily of a steadfast refusal to gratify male desire. Well might the sight of her eyes, lips, and breasts arouse his senses: her role was to lead him beyond mere appetite to an appreciation of her soul.

No one struggled more verbally with the conflict between sexual desire and Christian virtue than Sir Philip Sidney (1554–86) in *Astrophel and Stella*. To the radiant Stella he complained: ". . . while thy beautie drawes the heart to love, . . . Desire still cries, 'give me some food.' " Beauty, which should lead to chaste admiration according to the conventions of courtly love, founders on the shoal of lust. For the writer whose inner state was mirrored in this poem, the eroticized female body triggered an experience of conflict that only the sacrament of marriage could satisfactorily resolve.

Sight, then, is a dangerous sense when it fixes on a female form, dangerous for the male in terms of his psychological well-being, and even more dangerous for the woman who risks losing her "virtue" and even her life. Literary critic Nancy Vickers has analyzed the progression from gazing to rape that occurs in certain Elizabethan texts.[54] She cites one powerful example from Shakespeare's *Rape of Lucrece*, when the brutal hero Tarquin finds Lucrece asleep and lays his lustful hand "On her bare breast, the heart of all her land." Tarquin quickly violates Lucrece, leaving her "round turrets destitute and pale." However dazzling the language, the subject is nothing more nor less than rape at the hands of a ruthless predator.

Just as Shakespeare saw the female body as a site to be conquered and ravaged, so too Renaissance explorers viewed the New World as virgin territory awaiting the penetration of a robust male. The network of associations between woman's body and the conquerable earth was firmly entrenched in the psyche of that ultimate explorer, Christopher Columbus, as seen in his journal entries. One entry compares the earth to a pear-shaped woman's breast, at one part of which "was placed something *like a woman's nipple [una teta de muger]*."[55] Penned in 1498, when Columbus had first sighted the landmass of South America, these words present the New World as the best of the breast—an "Edenic nipple" projecting out from a mammary globe.[56]

The identification of woman as land has a very long history. Renaissance writers drew from classical antiquity the equation of woman and Nature, with woman often placed in Arcadian settings or in a garden, or becoming the garden herself. In Elizabethan poetry, the words "land" and "garden" conventionally referred to the female body, with "hills" and "mountains" evoking the breasts, and "dale" the cleavage between the breasts.

Michael Drayton, for example, transformed his mistress's chest into a pastoral landscape replete with meadows and rivers: "Thy full and youthful breasts, which, in their meadowy pride / Are branch'd with rivery veines meander-like that glide." Conversely, it was also common to imbue Nature with mother's milk, as in Sir Walter Raleigh's memorable lines: "Nature, that wash'd her hands in milk / And had forgot to dry them." But the British were never able to immerse themselves completely in the Mediterranean picture of woman as beneficent Nature; too long, too entrenched was the tradition of Nordic-Christian hostility to sensual delight.

Such hostility sometimes erupted in vilification or mutilation of the female body. Like the mysogynistic underside of French art and poetry, so, too, Elizabethan poetry provided a medium through which men could express their negative feelings toward feminine flesh. Consider Shakespeare as a prime example. The women in his plays are frequently attacked in the breast, both literally and figuratively. From the tragic misunderstandings of *Romeo and Juliet* ("This dagger hath mista'en . . . / And is mis-sheathed in my daughter's bosom!") to the serpent-breast suicide of *Antony and Cleopatra* ("Here on her breast there is a vent of blood"), the list of wounds inflicted to the breast is long and imaginative. Violation, suicide, and murder occur at the very locus of male desire, as if the mutilation of the breast would put an end to his psychic dissonance. Sometimes the breast attack is merely metaphoric, though nonetheless potent, as in these ominous words about Hamlet's mother: ". . . leave her to heaven / And to those thorns that in her bosom lodge / To prick and sting her."

Shakespeare's most forceful use of negative breast imagery is found in *Macbeth*, in connection with Lady's Macbeth's "unnatural" manliness. Who can forget her enraged speech to Macbeth urging him to kill the king?

> . . . I have given suck, and know
> How tender 'tis to love the babe that milks me;
> I would while it was smiling in my face
> Have plucked my nipple from his boneless gums
> And dashed the brains out, had I so sworn as you
> Have done to this.

Macbeth, she fears, is "too full of the milk of human kindness" to perform the deed that would grant him the crown. Murder, she reflects, requires a different kind of nourishment: "Come to my woman's breasts / And take my milk for gall. . . ." According to long-held notions that maternal milk carried with it the mother's character traits, Lady Macbeth would have conveyed to her offspring (or her husband) her own vengeful nature.

This portrait of a woman wishing to transform her milk into gall so as to incite her husband to murder, or dashing out the brains of her nursing babe for fear of cowardice, betrays a primitive fear that the nurturant breast can change into an agent of destruction. Poison and gall become symbolic substitutes for milk—toxic fluids at the very heart of femininity. Lurking beneath the erotic and the maternal body lies the figure of the warrior woman—Amazon or Lady Macbeth—who strikes terror in the hearts of men.

Unfortunately, there are no Englishwomen's poems from this period that offer an alternative perspective on the female body. Two, however, attributed to none other than Queen Elizabeth, do indeed refer to the breast, though not as a site of physical arousal. As in the poetry of the two Frenchwomen cited earlier, the breast is equated with the heart, offering an internal and emotional, rather than external and sensual, view. In the following poem, the breast is described as tender and vulnerable, an easy mark for Cupid's arrows or reproaches, and here it is the latter, for Elizabeth has scorned love's alliances and lived to regret it, at least in poetry:

> When I was fair and young, and favor graced me,
>   Of many was I sought, their mistress for to be.
>   But I did scorn them all, and answered them therefore,
>   "Go, go, go, seek some otherwhere,
>   Importune me no more!"
>
> . . .
>
> Then spake fair Venus's son, that proud victorious boy,
>   And said, "Fine dame, since that you be so coy,
>   I will pluck your plumes that you shall say no more,
>   "Go, go, go seek some otherwhere,
>   Importune me no more!"
>
> When he had spake these words, such change grew in my breast
>   That neither night nor day since that I could take
>   any rest.
>   Then lo! I did repent that I had said before,
>   "Go, go, go, seek some otherwhere,
>   Importune me no more!"

This female lament of love's lost opportunities must, of course, be seen within the context of a male poetic discourse: men had been telling women for more than a century to gather their rosebuds while they may, and Elizabeth, having lived beyond the advantages of youth, seems to be saying they were right. On the other hand, this poem may be nothing more than a conventional bow toward the dominant discourse. Elizabeth reigned into her seventieth year, and nothing—no personal attachment or pain within her breast—ever eclipsed the role she had set for herself as both king and queen, without the interference of a connubial prince who might have undermined her authority.

Another poem attributed to Elizabeth, "On Monsieur's Departure," expresses the queen's sadness after the visit of one of her suitors. Whether or not she truly regretted his absence is open to conjecture, yet one verse, at least, sounds authentic: "No means I've found to rid him from my breast." Like Louise Labé, Elizabeth conceptualized the breast internally as the seat of pain and regret. This is a far cry from the ripe apples and round turrets, ivory globes and Orient pearls, that proliferated among male poets, one might even say for poets. Were their poems really intended to be read by the women whose bodies they celebrated?

One thing is sure: for the first time in history, there was a reading public in much of Europe that extended beyond a thin upper crust. With the invention of the printing press in fifteenth-century Germany followed by Caxton's English editions, English men and women began to have greater access to the published word. Between 1500 and 1600, there was a large increase in reading, due not only to the development of printing but also to the spread of the Protestant Reformation, which encouraged Bible reading.

In England, book ownership extended beyond the titled and propertied few to include members of a rising middle class. Though more men were able to read than women, female readers had reached such numbers by the last quarter of the sixteenth century that many authors were making an open appeal to them.[57] Among authors targeting women as their audience, one finds the names of John Lyly, Thomas Lodge, and Robert Greene—all cited above for their mammary effusions. Women read all sorts of literature, ranging from chivalric romances to books of piety, and were by no means untouched by the erotic outpourings of the poets. They knew that their breasts were objects of desire, just as twentieth-century women recognize their erotic value from magazine covers, television, film, advertising, and jokes. Some undoubtedly flaunted them in loosely laced bodices, much to the dismay of churchmen who continued to rail against the "gates of Hell." Since full breasts were considered a sign of fertility and a potential source of milk, it would have been in the interest of nubile women, especially in the country, to let their healthy breasts be seen.

During the Elizabethan period, most British infants were breast-fed at home by their mothers, though many affluent women in England and Scotland did employ wet nurses.[58] There were significant differences between fundamentalist Protestants, who regarded the practice of wet nursing as sinful, and Catholics, who did not. Puritan sermons and tracts promulgated the view that women who did not breast-feed were derelict in their duties toward their children and toward God. Consequently, women of the stricter Protestant sects were more likely to breast-feed their children than were Catholics and moderate Protestants.

Some mothers were undoubtedly obliged to forgo breast-feeding on the grounds of ill health. Others employed wet nurses as a status symbol. One historian, commenting on the increased use of wet nursing among the wealthy in the late sixteenth and early seventeenth centuries, concluded that "Tudor and Stuart ladies so rarely breastfed their babies that to do so was interpreted as a mark of poverty, or an out-of-the ordinary commitment to the child."[59] Another constraint came from authoritarian husbands, who forbade their wives to breast-feed because it interfered with sex.[60] With the increased accent on the erotic rather than the maternal breast, many genteel women had to choose between giving their breasts to their husbands or their infants. Unfortunately, Elizabethan women themselves have left scant evidence of their own feelings on these matters.

In the seventeenth century, British women began to be more outspoken. Several women have left testimonials, both in private letters and published works, expressing their support of breast-feeding. Among them, Elizabeth Clinton (1574–1630?) traced this "duty" to biblical precedent: "Now who should deny the own mother's suckling of their own children to be their duty since every godly matron hath walked in these steps before them: Eve, the mother of all the living; Sarah, the mother of all the faithful; Hannah, so graciously heard of God; Mary, blessed among women . . ." (*The Countess of Lincoln's Nurserie*, 1622). No less a person than Queen Anne, the wife of James I (1566–1625), lined up with the breast-feeders, though her personal example was based more on a sense of difference from other women than similarity with them. Indeed, she argued against wet nursing on the grounds that she did not want her royal child to imbibe a wet nurse's base characteristics along with her milk: "Will I let my child, the child of a king, suck the milk of a subject and mingle the royal blood with the blood of a servant?"[61] Whatever their reasons, some high-status women became vocal adherents of maternal breast-feeding in an effort to persuade other mothers to follow their lead.

Another subject on which Englishwomen became more outspoken concerned their erotic feelings. This represented a daring incursion into what had traditionally been male territory. One poet, known as "Eliza," wrote an ironic address titled "To a Friend for Her Naked Breasts." In it she praises her friend for uncovering her breasts, in keeping with a short-lived fashion. But the deeper meaning of the poem suggests that her friend hoped to seduce "some wanton Lover." Be careful, says the poet, of that all-seeing God, "Lest he through your bare breast see sin, / And punish you for what's within" (*Eliza's Babes*, 1652).

A more famous seventeenth-century woman poet and playwright, Aphra Behn (1640–89), advanced the cause of female eroticism as no woman in the English tradition had done before her. This earned her the reputation of being a "lewd harlot."[62] In her poem "On a Juniper-Tree, Cut Down to Make Busks," she presented a conventional picture of the shepherdess yielding to the shepherd, "His panting Breast, to hers now join'd," with the ironic twist that the tree shading the couple during their amorous rapture would ultimately be felled and made into busks for women's corsets. This was thoroughly in keeping with the frivolous and sometime cynical tone that crept toward the center of seventeenth-century breast culture. The ladies of the English Restoration (1660–88) and the French court of Louis XIV (1643–1715) may have been entertained, but I suspect that some just heaved their bosoms with a weary sigh as they listened to the ironic monologues, clever madrigals, and cerebral enigmas devoted to their chests.

A follower of Aphra Behn known as "Ephelia" came a little closer to expressing authentic female desire in her poem "Love's first Approach." Assuming the position of the viewer rather than the viewed, she remembered how *his* looks had affected *her* heart, and pleaded with the deity of Love "To make his frozen Breast as warm as mine" (*Female Poems*, 1679). Here both male and female breasts offer reciprocal possibilities.

The persistence of competing claims on the bosom deriving from erotic as well as maternal sources can be summed up by two mid-seventeenth-century English texts. The first are lines from "Upon Julia's Breasts" by the Cavalier poet Robert Herrick (1591–1674):

> Display thy breasts, my Julia—there let me
> Behold the circummortal purity:
> Between whose glories, there my lips I'll lay,
> Ravished in that fair *Via Lactea*.

The second is a tombstone that bears these words:

IN MEMORYE
OF ESSEX COVNTESSE OF MANCHESTER
DAUGHTER TO S THOMAS CHEEKE
& WIFE TO EDWARD EARLE OF
MANCHESTER
SHEE DYED THE 28 OF SEPTEMBER
ANN DOM 1658 & LEFT
8 CHILDREN 6 SONNS &
2 DAVGHTERS 7 OF THEM
SHEE NURSED WITH HER OWNE BRESTS
Her children shall rise up & call
her blessed.[63]

The Renaissance erotization of the breast must be understood within the context of a new wave of sexual liberation, a phenomenon that has subsequently crested several times.[64] For the first time in Judeo-Christian history, man, rather than God, was proclaimed as the measure of all things. The human body took precedence over the divine body, and physical pleasures were granted the status of universal rights. Once the Italians and French had caught the fever, all of Europe became infected. Even the German states, if we are to believe the fulminations of Luther, became hotbeds of illicit sexual behavior: "The women and girls," he asserted, "have begun to go bare before and behind, and there is no one to punish or correct them."[65]

Between the fourteenth century, when the Italian Madonna took out one miniature breast as a symbol of divine nurturance, and the sixteenth century, when nude breasts proliferated in painting and poetry, Europe underwent a radical social and cultural revolution. The old religious worldview succumbed to secular appetites, whetted by new political, economic, and geographic realities. The breast became yet one more object to be conquered by enterprising men, one more object to be wrested from the hands of priests and preachers, not to mention women and babies. Kings, courtiers, painters, poets, explorers, and pornographers—all believed they had a claim to the breast. Each thought of himself, in some way, as its owner. Women's breasts, shorn of their religious associations, became blatant emblems of male desire. The hand on the breast—a common motif in Renaissance art—spoke for the sense of possession that men believed was their due.

In allegorical paintings devoted to the five senses, it was standard practice throughout Europe to represent the sense of touch by a male hand on a fe-

33. Hans Baldung Grien. *Old Man and Young Woman.* 1507.
The old man proudly places his hand on the young woman's breast, while she
slips her hand into his purse.

male breast. Among German artists, the heterosexual couple was frequently
depicted as an old man and a young woman, with his hand on her breast and
her hand in his purse (fig. 33). Such works injected a moralistic message into
erotic art, equally condemning his lust and her venality.[66] French and Italian
paintings teemed with nude goddesses and nymphs caressed by gods and cu-
pids—any area above the waist was considered fair play. (There was also a
market for pornography, which had no bodily barriers.)

That men should place their hands on women's breasts as a sign of possession and dominance was not out of keeping with the Christian injunction for
wives to be subservient to their husbands—an injunction that was generally interpreted as "natural" law.[67] Historian Joan Kelly Gadol, relying largely on Italian sources, argued that women lost ground during the Renaissance, because,
though their beauty inspired love, "the lover, the agent, was man."[68] But
French and English sources suggest a somewhat less negative reality. We cannot assume that women were necessarily passive in their intimate relations. For
one thing, whatever the public discourse, we can never know what transpired
in the privacy of the bedroom and the bower. Given the delicious erogenous
pleasure one can experience when the breasts and nipples are stimulated, it is
likely that many women then, as now, enjoyed the hand on the breast, and
probably guided its explorations, with or without the sanction of marriage.

As for agency in a more public arena, there were indeed some elite
women who knew how to take advantage of the magnetic force issuing from
their bodies so as to draw themselves to the center of court life and the back-
stairs of government. Their eroticized breasts were symbols of power, as they
continue to be today in many Western nations. Paradoxically—if we are to believe the poets—women, especially Englishwomen, were expected to inspire
men's love through the beauty of their bodies, while convincing them that
what really mattered was their souls. It must have been a difficult balancing
act to attract and repel in just the right doses, or, in breast language, to reveal
and conceal in just the right amount.[69] Surely Joan Kelly Gadol is right in
maintaining that the Renaissance was not the same for women as for men,
and it is indeed possible that women lost some of the power that medieval
courtly love had conferred upon them at the highest levels, yet we have no
reason to believe they were helpless in the face of men's desires. Except in the
case of outright rape, many women had some say in determining whether
they would or would not, and with whom.

Since the late Middle Ages, the cult of the erotic breast has steadily
marked Western civilization. The only notable change over time has been a
transformation in the ideal volume, shape, or function. Medieval painters
and poets expressed a preference for small breasts, perched high above a large
stomach suggesting pregnancy. The French carried their preference for small
breasts into the late sixteenth century, along with slim, elongated bodies. The
Italians of the high Renaissance allowed for wider chests and somewhat fuller
hips and thighs. Elizabethan men seem to have been less concerned with

size than with oral satisfaction: breasts called up images of apples, cream, and milk, or bountiful gardens.

On the whole, since the late Renaissance the trend in male preference has favored larger breasts. The small, pubescent mounds of the late Middle Ages have given way, five hundred years later, to the Jane Russells of the 1950s, the Carol Dodas of the 1970s, and the Cindy Crawfords of the 1990s. Women eager to exploit this male ideal have enlarged their bosoms with padded bras and silicone implants, the latter often causing them to lose the erogenous sensations which contributed to the sexual value of the breast in the first place.

Historically speaking, the erotization of women's breasts has been predominantly a male affair. A history based on the records of women's subjective experiences would look very different, but unfortunately such records are virtually nonexistent before relatively recent times. Certain conventions were established during the Renaissance that have by no means disappeared from Western civilization. In the graphic arts and in literature, breasts were offered up for the pleasure of a male viewer or reader, with the intent of arousing him, not her. When breasts became overeroticized, their sexual meaning began to overshadow their maternal meaning. The fight to restore the breast's nurturant significance would be taken up at regular intervals during the centuries to come by individuals and groups opposed to the absolute reign of the sexualized breast.

Three

THE DOMESTIC BREAST:
A DUTCH INTERLUDE

T H E N E T H E R L A N D S in the seventeenth century represented, in the felicitous words of Simon Schama, an "embarrassment of riches."[1] Having at last thrown off the yoke of Spanish rule and formed a republic in 1581, the new nation rose quickly to a level of prosperity that astonished even its own inhabitants. The young commonwealth—a democratic exception among rival kingdoms like France, England, and Spain—soon became known for its thriving commerce, medical progress, political freedom, religious tolerance, cultural productivity, and the much-vaunted Dutch qualities of cleanliness and thrift. Many of these attributes were present in the breast culture that flourished during the Dutch golden age.

To think about the breast in the Netherlands, we have to imagine a very different setting from those we have encountered thus far. We must leave behind all memories of pagan shrines and Catholic churches, allegorical gardens and eroticized boudoirs, and move into the orderly space of a bourgeois household. Our eyes must adjust to the oblique light filtering through a lead-paned window to reveal—but scarcely—a few choice objects of everyday use: a metal pitcher, a sturdy chair, a basket or spinning wheel. In front of the fireplace sits a mother holding a baby, who sucks contentedly at her breast. We have come upon a scene of simple domestic happiness.

Pieter de Hooch's *Woman Nursing an Infant, with a Child* helps us visualize that scene (fig. 34). From the light of an overhead window, we see a burgher mother gazing with love at her nursing babe. The emphasis is less on the breast itself, which is hardly seen, than on the aura of calm sweetness generated by the act of suckling. Everything is as it should be in this idealized picture of familial harmony.

It is impossible to know the extent to which this kind of painting mirrored real domestic life. As art historian Wayne Franits has shown, both art and literature from this period served the purpose of providing guides to the upbringing of virtuous children and the conduct of righteous adults.[2] Such works presented children as gifts from the Almighty, to be raised in an atmosphere that would engender religious piety and social stability. The home was the principal setting for molding children according to this lofty vision, followed by the church and the school. And in the home, it was the duty of the

34. Pieter de Hooch. *Woman Nursing an Infant, with a Child.* 1658–60.
A Dutch mother nurses a bonneted infant, flanked on one side by an older child and a dog, the symbol of fidelity.

mother to nurture her offspring in every respect—from their first drops of milk to their first trusting prayers.

Dutch medical, religious, and moral authorities were all staunch advocates of maternal breast-feeding. As in England, strict Protestants were the most outspoken, for they believed that a nursing mother was pleasing to God and that a woman who refused to nurse was an abomination in the eyes of the Lord. A mother was expected to nurse the baby to whom she had given birth, according to the ancient notion that Nature nourishes what it creates. One of the aphorisms of the prolific writer and magistrate Jacob Cats (1577–1660) summed up this attitude:

> One who bears her children is a mother in part,
> But she who nurses her children is a mother at heart.[3]

The true mother was the one who nursed her babe. More than any other factor, maternal nursing was *een merck-teecken van een vrome Vrouwe*—the hallmark of a pious mother.[4]

Medical treatises added their weight to the debate. Following the contemporary belief that maternal milk was formed from the blood that had nourished the fetus in the womb, it was considered important for the baby to continue imbibing the same substance—i.e., the same mother's blood that had been transformed into milk. There were many fears surrounding the "blood/milk" of a stranger, not the least of which was the fear that the baby would acquire the wet nurse's personality traits along with her milk. Jacob Cats expressed this widespread view in one of his many doggerel pronouncements: "How many a nice child, healthy and lively, / Has lost its own nature through a wicked wet nurse!"[5] The fear of the wet nurse's negative influence was certainly a standard theme in seventeenth-century Dutch moral and medical literature, as it was in England and France.

What is more difficult to determine is whether Dutch mothers actually employed wet nurses any less than their English, French, and Italian counterparts. At least one authority believes that wet nursing was less common in the Netherlands and that Dutch families might have provided an exception to the extremely high infant-mortality rates found in countries where infants were regularly farmed out to wet nurses.[6] But other authorities disagree. In the absence of statistics on this subject, we must fall back upon such cultural artifacts as literature and paintings, which at least offer glimpses of what was distinctive in Dutch society, as compared with the rest of Europe.

The Dutch vision of the domestic breast found in a poem by Jacob Cats offers a clear contrast with the erotic paeans found at this time in France and England:

> Employ O young wife, your precious gifts
> Give the noble suck to refresh your little fruit
> There is nothing an upright man would rather see
> Than his dear wife bid the child to the teat
> This bosom that you carry, so swollen up with life
> So finely wrought, as if't were ivory orbs.[7]

Despite the by-now banal metaphor of "ivory orbs" and the undertones of subversive sexuality, there are distinctly new meanings attached to the bosom. The male figure in the poem entreating his "dear wife" to give suck is by no means a selfish lover concerned with his own pleasure, and therefore hostile to the notion of lactation, since it was commonly believed that sexual activity would curdle a nursing woman's milk. He is a husband and a father, an "upright man" dedicated to the well-being of his child and, by extension, to the community of burghers of which they were a part. The family unit, seen as a microcosm of the larger political macrocosm, was judged to be best served when the mother undertook to breast-feed with the same dedication she brought to her rigorous housecleaning. Naturally, her husband was expected to support this vital activity and to share the parental love symbolized by the act of suckling. We are a century removed from the "little ball of ivory" that titillated Marot, and a century ahead of the Rousseauist breast that would ostensibly return a corrupt society to Nature and good citizenship.

Nowhere is the Dutch respect for the maternal breast more evident than in its art. Pieter de Hooch was only one of many popular artists who made the nursing mother a favorite theme in the countless genre paintings they produced for the Dutch market. These found their way into affluent and even less affluent bourgeois homes, reflecting the values of a society that prized pictures of its own well-being. Only in seventeenth-century Holland could one find a hundred paintings, or more, in a middle-class home, with preference given to realistic scenes from everyday life.[8] Many of these paintings show mothers with their breasts exposed, not only while they were nursing but before and after they suckled. A burgher woman is shown chatting with a young boy outside her window, a peasant woman sits outdoors with two children—each woman with an uncovered breast and obviously at ease. As long as there was a baby in the picture, the naked breast needed no other excuse.

Especially in the Protestant north, where the Catholic Madonna was no longer considered a fitting subject, Dutch painters sought inspiration from real-life mothers and infants in their natural settings: nursing, eating, drinking, dressing, playing, even wiping the baby's bottom found their way into Dutch art. This thematic transition from the sacred to the secular mother was consecrated in the Netherlands a full century before it emerged in other European countries.

Schama points out that the Dutch abolished images of the Virgin and Child from their churches "only to reinstate them . . . as simple nursing mothers in paintings of church interiors."[9] The nursing mothers in these paintings are usually tiny figures, dwarfed by the edifices that surround them. One has to look very hard to find the mother discreetly nursing at the foot of a thick church pillar, twenty times her size. Many of these paintings were hung within real churches as semireligious icons (fig. 35). The message for the Protestant Dutch would have been clear: what was worthy of worship was not the celestial Queen, but the natural act of piety that a flesh-and-blood mother performed when she breast-fed and cared for her young.

Nursing in Dutch art, as in life, was always understood within the context of the larger social unit. What the mother did or did not do was enacted according to strictly gendered family roles. A 1632 illustration in one of Jacob Cats's books shows the mother breast-feeding while the small daughter at her feet spanks her doll and the father instructs his son.[10] The family was best served, so said the picture, when females took care of children's physical needs, and males transmitted learning. A lower social level is exemplified by such paintings as Pietr van Slingeland's *The Carpenter's Family* (London, Collection of Her Majesty the Queen), in which the mother nursed and the father exercised his craft in the back room.[11] Parental duties were clearly sex-segregated: the father provided for his family by practicing his trade, the mother provided the very substance of her body. Though both parents were responsible for the moral training of their offspring, the mother carried the major burden for the child's first years. Mothers were then, as they are today, the primary parents of infants. A proper upbringing was supposed to begin with the mother's milk and to flourish within a carefully controlled environment distinguished by the homely virtues of modesty and affection.

35. School of Gerard Houchgeest. *Church Interior with Nursing Mother.* Mid-seventeenth century.

One has to look very hard to see the nursing mother seated at the base of a towering column.

36. Paulus Moreelse. Sophie Hedwig, countess of Nassau-
Dietz, duchess of Brunswick-Wolfenbüttel, portrayed as
Caritas (Charity). 1621.
In a pose that is reminiscent of the nursing Madonna and
symbolizes Charity, Sophie Hedwig presses two fingers around
the nipple of her naked breast to facilitate the flow of milk.

A number of Dutch artworks from this period presented suckling as synonymous with love. Herman Saftleven's engraving of a peasant woman nursing a healthy-looking babe bears the one-line inscription *Liefde* (*Love*).[12] No
less a person than Sophie Hedwig, the duchess of Brunswick-Wolfenbüttel,
commissioned a Dutch painter to portray her with her breast exposed in the
presence of her three sons, to symbolize Caritas—Charity (fig. 36). Though
religious images of anonymous nursing mothers representing the theological
virtue of Charity were common, it was rare for a real-life person—especially
a duchess—to be pictured in this manner.

More humble mothers with babies at the breast were also portrayed allegorically, often with the didactic intent of contrasting breast milk to lesser forms

of sustenance. Art historian Mary Durantini has drawn attention to paintings that show a baby distracted from nursing by the sight or sound of a rattle, or another frivolous object, in the hands of someone outside the mother-baby dyad.[13] She also cites the work of Johannes a Castro in his *Zedighe Sinne-beelden* (1694), where the mother is shown offering the baby a choice between the rattle and the breast, while the accompanying text compares the mother's breast to the spiritual nourishment of God. It was the mother's job to see that the baby was not seduced by trivial temptations and drawn away from her bosom, since the breast was considered the fount of religious and moral edification.

Mothers were also responsible for the management of all aspects of the Dutch home, which was known for its cleanliness and thrift. The great Dutch historian Johan Huizinga was proud to claim cleanliness as a national quality, noting that the Dutch word *schoon* evokes not only cleanliness but also purity and beauty.[14] It also conveys the sense of the English word "proper." A Dutch home worthy of being called *schoon* would begin at a milky-white maternal breast and radiate cleanliness to every nook and cranny, including the proverbially immaculate stoop in front of the house. The mother was enjoined to breast-feed with the same rigorous concern for cleanliness and thrift that she brought to her other domestic chores, such as sweeping, sewing, spinning, and churning. Thrift, we recall, means frugal economic management, and what could be more "thrifty" than using the mother's own milk instead of paying for an outside source? Of course, proponents of maternal breast-feeding did not base their arguments on the economic benefits provided by a nursing mother's milk; they came up with far more grandiloquent medical, religious, social, and moral reasons. Yet it might not have escaped the notice of Dutch homemakers and their husbands that it was an unnecessary expense to pay for a wet nurse when one already had a free flow of milk in the biological mother's breasts.

Though it is true that Dutch women were nominally under the control of fathers and husbands, it is also true that they exercised a great deal of authority within the domestic realm. Submission to the paterfamilias often seems to have been diluted by a good dose of affection, and, in the case of wives, by an ethos of mutuality way ahead of the ideal of companionate marriage that would be honored in England and France a century later.

The lovely painting by Rembrandt of *The Couple*, also known as *The Jewish Bride*, is a good example of this admixture of paternalism and mutuality (fig. 37). The husband's hand on his wife's chest can certainly be interpreted as the mark of possession, yet the feeling the painting exudes is unlike any of the other "hand-on-the-breast" paintings we have seen. There is a sense of sharing rather than ownership, a gentle aura of intimacy and friendship, tenderness and respect, which suggests that the breast to be shared also contains a heart.

Men's hands on women's breasts are found in any number of Dutch paintings representing all classes of society. Among respectable folk like the Jewish couple, the gesture is affectionate rather than overtly sensual or lustful. Sometimes the woman returns the caress by placing her hand on the man's hand or face. But in scenes representing lower-class people, many of which take place in taverns, the hand on the breast is part of the general atmosphere of sexual license. A leering youth reaches his hand inside the cleavage of a rustic woman while a group of appreciative revelers eggs him on, or an older man makes a suggestive offer to a buxom lass by pointing to her breasts. In such scenes, the woman usually enters gamely into the play.

Even scenes with prostitutes are notable for the playful reciprocity between woman and client. Vermeer's *Procuress*, for example (fig. 38), which shows a male hand cupping a female breast, bespeaks an ease and familiarity

37. Rembrandt van Ryn. *The Jewish Bride*. 1665–67.
The male hand on the female breast in this portrait of a respectable bourgeois couple is a sign of companionate affection.

38. Jan Vermeer.
The Procuress. Mid-
seventeenth century.

Vermeer's procuress holds
up her palm to receive her
client's money with the
same self-assurance, and
lack of guilt, she would
manifest if she were lifting
up a pitcher of milk.

between the brothel patron and the mistress of the establishment that is not
so far removed from the mutuality of Rembrandt's Jewish couple. In the
Netherlands, prostitutes were allowed to have a "homey" side, even a maternal aspect, despite the public condemnation of their trade. The respectable
burghers who administered their cities conceded in private that prostitution
was a practical necessity, especially in the case of lustful sailors arriving in
Dutch ports after heterosexless months on the high seas.

More often, it is true, procuresses—former prostitutes who have taken on
the management of younger ones—were represented in art as unsavory creatures: old, ugly, and avaricious. And younger prostitutes were frequently depicted as licentious, their ample breasts overflowing from low-cut bodices,
their sensual appetites equal to those of their male clients. Many Dutch genre
paintings leave little to the imagination, suggesting the sensual excesses that
lurked beneath or beyond bourgeois sobriety and that proper Dutch society
was anxious to disown.

When one spends any length of time among seventeenth-century Dutch
paintings, one comes away with a dizzying sense of contradiction. On the one

hand, there are all those portraits of stolid citizens, ruffed and capped, the men administering the world and the women dutifully tending their households. These burghers are models of sobriety and social harmony. On the other hand, there are hundreds of scenes that portray the Dutch in less dignified poses—scenes of brawling and merrymaking, men and women carousing and drinking, flirting and pawing each other, children and cats and dogs underfoot and out of control. Half of the people are made to look like village idiots. What does this say about Dutch society? Was it so heavily repressed by its Protestant denial of erotic pleasure and its heavy work ethic that all manner of license had to be projected onto the lower classes? The bourgeoisie seems to have found the depiction of sexual desire acceptable only when it was restricted to a different social milieu.

The world of Jan Steen (1626–79) has become synonymous with the unruly revelry enjoyed by members of the popular classes. He shows common folk carrying on in their homes and taverns, oblivious to the moral standards

39. Jan Steen. *As the Old Sing (Soo de Ouden Songen)*. Mid-seventeenth century. The rosy breast at the center of this roisterous scene is in danger of being corrupted by bad company.

of more proper folk. Yet there is often a moral hiding within the drunken play. A skull recalling death or a boy blowing bubbles to evoke the adage that "man is a bubble" reverses the painting's surface meaning: the viewer is reminded that such merrymaking is only an illusory bulwark against deeper, more tragic realities.[15]

Several of Steen's paintings bear the title *Soo de Ouden Songen* (*As the Old Sing, So the Young Chirp*), which carries the implicit message that children will follow the bad example of their elders. These works show adults and children holding up glasses, jugs, and pipes. Some of the revelers play flutes or bagpipes. Everyone seems to have something in or near the mouth. And in the very center of one very "oral" painting (fig. 39) is the uncovered globular breast of a mother, who is holding a fat baby, who is holding a clay pipe. The fully exposed breast seems out of place in such a ribald setting. On one level, it could be accounted for as just another expression of the license permitted in the inebriated world of Jan Steen. But at a deeper level, the painting contrasts the "natural" breast—the original source of sustenance and moral development—with the "unnatural" substances that have befuddled the minds of Steen's tipplers and smokers. From this moralistic point of view, one is well advised to keep the breast away from corrupting influences.

Popular literature also warned that the breast could be perverted for carnal purposes. Future prostitutes were portrayed in their earlier lives as housemaids, slyly exposing their bosoms as they went about their work so as to snare male family members. A poem begins: "My master's eldest son was always pawing at my breasts. . . ."[16] The home, if not managed with scrupulous surveillance, could become a way-station to the brothel. Such texts were intended to warn working-class young women against the temptations of the flesh and the irreparable loss of virginity. They also served as warnings to middle- and upper-class young men to resist lower-class temptations.

If one considers only their size, those fleshly temptations were very great indeed: Dutch women had the reputation for very hefty bosoms. By midcentury, Dutch and Flemish women began to inspire a totally new breast ideal among the artists. For the first time in art history since the ancient goddesses, big breasts became fashionable. The Flemish painter Rubens (1577–1640) launched the mode of cushiony women, and after his death, other Dutch and Flemish painters expanded the mammary dimensions of their subjects to unheard-of proportions. Commenting on this new model, Anne Hollander notes that after 1650 Dutch art abounds in "ladies with very emphatic breasts escaping from their necklines—breasts that seem larger, rounder, and shinier than those unveiled in earlier centuries."[17]

Despite the Calvinist and Baptist emphasis on spiritual truths, neither the Protestant Dutch in the north nor the Catholic Dutch in the south ever fully repressed their sensual delight in earthly realities. Their appreciation for the shapes and colors of the visible world was as evident in the Dutch obsession with tulips (which produced a national economic fiasco in the seventeenth-century speculation in tulip bulbs!) as in their loving paintings of landscapes, still lifes, and female bodies with luscious curves. The "embarrassment of riches" produced by the rise of the Dutch bourgeoisie and colonial expansion could count among its assets not only cheeses, fruits, and flowers, but also well-fed, well-endowed bodies.

Visitors to Holland in the seventeenth century were impressed by the buxom charms of Dutch women, and by their freedom to act in ways that would have been unthinkable for respectable women in other European countries. "Public kissing, candid speech, unaccompanied promenades, all struck foreigners, and especially the French, as shockingly improper, even though they were repeatedly assured of the impregnable chastity of the married woman."[18] Dutch women's visible curves and free manners were clearly

40. Adriaen van de Welde. *Seated Peasant Woman*. Before 1671.
Dutch peasant women propped up their proverbially ample breasts with external bodices.

not synonymous with the sexual license that foreign men would have read into their own women.

As the century progressed and the Dutch became a major colonial power, fashion reflected the nation's increased wealth and the growing influence of foreign styles. Initially, during the first part of the century, Spanish ruffs covering the neck were ubiquitous among the ladies, whose heads seemed to sit on the ruff like pumpkins on platters. Toward midcentury, the ruff relaxed and gave way to the softer collar, often pointed or scalloped, and embroidered in lace. Still later, following French and English styles, the neckline dropped lower and allowed for a show of the area between the clavicle and the swell of the bust, sometimes as far down as the edge of the nipple. How much of a show a woman would make was determined by such variables as class, religion, and age, not to mention personal preferences. Many austere Protestants continued to wear oversized collars that formed a tentlike structure around their necks and shoulders, as well as tight caps on their heads, when it had already become fashionable for women of the better classes to show a good stretch of breast and a head of curly hair. As in France and England, which set the pace, corsets became a mainstay of middle- and upper-class women. This foreign-born garment, which lifted the breasts to unnatural heights above the neckline, was of course condemned by preachers and moralists, who admonished Dutch ladies to lower their breasts and keep them modestly under wraps.

Less privileged women, such as maidservants and farm workers, wore only an external bodice laced in the front, with a chemise underneath (fig. 40). The laces could be easily loosened and the chemise opened to reveal the breasts. Prostitutes wore either inner corsets or outer bodices to prop up the bust and achieve the desired cleavage expected in their trade.

The reputation enjoyed by Dutch women's emphatic bosoms did not die with the golden age. The eighteenth-century French *philosophe* Diderot, in an ungallant statement that does him little credit, once remarked that the whole of a Dutch woman's person "removed the incentive to discover whether the reputation of their prodigious bosoms was true or false."[19] Diderot is, of course, better remembered for his contributions to the Enlightenment, when he and his colleagues discovered and espoused the republican virtues that Dutch society had been practicing for quite some time. It took the English and the French a century longer than the Dutch to link domestic harmony and good government to maternal nursing. And when they did, breasts would become the emblems of a new social order.

Four

THE POLITICAL BREAST:
BOSOMS FOR THE NATION

A T NO TIME IN HISTORY —barring our own age—have breasts been more contested than in the eighteenth century. As Enlightenment thinkers set out to change the world, breasts became a battleground for controversial theories about the human race and political systems. Before the century was over, breasts would be linked, as never before, to the very idea of nationhood. It is not too far-fetched to argue that modern Western democracies invented the politicized breast and have been cutting their teeth on it ever since.

These political connections would not have been obvious from women's fashions, which featured breasts solely as aesthetic and erotic ornaments. In France and England, which set the style for the rest of Europe, corsets and bodices were designed to force the shoulder blades backward and project the chest forward, with the nipples on the verge of exposure. If we are to believe the colorful language of one fashion historian, an English coquette would have taken "every opportunity to display a nipple in the twinkling of a rake's eye."[1]

Certainly one had little inkling of the breast's political ramifications at the court of Louis XV (reigned 1715–74), a court notorious for its libidinous displays. Responding to the appetite for erotica, French painters covered their canvases with voluptuous women in various states of undress. Cleavage was no small matter for Louis XV, who berated one of his ministers for not noticing if his future daughter-in-law, Marie-Antoinette, was well endowed. "And her breasts? That's the first thing one looks at in a woman," he is rumored to have said.

The high culture ideal was still that of the "unused" bosom, dependent on wet nursing for its youthful preservation. In 1700, less than half of British mothers breast-fed their own children, with the remainder fed by wet nurses or by the "dry-feeding" method using semiliquid food.[2] In France, the incidence of wet nursing was even higher: what had been only an aristocratic practice during the sixteenth century won over the bourgeoisie in the seventeenth and even extended to the popular classes in the eighteenth. Working women and aristocrats were equally dependent on mercenary milk, the former so as to be able to ply their trades, the latter to be free for the numerous social obligations incumbent upon highborn ladies.

By midcentury, around 50 percent of all Parisian children were sent to the country to be raised by wet nurses. In 1769, a Wet Nurse Bureau was set up in Paris with the aim of assuring that wet nurses be paid in advance.[3] By 1780, of approximately twenty thousand babies born in Paris, as few as 10 percent were being nursed in their own homes. The other 90 percent were placed by their parents or by foundling hospitals with wet nurses.[4] Yet, by 1801, it has been estimated that half of all Parisian babies and two-thirds of English babies were nursed by their mothers.[5] What caused this striking change?

A virulent outcry against wet nursing began to be heard throughout Europe in the mid-eighteenth century from the ranks of moralists, philosophers, physicians, and scientists. Speaking in the name of Nature, they set out to prove that what was natural in the human body was basically good for the body politic. Physical health offered a metaphor for the health of the state, with breasts metonymically targeted to carry the germs of disease or well-being.[6] In this new discourse, breasts were divided into two categories: the "corrupted" or "polluting" breast, linked to wet nursing; and the maternal breast, linked to familial and social regeneration.

In England, the campaign against wet nursing began with a number of essays proclaiming that maternal breast-feeding was necessary for the good of the individual child and the entire nation.[7] The birth mother's milk was seen as a natural antidote to the extremely high mortality rates for infants sent from middle- and upper-class homes into the homes of lower-class wet nurses. There was no dearth of wet-nurse applicants, since wet nursing was one of the few occupations that allowed a working-class woman to earn as much as her husband if he was a laborer, especially if she nursed more than one child, as many did. Few inquired about the negative effects of this occupation on the wet nurse's own babe, who might be deprived of its full share of maternal milk for the sake of a take-home baby and take-home pay.

Before the middle of the eighteenth century, the main argument against wet nursing was that the suckling would imbibe the nurse's bad character and physical defects along with her milk. The novelist Daniel Defoe (1660–1731) railed against the mother who allowed her child to "suck in the life blood of a dairy-wench or a wool comber" and who did not "trouble to enquire into the temper, nay, indeed the very soul of the woman whose milk he sucks, not to speak of her bodily infirmities."[8] Defoe, for all his imaginative brilliance, had obviously not escaped middle-class prejudice against the working class.

But the greatest ammunition in the English crusade against wet nursing came not from novelists like Defoe but from doctors, and in particular Dr. William Cadogan. His influential 1748 *Essay upon Nursing*, which went through numerous English, American, and French editions before the end of the century, called upon mothers to follow the laws of "unerring Nature" and accept their breast-feeding obligations. Lest the father feel left out of the mother-child dyad, Cadogan assigned him the role of watchdog: "I would earnestly recommend it to every Father to have his Child nursed under his own Eye."[9] The production of milk for British babies was considered too important a matter to be left in the hands of women, given that "most Mothers, of any Condition, either cannot, or will not undertake the troublesome Task of suckling their own Children."

Cadogan argued that breast-feeding was troublesome "only for want of proper Method; were it rightly managed, there would be much Pleasure in it, to every Woman that can prevail upon herself to give up a little of the Beauty of her Breast to feed her Offspring." Moreover, as a recent father, Cadogan assured prospective mothers that there should be "no fear of offending the Husband's Ears with the Noise of the squalling Brat. The Child, was it nurs'd in this Way, would be always quiet, in good Humour, ever playing, laughing or sleeping." The breast-feeding method he recommended had apparently worked wonders in the Cadogan household.

The nursing mother was seen as fulfilling her duty first to her family and then to the commonwealth, which, according to the reigning platitude, treasured the multitude of its inhabitants as its greatest strength. With war a recurring reality in eighteenth-century Europe, Cadogan shared a fear of depopulation with many other nationalist and colonialist thinkers.

As a medical man, he also reflected the values of a rising middle class, for whom the employment of a wet nurse constituted a frivolous status symbol. Conversely, he eulogized "The Mother who has only a few Rags to cover her Child loosely, and little more than her own Breast to feed it." The child of such a woman, he claimed, would usually be "healthy and strong"—as if poor folk were somehow immune to the ills of the affluent. In the ideal society which Cadogan envisioned, women from all classes would breast-feed. Each familial unit would constitute a domestic haven, and each would contribute to the overall "publick Spirit." By the mid-eighteenth century, maternal breast-feeding had become a tenet of egalitarian politics. It would take another generation or two for infant nurture to change substantially, and when it did, around 1800, one cannot say that it altered the British class structure.

Across the ocean in America, wet nursing does not appear to have been as popular as it was in the mother country. Colonial women were expected to nurse their babies themselves, usually for about a year. Many nursed even longer, for a variety of reasons, including the conscious use of lactation as a form of birth control.[10] Because infant mortality was very high—estimates suggest that one-quarter of all children died before the age of one, and one-half before the age of five—mothers undertook to breast-feed with a set of realistic anxieties about the survival of their children.

Yet, if we judge by the many eighteenth-century newspaper advertisements that offered breast milk as a commodity available in the nurse's home or at the infant's residence, wet nursing was by no means rare. There were always newly arrived immigrants and Native Americans willing to serve as wet nurses, and, in the South, black slaves, who had no say in the matter. Their services were most likely to have been used immediately after childbirth, while the mother was recuperating, or as a supplement to a sickly mother's milk supply, or as a replacement for a mother who had died.[11]

Back in Europe, the wet-nurse controversy drew in some of the finest minds of the age, among them the Swedish physician and botanist Carolus Linnaeus (1707–78). In his 1752 Latin treatise titled *Nutrix Noverca* (roughly translated as *Step-Nurse* or *Unnatural Mother*), he insisted that wet nursing violated the laws of nature and endangered the life of both mother and child, who needed each other for reasons of health. It was not as a wet-nursing abolitionist that Linnaeus would make his greatest mark on breast history, however, but as a zoological taxonomist who coined the term "Mammalia" from the Latin *mammae* (milk-secreting organs) to distinguish suckling animals from all other creatures. Mammalia—literally meaning "of the breast"—embraces all viviparous creatures with hair, three ear bones, and a four-chambered heart.

The historian of science Londa Schiebinger has questioned Linnaeus's choice of this term: "The presence of milk-producing mammae is, after all, but one characteristic of mammals," and one that is found in only half of human beings.[12] A few of Linnaeus's contemporaries, like the naturalist Buffon, objected to the term on the grounds that some mammals do not have teats (e.g., stallions), but so great was the eighteenth-century fixation on female breasts that the new nomenclature for the class of animals previously called quadrupeds rapidly gained worldwide acceptance.

The class Mammalia was adopted by the English as "mammals" and by the French as *mammifères* (breast-bearers). The Germans changed the focus somewhat with the term *Säugetiere* (suckling animals), which emphasizes the role of the infant rather than that of the mother. Indeed, following the German model, it might have made more sense to coin a generic phrase for "sucklings," since that category applies to both males and females. The ramifications of Linnaeus's taxonomy were far-reaching: his privileging of the *mammae* dovetailed with eighteenth-century politics favoring maternal breast-feeding and an exclusively domestic role for women. It is interesting to note that Linnaeus's scientific appropriation of women's breasts had already been foreshadowed in an earlier treatise, his 1746 *Fauna Suecica*, which had as its frontispiece a four-breasted human female, chosen to symbolize the animal kingdom (fig. 41).

Like many Enlightenment thinkers, Linnaeus believed that breast-feeding was simply a matter of maternal instinct. Nursing and maternal sentiments were thought to be inborn in animals, including humankind. A mother did not have to be taught to suckle her offspring—it would come to her naturally. Oddly enough, even during the Middle Ages it was known that some women, mainly from the nobility, did not possess this "instinct." Several medieval French poems describe the plight of the first-time mother who "did not know how to nurse" because she "had never learned" or because she was "scarcely skilled in this *métier*."[13]

Today we have ample evidence derived from medical and anthropological studies that breast-feeding is not instinctive in human mothers: like any other social behavior, it must be learned through observation or information. Among the higher mammals, even chimpanzees and gorillas when raised in zoos sometimes have to be taught to nurse their offspring.[14] What would Linnaeus have thought of human mothers breast-feeding in front of a cage of primates to teach them how to nurse! Had Linnaeus not been so embedded in eighteenth-century maternalist thought, and had he not been the father of seven children, we would probably be calling ourselves something other than mammals.

In France, the breast-feeding issue was to have the most revolutionary consequences. There, *philosophes*, political writers, and government offi-

41. Linnaeus. *Faunus Suecica*. 1746.

The multibreasted statue that appeared on the frontispiece of Linnaeus's 1746 treatise reflects the entire century's preoccupation with women's breasts. Linnaeus made the breast the foremost identifying feature of the class of animals previously called "quadrupeds," which he rebaptized as "mammalia" in 1752.

cials, as well as physicians, led the campaign against wet nursing, and no one more influentially than Jean-Jacques Rousseau (1712–78). His 1762 treatise on education, *Émile*, argued that breast-feeding would attach mothers more firmly to their babies and their families, and provide the basis for societal regeneration. "Once women become mothers again"—and by that he meant breast-feeding mothers—"men would once again become fathers and husbands."[15]

However seductive his language and however influential his ideas, Rousseau's position has come under the fire of latter-day critics offended by his view that women were put on earth for the sole purpose of pleasing their husbands and nurturing their children. Men, he suggested, were given minds for thinking, and women breasts for suckling. If men found women's breasts attractive, this was ultimately in the interest of perpetuating the species and preserving family ties. Behind the poetics of mothers as a redemptive social force and the politics of egalitarian breast-feeding lay a sexist worldview so deeply entrenched in Western culture that few recognized it as such. The Rousseauist idea that woman was by nature a giving, loving, self-sacrificing, contingent creature was to form the basis for a new ideology of idealized motherhood, and one that would find currency in Europe and America for much of the next two centuries (fig. 42).

Two facts of Rousseau's personal life make his writings on breast-feeding doubly problematic. For one, he lost his own mother in childbirth and was raised by his father, with the aid of a wet nurse. Latter-day commentators, especially those with a psychoanalytic bent, have seen in this early loss the origin of Rousseau's permanent longing for the breast. Certainly he left behind considerable evidence of an obsessive, sometimes comical interest in women's breasts. In the seventh book of his *Confessions* he tells the story of his sexual fiasco with a Venetian courtesan called Giulietta. First he was unable to perform out of sheer overexcitement. Then, when he was about to delight in her beautiful body, he discovered that one breast differed from the other: it seems to have had a malformed or inverted nipple. This was enough to put a definitive end to desire, and, in retrospect, to merit the ugliest invective. Rousseau got his revenge on Giulietta for his own impotence by calling her "some kind of monster, rejected by Nature, men, and love."[16]

A more troubling set of facts surrounds Rousseau as a parent. From his long-term liaison with Thérèse Levasseur he fathered five children, all of whom were abandoned to the Foundling Hospital. This facet of his life was unknown before the publication of the second part of the *Confessions* in

42. Auguste Claude Le Grand. *Jean-Jacques Rousseau ou l'Homme de la Nature.*
Engraving. Ca. 1785.

No one did more than the Swiss philosopher Rousseau to popularize maternal breast-feeding in the eighteenth century. The caption on this engraving reads: "He restored women to their duties and children to happiness."

1788, by which time he had won over swarms of women who followed the advice of *Émile* and breast-fed their babies, turning their backs on the fashionable practice of wet nursing and occasionally opposing the express wishes of their husbands.

The mounting popularity of Rousseau's "back-to-Nature" doctrine with its special emphasis on breast-feeding reached as far as the court of Louis XVI and Marie-Antoinette. At Versailles, the queen lived out the fantasy of bucolic life at the hamlet she adapted for her personal use, replete with its dairy, milkmaids, shepherdesses, and lambs. In homage to the lactating mother, she commissioned from the manufacturer of Sèvres two porcelain bowls in the form of a pair of perfect breasts (fig. 43).

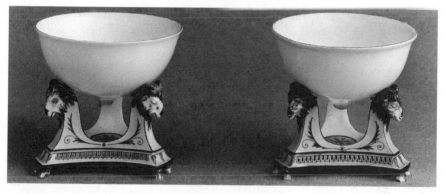

43. Porcelain bowls from the dairy at Rambouillet. Produced by Sèvres for Marie-Antoinette.

Legend has it that these two breast-shaped bowls commissioned by Marie-Antoinette were molded on her own breasts.

Women recalling this period of history sometimes referred with pride to the fact that they nursed their babies themselves. Madame Roland, for one, an enthusiastic follower of Rousseau's domestic philosophy and one of the most intellectual women of her day, summed up her maternal happiness with the words "I was a mother and a nurse."[17] She had been determined not to give her daughter to a wet nurse, even after her milk had dried up and she had to feed her baby by hand. To everyone's surprise, she was able to resume breast-feeding after a dry spell of almost seven weeks.

A considerably less educated woman, Élisabeth Le Bas, remembered that the question of breast-feeding had been used by her future husband as a kind of character test. As a staunch republican and close associate of Maxi-

milien Robespierre, the deputy Philippe Le Bas wanted to make sure that
Élisabeth would be willing to follow the party line on breast-feeding; he even
tried to trick her into admitting countersentiments, but she was too clever to
be taken in by such a ploy. Before long she was indeed married to Le Bas, and
was indeed nursing a baby, though under circumstances she would never
have chosen. Le Bas lost his life in the 1794 coup against Robespierre, and
Élisabeth was thrown into jail with her five-week-old baby, whom she nursed
for nine months in the squalor of a prison cell. Her husband's last words to
her were: "Nourish him with your own milk. . . . Inspire in him the love of his
country."[18]

Though it is understandable that Madame Roland and Madame Le
Bas—both bourgeois women with ardent republican sentiments—chose to
breast-feed in keeping with the dictates of the revolution's most honored ora-
cle, it is less easy to comprehend Rousseau's popularity among aristocrats and
royalists. Yet the passion for breast-feeding he inspired cut across class status,
political loyalties, and national frontiers.

In Germany, as in France, the breast-feeding mother became the subject
of sentimental poems and paintings. Sometimes, as in the lovely 1779 pastel
by Johann Anton de Peters known as *Die Nähreltern* (*The Nurturing Parents*),
the mother's breast was the focal point of an intimate family scene—mother,
father, and child drawn together around the breast as if it were an open
hearth.[19] The simple pastoral types in this picture were ostensibly more loving
parents than their sophisticated city counterparts.

A quite different threesome is found in an English picture that satirizes
upper-class ladies pressed by fashion to nurse their infants. Their breasts were
in it, but not their hearts, if we are to believe James Gillray's 1796 satire, *The
Fashionable Mamma*, depicting an elegantly dressed mother rigidly seated
on the edge of a chair while a maid holds out a baby to her bosom and a car-
riage waits outside to whisk the mother away (fig. 44).

By the last years of the eighteenth century, breast-feeding had taken on
the aspect of a cult. Consider this example of a women's philanthropic organization, La Charité Maternelle, founded in 1788 by affluent French ladies to
provide aid to poor Parisian mothers. The rules for prospective recipients
were the following: that they be married, that they have certificates of good
conduct from their parishes, and that they nurse their children themselves.
The breast-feeding provision, designated as "the fundamental principle of the
Maternal Charity," was seen as a means of "strengthening family bonds, at-
taching mothers to their duties, forcing them to remain indoors and, in that

44. James Gillray. *The Fashionable Mamma.* 1796. The baby's strained position between the maid and the mother—its head stretched uncomfortably to the maternal breast and its bottom propped up in the attendant's arms—makes a mockery of the fashionable cult of breast-feeding.

way, of preserving them from disorderly conduct and begging."[20] Enforced nursing thus became a form of social control exercised by wealthy ladies over members of the popular classes.

It was not only elitist ladies who restricted their largesse to mothers who would breast-feed. The French government itself decided, by the Convention decree of June 28, 1793, that if a mother did not nurse her child she and the child would not be eligible for the state support offered to indigent families. A separate provision was added for unmarried mothers: "Every girl who declares that she wants to nurse the child she is carrying, and who has need of the help of the nation, will have the right to claim it."[21]

A year later, the Germans followed suit and even upped the ante: a Prussian law of 1794 required all healthy women to breast-feed.[22] Yet, if the records from Hamburg are indicative of wider German practices, few ladies took to nursing their young. In Hamburg in the last decade of the eighteenth century, the demand for wet nurses to serve in prosperous homes was substantially the same as before. When, in 1796, the Hamburg Poor Relief opened a lying-in ward for unwed mothers to be delivered free of charge, it was with the understanding that they would become wet nurses after childbirth. "Indeed, unless they were physically incapable of nursing a child, the Relief *required* these women to accept the opportunities offered them."[23] As for the wet nurse's own child, it was either nursed alongside her paid charge or farmed out to rural peasants. Whereas poor Frenchwomen received subsidies only if they breast-fed their infants, here the situation was quite different: poor Hamburg mothers were supported only if they were willing to breast-feed the babes of others. Both instances reveal the intrusion of the state into domestic practices, not only in France but in neighboring European nations. Since France was the trendsetter both in politics and fashion, whatever upheavals happened on French soil were sure to send seismic vibrations beyond the national borders, or, as it was later put: whenever France sneezed, all of Europe caught a cold.

The revolution touched Frenchwomen's breasts in many ways. Some took up nursing with rhetorical fervor, as can be seen from the letter of an expectant mother eagerly awaiting the moment when she would take her baby to her breast "and fill it lavishly with a nourishing and healthful milk."[24] Some had to choose between nursing their babies or following their husbands into exile, prison, or war. One woman, the aunt of the future poet Alphonse de Lamartine, described how breast-feeding proved a boon to her sister, whose "husband had been put in prison, but as she was nursing, they let her go free."[25] On the whole, the nation's overt concern with healthy children allowed for numerous concessions to pregnant women and nursing mothers alike. When women looked back on the revolution, they did not consider their breast-feeding stories trivial or irrelevant, since nursing had been raised to a quasi-mythological level.

In the revolutionary discourse, the pure milk of loving mothers was implicitly compared with the tainted milk of *ancien-régime* aristocrats, most of whom were raised by wet nurses. This pairing of maternal nursing with republican virtues and wet nursing with royalist decadence allowed women a "patriotic" choice: those who chose to suckle their young could be seen as making a political statement in favor of the new regime. In this vein, the women citizens of Clermont-Ferrand wrote the following words to the National Assembly: "We see to it that our children drink an incorruptible milk that we clarify for that purpose with the natural and agreeable spirit of liberty."[26] Nursing was no longer a private matter with ramifications only for the infant and its family. It had become, as Rousseau had hopefully envisioned, a collective manifestation of civic duty.

An official handbook of prayers and rituals exhorted women to offer their bosoms to their husbands for repose and to their children for nurturance. And all the infants of the nation were assured that "The fatherland has heard your tender cries; for us it has become a second mother."[27] The fatherland was pleased to represent itself as a mother offering her breasts to all her children, even former black slaves from the French colonies (figs. 45 and 46).

The iconography of the French Revolution quickly became peopled with bare-breasted women. Following classical models, female figures dressed in tunics with one or two breasts exposed became common symbols for the new Republic. Sometimes the Republic was a warrior woman with one breast uncovered, an Athena-like helmet on her head, and a spear topped by a Phrygian cap. Elsewhere, reviving the model of the multibreasted Artemis, she displayed as many as a dozen breasts to represent popular ideals, such as Nature and Reason (fig. 47). Countless paintings, engravings, medals, reliefs, and statues transformed the breast into a national icon.

Picture the celebration of the Festival of Regeneration on August 10, 1793, at the site of the old Bastille. Here, at the first of six stations strung throughout Paris, a fountain was erected in the form of an Egyptian goddess, with jets of water streaming from her breasts. Louis David, the author of this project, waxed eloquently about the supreme moment when "our common mother, Nature, presses from her fecund breasts the pure and salutary liquid of regeneration."[28] A crowd of astonished Parisians watched as each of eighty-six commissioners drank a cup of water from the goddess's flowing breasts, and the president of the National Convention, Hérault de Séchelles, proclaimed: "These fecund waters which spurt from your breasts . . . will consecrate the oaths that France swears to you on this day." The women in the crowd were encouraged to breast-feed so that "military and generous virtues could flow, with maternal milk, into the heart of all the nurslings of France!"[29] This Hollywood-like spectacle effected a stunning propagandistic merger of the new Nation with the twin images of Mother Nature and real mothers, all honored as breast-feeders.

Paradoxically, it drew women into the picture at the very moment they were being definitively written out of public life. The new laws that granted civil rights to religious minorities and even to former slaves did not extend to

45. *La France Républicaine.
Ouvrant son sein à tous ses
citoyens.* Ca. 1790.

The new French Republic was
frequently represented as a woman
"opening her breasts to all her
citizens." In this engraving, a
carpenter's plane dangles in her
cleavage to indicate equal access to
everyone.

46. Nature, as an egalitarian
mother. Ca. 1790.

During the campaign to liberate the
slaves of the West Indies, the French
Nation was portrayed as a generous
mother nursing both a white and a
black child.

47. Monument erected to Nature in the Temple of Reason in Strasbourg. 1793.
Multibreasted statues, harking back to Greek antiquity, became national icons during the
French Revolution.

women. But female breasts were enlisted to convey a wide array of republican ideals, such as liberty, fraternity, equality, patriotism, courage, justice, generosity, and abundance. The idea of the Republic as a bounteous mother, her swelling breasts accessible to everyone, has been a mainstay of liberal politics ever since.

It can be argued that the new iconography was in some ways related to the clothes real women wore in the revolutionary period. In the 1780s, the chemise dress made its first appearance, its light fabric and loose fit contrasting to the rigidity of earlier apparel. Heavy corsets and fabrics were abandoned for simpler forms as part of a widespread classical trend that looked to the ancient Greeks and Romans for their philosophy, politics, and styles. The "politically correct" chemise dress became, alongside Jacobin trousers for men, signs of the new egalitarian society.

During the Directoire (1795–99), according to literary critic Barbara Gelpi, women's dress on both sides of the Channel showed "a negligence and simplicity appropriate for the comfort of a pregnant or nursing mother. Breasts were emphasized and their availability [was] heightened."[30] For a brief period at the end of the century, corsets were discarded and clothes were so light and transparent that they weighed only a couple of pounds.[31] An article in *La Petite Poste* of June 22, 1797, provides this revealing picture:

> Two women get out of a pretty cabriolet: one dressed decently, the other with her arms and throat naked, and a gauze skirt over flesh-colored pants. They scarcely take two steps before they are surrounded and squeezed. The half-naked woman is insulted. . . . No one could see, without indignation, the indecent attire of that lady of the 'new' France.[32]

An English magazine editorial from the early 1800s noted that young ladies were now "covered with nothing more than transparent shawls that float and flutter over their breasts, which are clearly seen through them."[33] This scant attire was considered appropriate for young mothers as well as single women. The breasts that had been separated during the Renaissance into two groups—one for nursing, the other for sexual gratification—were now reunited into one multipurpose bosom. Lactating breasts had become sexy (fig. 48).

From this point on, the maternal breast with erotic overtones would be called upon to serve various national interests. In France, throughout the

48. Marguerite Gérard. *Les Premiers Pas ou la Mère Nourrice*. Ca. 1800.

In the years following the revolution, the nursing mother acquired sexual as well as civic connotations.

49. Eugène Delacroix.
Liberty Leading the People.
1830.

In the midst of slain bodies and
unfurled banners, Delacroix's
bare-breasted Liberty leads the
people to victory. Here naked
breasts have become symbols
of defiance, as urgent and as
aggressive as revolution itself.

nineteenth and twentieth centuries, the allegorical figure with one or two
breasts uncovered continued to represent the Republic. Often she was identified with the idea of Liberty, as in Delacroix's famous painting *Liberty Leading the People*, which was not about the revolution of 1789, as most people
assume, but the bloody uprising of 1830 (fig. 49).

In contrast to the "accidental" exposure of women's breasts in Renaissance or eighteenth-century erotic art, this Liberty uncovers her breasts de-
liberately in an attempt to inspire political rather than sexual feelings.[34] More

than a hundred years later, at the time of the Liberation of Paris following World War II, the popular French singer Anne Chapel jumped up on top of a car, tore open her blouse, and, "like Delacroix's *Liberté*, exposing her superb breasts, she belted out the national anthem."[35] Life, taking its cues from art, had no better symbol for freedom than unfettered breasts.

Around 1850, the bosomy incarnation of the French Republic acquired a name—Marianne. With her youthful face, Phrygian cap, and uncovered breasts, Marianne has been featured since then in countless paintings, works of sculpture, posters, cartoons, and pieces of money to suggest the qualities of daring, dynamism, solidarity, and sexual attraction, which the French claim for their national character.[36] Though other nations have sometimes adopted aspects of the Marianne figure in their national emblems—for example, in the American Columbia, the British Britannia, and the Prussian Germania—these counterparts have never displayed their breasts with the effrontery of the French.

FRANCE HAD SET THE TONE during the eighteenth century and would cling to a belief in its political superiority long after it had become a lesser international force. But the rising tide of British imperialism and the growing power of the United States shifted the center of influence to the English-speaking world. For most of the nineteenth century, it was Queen Victoria, with her beloved husband, Prince Albert, and their nine children, who offered the supreme model of familial and civic devotion.

In both England and America, only the maternal breast was publicly honored. Mothers were encouraged to nurse their babies and to assume all the duties related to their general well-being. Increasingly, an awareness of the psychological importance of the intimate relationship between mother and child added further weight to the mandate to breast-feed. Mothers who refused to nurse their babies were seen as personally selfish and socially subversive. At the least, the practice of sending British babies to the country declined, and a wet nurse was increasingly expected to reside in the home, where the mother could supervise her.

Most American women breast-fed their babies. Even in the antebellum South, where slave nurses were an option, only 20 percent of mothers used a supplemental or replacement wet nurse.[37] When black mammies were recruited to suckle white children, it was often at the expense of their own babies, as can be seen in this story told by a slave in North Carolina.

My Aunt Mary b'longed to Marse John Craddock and when his wife died and left a little baby—dat was little Miss Lucy—Aunt Mary was nussin' a new baby of her own, so Marse John made her let his baby suck too. If Aunt Mary was feedin' her own baby and Miss Lucy started cryin' Marse John would snatch her baby up by the legs and spank him, and tell Aunt Mary to go on and nuss his baby fust.[38]

The tensions inherent in white ownership of the black breast erupted into one of the most dramatic moments of abolitionist history. It occurred in Indiana in 1858, when Sojourner Truth, an antislavery activist and former slave, was addressing a mostly white audience. At the close of the meeting, a group of proslavery sympathizers challenged her sexual identity. They sought to prove that she was not a woman. As Nell Painter has shown in her biography of Sojourner Truth, this charge of imposture, meant to undermine Truth's authenticity, was turned against her accusers to impugn their authority.[39]

This is how the incident appeared in *The Liberator* of October 15, 1858:

Sojourner told them that her breasts had suckled many a white babe, to the exclusion of her own offspring; that some of those white babies had grown to man's estate; that, although they had suckled her colored breasts, they were, in her estimation, far more manly than they (her persecutors) appeared to be; and she quietly asked them as she disrobed her bosom if they, too, wished to suck! In vindication of her truthfulness, she told them that she would show her breast to the whole congregation; that it was not to her shame that she uncovered her breast before them, but to their shame.

Uncovering one's breasts for political effect would have more numerous adherents a century later, among 1970s and '80s feminists, but never more poignantly than on that Indiana platform in 1858 when the moral question of slavery was about to rend the entire nation. Sojourner Truth's bared breasts, like her equally famous "arn't I a woman?" speech, left no doubt about her womanhood and her personhood. How could those breasts, which had reputedly suckled both black and white babies, not be seen as fully human? Yet black slave bodies were treated as considerably less than human—both on the slave block, where their teeth and muscles and breasts were openly ex-

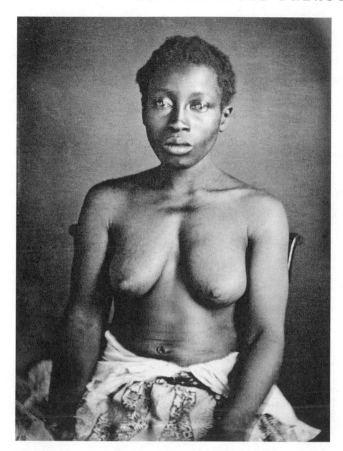

50. J. T. Zealy. Daguerreotype. March 1850. Delia, country born of African parents. Daughter of Renty, Congo. Plantation of B. F. Taylor. Columbia, South Carolina.

Early American photographers documented black women as "property." This black woman's fully exposed breasts were treated as an intrinsic part of her worth as a slave.

amined by prospective buyers, and in their subsequent homes, where they belonged to their masters like dogs or cows (fig. 50).

Truth's struggle to free the black body from white exploitation was far removed from most middle-class concerns. While slave women were being
treated like animals, American and British white women were being idealized as domestic angels. Coventry Patmore's poem "The Angel in the House"
(1854–56) gave expression to this high-culture view of the mother as an ethereal good fairy, selflessly devoted to her family.

The erotic breast was largely banished from Victorian literature, except
in covert form, as was evident in the poetry of that proper Victorian Alfred,
Lord Tennyson.[40] Whenever the "b" word was named directly in Tennyson's
poems (rather than "rounded forms" or some other euphemism), it always be-
spoke catastrophe. The narrator of "Tiresias" was made blind by viewing the

breasts of Pallas Athene as she stepped from her bath. "The breasts of Helen" of Troy called up the vision of widespread destruction ("Lucretius"). And Cleopatra's suicide was, of course, dramatically effected by "the aspick's bite" at her breast ("A Dream of Fair Women").

Conversely, the good breast was understood to be the nursing breast. In England and the United States, as in France and Northern Europe, mothers were not ashamed to be seen in their homes as they nursed their babies; indeed, it was even permissible to breast-feed in such public places as parks and railroads, especially among the popular classes.[41] This was true even for middle-class women in rural England, where babies were breast-fed as a matter of course, for example, in church, without the prudery one usually associates with Victorian society.

For those hostile to wet nursing and the rising trend in bottle-feeding, the nursing mother had to be protected like an endangered species. Following Pasteur's discoveries, it was understood that heating milk sufficiently could make bottled milk safe for infants, and by the 1880s bottle-feeding had become common in British cities. In rural areas, however, bottles were still very rare. Flora Thompson wrote in her autobiographical evocation of life in Oxfordshire that "when a bottle-fed baby was brought on a visit to the hamlet, its bottle was held up as a curiosity."[42]

The glorification of the maternal breast stretched westward from London to the New World and eastward as far as Russia. To foster a growing nationalistic spirit, Slavophiles evoked the image of Mother Russia, who was simultaneously identified with Mother Earth and the peasant nurses who suckled Russian babies. Great writers like Pushkin and Dostoevsky championed Mother Russia alongside, and even above, Father Tsar; both symbolic and living female nurturers were invoked as the source of male redemption and societal rebirth. In the context of the 1860s Russian debate on women's social role, the novelist Nikolai Leskov celebrated the maternal breast as the sustainer of traditional order and as a "vehicle of feminine civic virtue."[43]

The great majority of Russian infants were nursed at the breast, either by their mothers or, in the case of the nobility, by wet nurses, but by the late 1870s, a large number of children were already being bottle-fed.[44] Tolstoy, raising a challenge to wet nursing and bottle-feeding alike, made maternal breast-feeding the cornerstone of his vision of marriage and communitarian society. First and foremost, it was the duty of his wife, Sonya, to nurse their children, an event that occasioned bitter duels. From Sonya's diaries we learn that she had suffered from painful mastitis and would have given up nursing had it not been for Tolstoy's adamant insistence. In the words of one literary historian: "Tolstoy won out: Sonya nursed through her pain, in a victory that is, again, hard not to see as symbolic of men's control of women's bodies. In this skirmish as in the novel he wrote ten years later [*Anna Karenina*], Tolstoy appropriated the breast . . . to his own ideological ends."[45]

Tolstoy's personal victory resonated with traditional Russian patriarchal values, which expected women to be subservient to men, children to parents, and serfs to landlords. Coming from the pen of the most revered Russian writer of his age, Tolstoy's novels and tracts carried quasi-religious status. Who could doubt that the good mother in *Anna Karenina* was Kitty, who nursed her baby, and that the bad mother was Anna, who did not? Who would not be seduced by an idyllic vision of Russian society cemented by the mother-child nursing bond, as opposed to the commercial transaction of wet nursing, which forced women to "rent" their breasts and sell their milk? Tolstoy's pastoral picture of Mother Russia peopled by millions of breast-feeding mothers and idealized peasants was a last-ditch attempt to stop the clock, to prolong the agrarian dream of female nature and nurture.

It is worth noting that in 1895 the Russian empress, Alexandra Feodorovna, decided to nurse her first-born child, the Grand Duchess Olga. This was so contrary to standard practice that a group of wet nurses had already assembled at the palace, from which a final selection was to be made. Needless to say, the wet nurses went away disappointed.

The German empress, Auguste Viktoria, took an even more active role in promoting maternal nursing. Herself the mother of seven children, she lectured publicly on all the virtues that accrue from breast-feeding. In November 1904, she appeared before the Patriotic Women's League, an organization backed by conservative forces in government and medicine, who saw maternal breast-feeding as a bulwark against the declining birthrate and the growing participation of women in the labor force.[46]

That same year, the Prussian state granted funds for the first child-welfare clinic, voluntarily staffed by members of the Patriotic Women's League. Premiums were paid for breast-feeding, and mothers were encouraged to resist the moral decline that had been brought about by such reputed evils as bottle-feeding and birth control. The fear of depopulation that swelled to a crescendo before World War I played into German health politics and resulted in the creation of over one thousand child-welfare clinics by 1915. This alarm at the falling birthrate (though not so low as that of their

French neighbors) provided ammunition for Prussian politicians, who espoused breast-feeding as a panacea for all physical, moral, and social ills.

Others argued for purer bottled milk and better hygiene. The members of the League for the Protection of Mothers countered the government's pronatalist message with their own progressive program. They favored sexual liberation, the welfare of unmarried mothers, and other radical causes. During the next twenty years, until the advent of National Socialism, the League for the Protection of Mothers would pose an ongoing challenge to conservative factions.

THROUGHOUT THE TWENTIETH CENTURY, women's breasts have been politicized by various governments for a variety of causes, especially in times of war. During World War I, propaganda added new dimensions to the political use of the breast. In French posters, a bare-breasted

51. Bernard. *Honor to the 75th.* French poster. 1914. World War I French posters eroticized Marianne for patriotic purposes. Here she stands naked in front of a cannon, her hair blowing in the breeze and her upright breasts defying the German enemy.

52. G. Léonnec. *The Mail Carrier.* 1917.

The use of women as mail carriers during World War I gave rise to this image. Though the bare breasts and miniature soldier in the woman's hand are to be understood allegorically, her knee-length dress and uncovered legs attest to the historical shortening of skirts that had taken place during the war years.

Marianne raises her arms in an appeal for loans to the French government. Or, nude to the waist, she brushes off the Prussian eagle with the agility of a swirling dancer.[47] Elsewhere she boldly exposes her breasts and even her pubis (fig. 51). Other contemporary-looking females are shown backing the war effort in the roles of nurses, bus drivers, factory and agricultural workers, mail carriers, stocking knitters, frugal housewives, and prolific mothers (fig. 52).

The nudity or partial nudity of these feminine images harks back to a long French tradition of beautiful breasts — political during the revolution of 1789, erotic during the Renaissance, sacred in the late Middle Ages. The Germans saw this female nudity as further evidence of French decadence. They drew upon it for many caricatures of French women engaged in outrageous, sex-charged acts. In an anal reversal of the French breast fixation, one caricature

53. Ferdy Horrmeyer.
German poster. 1918.
"German women,
contribute to victory!"
This German poster, reflecting
the grim national mood of
1918, pictured women factory
workers with downcast eyes
and unshapely bosoms.

featured Marianne sitting atop the Arc de Triomphe, with enormous breast-like buttocks pointed in the direction of the military.[48]

German propaganda rarely made use of German women as inspirational figures. At best, they were pictured in traditional feminine roles, offering sustenance to men and children. In the early war years, pretty German women with full breasts and golden braids were shown offering flowers and drinks to servicemen. But as the war progressed, the images grew darker. Widows' veils and mournful faces became the visible reminders of the mounting dead (fig. 53).

Americans caricatured the German enemy as an inhuman monster, a circus-poster gorilla in a Prussian helmet, with canine teeth, a club in one hand marked "Kultur," and a helpless maiden in the other (fig. 54). This picture on a 1917 enlistment poster, with the caption "Destroy This Mad Brute," conveyed the message that Germans were beasts who violated female prey. The victim's uncovered breasts were signs of feminine vulnerability—not strength, as in the Marianne posters. Their soft beauty was intended to move the hearts of American youth and send them off bravely to defend Europeans, lest their own women be next in line. The poster was also not wasted on the Germans: it made such a powerful impression that, twenty-two years later, at the onset of World War II, the propaganda minister, Goebbels, used an exact reproduction of it to remind the Germans of the way they had been treated

54. H. R. Hopps.
American World War I
poster. "Destroy This
Mad Brute. Enlist.
U.S. Army."
The German enemy is a
gorilla monster
plundering helpless
women. With her
breasts cruelly exposed,
the victim covers her
eyes in a gesture that
speaks the shame of
nakedness and the
horror of rape.

earlier by their American and British enemies. The final words on the 1939 German poster read: "No second time!!!"

Uncovered breasts were generally not acceptable to the American war effort, except in scenes where women were being victimized by the enemy or, conversely, protected by American men. Another 1917 recruitment poster, carrying the caption "It's up to you. Protect the Nation's Honor," shows Uncle Sam standing vigilantly behind Miss Liberty, whose forward-leaning body exposes an enticing neck, uncovered shoulders and arms, and a good bit of nude breast. This melodramatic scene, designed by the Associated Motion Picture

55. "You Buy a Liberty
Bond Lest I Perish!" 1917.
With her bristling crown and
full draperies, Liberty is
desexualized in the mode of
a Greek Athena.

Advertisers, used blatant sexual imagery to rally American men against the potential rape of their country, symbolized by a vulnerable female.

Yet, if bare breasts were rarely a part of American self-representation except in scenes of victimization, there was, nonetheless, a rapid change during
the war from a fully covered Columbia or Liberty to a less clothed model. This
transition is clearly evident in a series of posters created to promote the sale of
Liberty Bonds between 1917 and 1919. The first of the series shows a statuesque
Liberty covered in heavy draperies from neck to toe (fig. 55). The second in
the series, issued a few months later, is radically different (fig. 56). She is softer,
more feminine; her arms are outstretched in a gesture of supplication; her face
is almost mournful; and her full breasts are clearly visible — indeed, literally
outlined by bands that cross over and under them. The third, fourth, and fifth
posters in the series, all created by Howard Chandler Christy, offer a younger,
more sexualized woman wearing something that is closer to a nightgown than
to classical drapery (fig. 57). Americans had learned the lesson that scantily

56. Maurice Ingres. American poster. 1917. "Let's End It—Quick—With Liberty Bonds." The artist Maurice Ingres gives Liberty a softer, more feminine form. He had learned from his Greek and French predecessors how simultaneously to conceal and reveal female rotundities.

clad females promote the cause of whatever it is one wants to sell to the public, be it Liberty Bonds, military service, or war itself.

Variations on the use of the breast in World War I propaganda can be charted according to national tastes and customs.[49] The Italians showed busty women exuding sex and power (fig. 58). The Austrians featured folk heroines with their breasts encased in national or mythological motifs.[50] The English relied heavily on their trusty Britannia, with her helmet, breastplate, sword, and shield.

Russian women were a special case, because some of them really did bear arms. By 1915, news of their heroic acts against the Germans had reached the British and American press, and by 1917, after the revolution had broken out, an all-female battalion of 250 Russian women served on the Northern Front.[51] The Bolsheviks themselves included in their 1917–18 propaganda some accounts of these "new women" who were taking their place beside men in the revolutionary struggle. Cartoonlike posters showing peasant

57. Howard Chandler Christy. American poster. 1918. "CLEAR—THE—WAY—!! *Buy Bonds.* Fourth Liberty Loan."

The wispy, almost see-through quality of the material barely covering Liberty's breasts, the hair flying in the breeze, the partially opened mouth in Christy's Liberty Bond poster, give the impression of a Hollywood starlet enlisted for the war effort.

women spearing Austrian soldiers with their pitchforks or exterminating Prussian cockroaches were intended to spread martial patriotism among the masses. But not everyone could take women soldiers seriously. Caricatures that made fun of the sexual possibilities offered by women warriors showed them with naked breasts sitting on the laps of their male comrades-in-arms, or fully nude in even grosser positions (fig. 59).

When the war was finally over, women, as a form of national propaganda, retreated from view. In France, Marianne held on to her pre-eminence, but less boldly than during the war years. Columbia and Uncle Sam continued to stand guard over the U.S., but somewhat less vigilantly than before. In Germany, a new monster was preparing to be born. Its self-images were overwhelmingly masculine, glorifying male bodies and fraternal bonds. When women did appear in Nazi propaganda, they were portrayed primarily as breeders and nurturers of Aryan children (fig. 60).

During World War II, the female figure on European and American posters changed dramatically. There were few images of women personifying the nation and many more pictures of real women in various work situations. In the United States, WACS, WAVES, and Army and Red Cross nurses were shown with perky hats and busy fingers dedicated to the war effort. Wholesome women, invariably white-skinned and often blonde, with sensibly high-necked clothing, were shown either as partners with men or as maternal figures protecting children and wounded soldiers. The old image of Columbia or Liberty had all but disappeared.

But breasts had by no means disappeared from the war effort. They emerged on the noses of airplanes in pictures of sexy women identified as

58. Luciano Achille Mauzan. Italian poster. "LIBERATION LOAN . . . and what was ours is ours again!"
The Italian woman featured on propaganda posters was a mature figure commanding loyalty and obedience. Her naked shoulders and full breasts covered by a diagonal sheath recall the one-bare-breasted Marianne, without offending propriety.

59. Enrollment for the
Russian Women's Brigade.
1917–18. Russian caricature.

A prospective member of the
Russian Women's Brigade is
examined by a male officer. With
her pants hanging down around
her knees, she flexes her muscle,
while he takes advantage of the
situation to lift up one of her
substantial breasts.

"Slightly Dangerous," "Mis-Behaving," and "Miss Laid" (fig. 61). Stripped to
the waist, like the bare-breasted figures on the prows of nineteenth-century
ships, these provocative fuselage figures imbued the fighters with a sense of
sexual power and destruction.

More commonly, and more benignly, breasts were the hallmark of millions of pin-up pictures enjoyed by servicemen throughout the world. In-your-
face bosoms appeared in glossy photos and magazine tear-outs sent free of
charge to "raise the morale" of U.S. troops. Over a four-year period, from 1942
to late 1945, some six million copies of *Esquire* featuring pin-ups by Alberto Vargas were sent to American soldiers.[52] The scantily clad "Vargas girl" was known
for her upward-thrusting breasts, her extra-long legs, and her overall airbrushed
perfection. Dressed in pseudo-uniforms, some were designated as mascots for
the air force, the infantry, the navy, and the marines. American GIs hung their
Vargas girls above their bunks and carried them, folded, onto the beaches of
Normandy. With their skimpy tops and clinging shorts, or strapless, backless
gowns, they projected a vision of paper-doll sexuality. When the men came
back from the wars, such breasts and legs would be waiting for them.

Another official purveyor of pin-up-girl pictures was the magazine *Yank*,
established in 1942 for enlisted men. For five cents per issue, American GIs

60. German poster. 1930s. "Germany grows from strong women and healthy children." To promote breast-feeding among German women during the Nazi period, this poster of mother and child mimicked the traditional image of the nursing Madonna.

could read well-written articles about the war and tear out the "pin-up girl" of the month for their private dreams. *Yank* pin-ups tended to be upbeat and smiley, like the girl next door, but some were sultry and sexy, with mammoth bosoms protruding through curve-enhancing blouses about to fall off the shoulders. Actresses Jane Russell and Linda Darnell were prominent among those whose careers were advanced in this fashion.

By 1945, when photographer Ralph Stein was sent by the army to Hollywood to make a series of pin-up pictures, he found the makeup women so accustomed to augmenting bosoms that the results were "overwhelming." As he tells the story: ". . . the makeup woman wasn't quite satisfied with the fullness of the starlet's sweater. She inserted a pair of felt pads about two inches in diameter, backed off, looked hard, and inserted two more. 'Enough?' she asked us. . . . We hemmed and hawed a bit. The makeup lady decided for us. 'What the hell,' she said, 'this is for the soldier boys' and put three more pads over each breast."[53]

What has come to be called the American breast fetish of the war and postwar years corresponded to very basic psychological desires. On the simplest level, breasts are biological signs of sexual difference that can be highlighted according to the historical moment. World War II was such a

61. "Slightly Dangerous." The Boeing B-17 Flying Fortress, at an English airbase.
August 12, 1943. 388th Bomb Group.
World War II fuselage art conflated breasts, danger, destruction, and victory.

moment. Men fighting overseas looked to the female bosom as a reminder of the values that war destroys: love, intimacy, nurturance. The breast's maternal and erotic functions took on added meaning for an entire generation of servicemen during the war and long afterward, when they returned to "normalcy."

Marilyn Monroe, Gina Lollobrigida, Jayne Mansfield, and Anita Ekberg incarnated the big-busted pin-up on the movie screen. Busts were the rage because they were the most obvious sign of femaleness. Men needed to be reassured that the nightmare of war was over and that the breasts they had dreamed of were now available to them. The emphasis on breasts also carried a clear message for women: your role is to provide the breast, not the bread. Four babies, two cars, and wall-to-wall carpeting were the rewards offered to visibly breasted women content with the status quo. It would take another generation to contest this vision of gendered fulfillment.

For most of this century, breasts have served national interests in a variety of ways—during the wars, as feminine icons inspiring male valor; afterward, as sexual and maternal emblems geared to pronatalist policies. Certainly one should not confuse graphic representation with the lives of real women, yet one cannot ignore the influence—indeed, the interchange—between the images of one's time and place and the experiences of flesh-and-blood people. The Frenchwomen of 1789, portrayed symbolically as breast-feeders, did indeed undertake to breast-feed their infants. The amply endowed pin-up girls of World War II launched a mode of torpedo bosoms for the rest of American womanhood. Both directly and indirectly, breast graphics have contributed to the spread of national ideologies.

As carriers of those ideologies, it is worth considering the use of female bodies on banknotes, a practice that has been around for about two hundred years.[54] Since banknotes circulate throughout the world, they disseminate carefully chosen national self-portraits. As far back as 1694, when the Bank of England chose Britannia for its seal, she has proclaimed the power and authority of the British crown. With her female face and male armor, she comes across like a desexed Athena. Characteristically, her breasts are never seen.

The French, as we have noted, have no scruples about exposing Marianne's breasts. This is in keeping with a deeply ingrained cultural eroticism—though sometimes erotic symbols can backfire. In 1978, for example, when France issued its hundred-franc notes showing the Delacroix Liberty with her swelling breasts, the image seemed so shocking that certain countries refused to accept them!

When France was a colonial power, she placed pictures of dark-skinned, bare-breasted women on the banknotes of French Indochina, West Africa, and New Caledonia. The money itself was a form of tourist publicity for the countries where one could presumably see the half-naked bodies pictured on the notes. The native women in many of these lands did go about with their breasts uncovered. But to represent such women realistically—not allegorically, as was the case for white women—does smack of racist exploitation. France was not, it should be said, the only offender. Some of the other colonial powers did the same. In Angola, a former Portuguese colony, a note issued in 1947 shows a bare-breasted black girl in the care of a fully draped white female. The girl's partial nudity is meant to suggest a primitive state of development that is best entrusted to the civilizing influence of a Western colonial power (fig. 62).

One more example, this time from Switzerland. The nursing woman on the Swiss fifty-franc note that circulated between 1955 and 1974 is part of an apple-harvest scene. This agricultural paradise stands for the great wealth of a small nation. It also acts as a subliminal reminder to Swiss women that lactating breasts, like edible apples, are another form of national wealth.

ON THE WHOLE, the United States has intervened less in matters of the breast than have many other countries. Certainly welfare mothers have never been forced to nurse their children in order to receive their stipends, as they were during the French Revolution. Nor were they ever paid premiums for breast-feeding, as they were at the turn of the century in Germany, and as they are today in French-speaking Quebec.[55] Perhaps the most extreme form of government intervention occurred during the Nazi regime, when German women were required to breast-feed at regular intervals and to undergo tests to establish exactly how much milk they were producing.[56]

In France during the same period, a government-sponsored program attempted to make breast milk available to babies who needed it as "medicine"; the program was located in a center for milk donors at the Baudeloque ma-

62. Fifty-angolar banknote from Angola, then a Portuguese colony. 1947. The nude breasts of dark-skinned females graced colonial banknotes, like this one, to suggest the need for external, white protection.

ternity clinic in Paris.[57] Four or five nursing mothers with their infants were housed, fed, and paid modestly, with the sole obligation of delivering their excess milk. Milk was extracted four times a day by special machines, similar to those used for cows, then refrigerated, and sold every morning and afternoon. Although this center and a few others had official support, they were never widely used, and disappeared with the beginning of World War II.

Government regulation of breast-feeding is currently very evident in Tasmania, part of a country in which the Nursing Mothers' Association of Australia has been enormously successful.[58] At present, mothers in Tasmania are required to sign a consent form if they want to give baby formula to their infants—a practice that would be unthinkable in the United States. Yet the history of breast-feeding in America has definitely had its own political agenda, with directives coming not only from the government but also from business, religion, medicine, and the overall sexual politics of the nation.

Consider these changes in American breast-feeding patterns during the twentieth century. As in the preceding centuries, maternal nursing was standard practice among American women until the 1930s. How, then, are we to understand the dramatic decline of breast-feeding between 1940 and 1970, when only 25 percent of American women nursed their babies, most of them for only the first weeks of life? A simple answer lies in the introduction of milk substitutes and their promotion by both industry and the medical profession. With millions of dollars' worth of baby formula sold each year, the growth of bottle-feeding can be attributed sheerly to the profits involved.

As for the part played by the medical profession, certainly many American doctors in those war and postwar years treated women as subjects to be managed by a technologically efficient, predominantly male establishment; they saw little need for women to participate actively in the birth process or to nurse their infants, especially since baby formula was considered a perfectly adequate—perhaps even superior—substitute for mother's milk. A 1975 study of the social forces surrounding breast-feeding concluded that American obstetrical care was structured in such a way that it denied women a real choice in the matter, and that late-twentieth-century American culture was intrinsically hostile to breast-feeding.[59] To support this last contention, the author quoted a story from *The New York Times Magazine* of July 27, 1975, to the effect that three women in a Miami park who were breast-feeding their babies were arrested for indecent exposure.

Women have been thrown out of various places—museums in Toledo, Ohio, shopping malls in Albany, New York, and department stores in California—all for the offense of nursing their babies.[60] Not until 1993 and 1994 did the states of Florida and New York allow women to breast-feed in public. The New York law of May 16, 1994, reads: "*Right to breast feed. Notwithstanding any other provision of law, a mother may breast feed her baby in any location, public or private, where the mother is otherwise authorized to be, irrespective of whether or not the nipple of the mother's breast is covered during or incidental to the breast feeding.*" One wonders how a mother can breast-feed without uncovering her nipple! "A bill affirming the right of California mothers to breast-feed their infants in public was finally approved by the State Assembly in July, 1997, after having been turned down the previous year. So far, thirteen states have voted similar laws that aim at preventing nursing mothers from being asked to leave stores, malls, restaurants, museums, and parks by officious managers and police officers."

Mothers in the 1990s are now encouraged to breast-feed by a wide variety of groups, like the World Health Organization and La Leche League. La Leche League, the oldest and most powerful of the breast-feeding organizations, argues that it is possible to work and nurse, without hiding its bias in favor of the nonworking mother. At best, the league validates women's desire to experience a uniquely female form of nurturance. At worst, the league induces guilt in women who do not breast-feed, and even in many nursing mothers who are made to feel that employment when children are small is not in the children's best interest. La Leche League is, in the words of one recent nursing mother, "a religion" that barely tolerates other practices.

Certainly La Leche League exemplifies a more subtle form of political pressure than that placed on women's breasts during the French Revolution or the Nazi period. In the United States, a mother's welfare subsidy is certainly not threatened by her refusal to breast-feed. If anything, her livelihood may be threatened if she *does* breast-feed, as some working women have learned to their dismay. Many women who have attempted to nurse in the workplace tell tales of harassment, lawsuits, and job dismissal.[61]

American women now face two sets of conflicting demands: that they nurse their babies, and that they compete with men for jobs without regard to sexual difference. This tension between nursing and earning one's keep shows up in the statistics: two-thirds of mothers with infants are now employed full-time, and barely 20 percent of all mothers breast-feed for as long as six months. With scarce on-site nurseries and paid maternity leave still very rare, the American Pediatric Association's recommendation to breast-feed for one year does not easily dovetail with the reality of most working mothers.

In America today, white mothers are the most likely to breast-feed. Statistics for 1987 showed that approximately 60 percent of white mothers nursed their babies in the hospital, as against 50 percent of Hispanic mothers and 25 percent of black mothers.[62] This differential breast-feeding pattern can be partially understood in terms of the greater education and income, and especially the more flexible work schedule, that white women generally enjoy, but it also has to do with complex ethnic histories. The black woman whose ancestors nursed generations of white babies as well as their own may indeed welcome bottle-feeding as a release from physical servitude and as a savvy response to the demands of late capitalist America.

In this connection, it is important to note that the United States is the only advanced industrial nation that does not have a maternity policy permitting mothers time off for childbirth and infant care. Over a hundred other nations, including Italy, Germany, Iraq, Uganda, Pakistan, and Argentina, provide an average maternity leave of twelve to fourteen weeks. Five or six months' leave with full or partial salary is increasingly the case in Northern Europe.[63] As far back as 1919, the International Labour Organisation voted to give mothers the right to two half-hour breaks a day for nursing, and this has since been written into the law of many countries. But in free-market economies, women are often afraid to demand these rights from their employers on the grounds that they will be discriminated against. This is the case not only in the United States, with its lack of protective legislation for mothers, but also in other industrialized countries such as Great Britain, where working women are still expected to "behave like men."[64] If they "behaved like men" and took two half-hour breaks to smoke cigarettes, one wonders if they would be equally penalized.

An interesting sign of the times appeared in a 1993 American advertisement that featured a woman in an unbuttoned velvet dress and hot pants who was nursing a baby. The outfit was clearly intended to be worn outside the home, perhaps at work or in an upscale restaurant. In a country that freely shows women's breasts in movies and on magazine covers, one might not have expected such an ad to cause a ripple. Yet, because the woman was shown in the act of nursing and in an outfit that was not designed for home use, there was indeed controversy. For one thing, the poster-sized versions of this ad began disappearing from Los Angeles bus stops, probably because some people loved them and because others found them "offensive."[65] As long as breast-feeding took place invisibly in the home, American society could condone it, even glorify it. But what if we were to see it all about us—

in parks and restaurants, courtrooms and offices? Will Americans resist such a scenario as too "messy" and too threatening to the overall separation between public and domestic life?

In Australia, where women can nurse in public places with notable ease, more than 50 percent of mothers are still breast-feeding three months after the birth of their babies. Everything in that country encourages breast-feeding, beginning with the five days in hospital during which mothers are taught how to nurse, what to do in the case of engorged breasts (cold cabbage leaves seem to work wonders!), and how to get assistance when they return home. Because of these supportive structures, it is rare for a mother not to breast-feed initially.

If it had been up to former American Surgeon General Dr. Joycelyn Elders (dismissed because of her outspoken pronouncements on sex education), 75 percent of American mothers would be breast-feeding by the turn of the century. In August 1994, she endorsed a global campaign to reduce reliance on baby formula.[66] Dr. Elders's statements recalled the "baby-milk scandal" some five years earlier, when it was discovered that a great number of formula-fed infants in developing countries had died because their mothers did not have access to clean water or refrigeration. In the wake of that scandal, such influential organizations as UNICEF and the World Health Organization tried to persuade third-world women to give up artificial formula and to breast-feed for as long as two years.

One 1989–90 UNICEF advertisement stated clearly: "Bottle feeding increases the risk of infection. UNICEF seeks various ways to protect and promote the practice of breast-feeding."[67] If all babies were breast-fed for at least the first half-year of life, they would be strengthened against diarrhea and the many diseases that now take a heavy toll on infants in poor countries. This would also reduce the cost of infant health care for UNICEF, whose support comes largely from Western industrial nations, like Britain and Italy, where breast-feeders are, ironically, in the minority.

Breasts, we have seen, began to take on political significance in the eighteenth century. Since then, women have been asked to offer up their breasts in the service of national and international interests. At certain historical moments, they have been mandated to breast-feed in order to increase the national birthrate, to reduce infant mortality, and to regenerate society. At other times, they have been directed toward bottle-feeding and milk substitutes. In times of war and revolution, they have been encouraged to pad their breasts "for the soldier boys" or to uncover them as symbols of freedom. Breast politics have emanated from a wide spectrum of governmental, economic, religious, and health-care sources—all traditionally male-dominated institutions not known for putting women's interests at the top of their priorities. Not until the late twentieth century would women themselves begin to have a significant say in the sexual politics controlling their breasts.

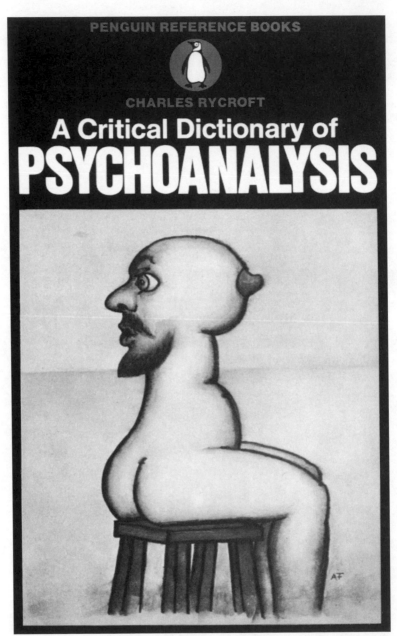

63. André François. Cover for Charles Rycroft, *A Critical Dictionary of Psychoanalysis*. 1972.

Psychoanalysis is represented as a man's face grafted onto a woman's body. A breast is symbolically placed at the back of the bearded analyst's head.

Five

THE PSYCHOLOGICAL BREAST:
MINDING THE BODY

BREAST   This word refers either to the anatomical organ
itself or to the idea (OBJECT-REPRESENTATION) of it existing in the subject's mind. 'The breast' is the object of
ORAL wishes, IMPULSES, PHANTASIES, and ANXIETIES
and is synonymous with 'the MOTHER' . . . 'Splitting of the
breast' refers to the psychological process by which the infant divides its image of a complete breast into two, one
part becoming 'the GOOD breast,' conceived to be perfect,
lovable, and all-satisfying, the other part being conceived to
be hateful and rejecting ('the BAD breast').

CHARLES RYCROFT, *A Critical Dictionary
of Psychoanalysis*, 1972 (fig. 63)

THOUGH CERTAIN FEATURES of breasts seem to be eternal,
such as their ability to produce milk and their vulnerability to disease, the meanings we attach to breasts are subject to considerable
variation. Indeed, as we have observed, we can pinpoint specific moments
when dramatic changes in breast lore took place—for example, when the
nursing Madonna appeared in the fourteenth century, when the erotic
bosom became dominant in the sixteenth century, and when the political
breast emerged in the eighteenth century. Another such seismic shift occurred at the turn of the twentieth century with the work of Sigmund Freud.

In the psychoanalytic scheme of things, breasts are the source of a person's deepest emotions. Freud posited that sucking at the breast was not only the child's first activity, but also "the starting point of the whole of sexual life."[1] His steadfast commitment to this principle was coupled with the belief that the father's penis—the phallus—cast its momentous shadow over the psychic development of both boys and girls. For Freud and his followers, human psychology was categorically constructed around the breast and the penis. These two body parts dominated the Freudian map of the mind, and established the reference points for psychoanalysis during its first hundred years.

In early analytic circles, Freud's disciples had the option of accepting his basic theses or of breaking off relations with the master. The Oedipus complex, which postulated that every boy lived in awesome fear of his father's penis and the threat of being castrated, was the ground-rock tenet to which Freudians swore allegiance. In the case of girls, "penis envy" was another not-to-be-contested principle.

From the beginnings, the breast stood behind the penis, somewhat obscured by phallic glory. Yet, like a half-buried goddess statue, the breast could claim that it had been there earlier and had never lost its power. Freud always acknowledged the significance of the breast, without ceding an inch of penis. Only latter-day Freudians, like Melanie Klein, would attempt to reorder the hierarchy and grant the breast pre-eminence.

Freud always thought of the breast as the child's first "erotogenic zone." From an initial oral stage at the breast, a normal child would inexorably proceed to anal and genital stages. The pleasurable erotic sensation of sucking at the breast was thought to persist in many unconscious forms throughout an individual's entire life. In one of those pithy expressions for which Freud is famous, he spoke of adult love as a return to the maternal breast: "The finding of an object is in fact a refinding of it."[2] From his earliest writings to his last, Freud was convinced that sexuality began at the breast and that the mother was in some way the child's "first seducer."[3]

Within this conceptual framework, dreams of spherical objects such as apples and pears could usually be interpreted as breasts. For example, a thirty-five-year-old man reported a dream he claimed to have had at the age of four. The dream involved two pears brought to the boy by a man who was in charge of his father's will. The boy's mother was also present, with two birds sitting on her head; one of them flew to her mouth and sucked at it. What does Freud make of this enigmatic vision? With characteristic certainty, he pronounced: "The dream must be translated: 'Give or show me your breast again, Mother, that I used to drink from in the past.' "[4]

Whenever there was the chance for Freud to see a breast hidden in the obscure thickets of his patients' thoughts, he rose to the occasion. Once, when he heard a young man free-associating from an account of his liaison with an actress to some lines of poetry, Freud declared: "There cannot be the faintest doubt what the apple-tree and the apples [in the poems] stood for. Moreover, lovely breasts had been among the charms which had attracted the dreamer to his actress."[5] Freud's dream interpretations, however far-fetched, are always presented with an air of papal infallibility.

Breasts figure prominently in Freud's basic theory of psychoneurosis, which has its roots in "perverse" sexual development. By "perverse" he means anything that does not lead to the primacy of genital functions over all other adult expressions of heterosexuality. The famous case of Dora, a "hysterical girl of nearly nineteen," offered a succession of perversions that moved along unconscious paths from infantile breast-sucking through childhood thumb-sucking and finally to an adult fantasy of sucking at the male organ—all of this intuited by Freud from her coughing and the irritation in her throat.[6]

In order to understand Dora, Freud drew upon the history of another patient, a young woman who had never stopped thumb-sucking, and who retained a childhood memory in which "she saw herself sucking at her nurse's breast and at the same time pulling rhythmically at the lobe of her nurse's ear"—the latter gesture suggesting masturbation. Following the thought trail leading from this unidentified woman to Dora's throat irritation, ostensibly caused by her wish to suck male genitals, and invariably back to the mother's breast, Freud asserts that it "needs very little creative power to substitute the sexual object of the moment (the penis) for the original object (the nipple)." "So we see," the good doctor concludes, "that this excessively repulsive and perverted phantasy of sucking at a penis has the most innocent origin. It is a new version of what may be described as a pre-historic impression of sucking at the mother's or nurse's breast."[7] The Freudian detective work, with its Victorian revulsion at oral sex, brings us full-circle: we are all glued to the maternal breast for life. Many later behaviors, and especially pathological symptoms, recall the nursing breast long after it has lost its original meaning.

To illustrate how early and later meanings attached to the breast can be confused, Freud often cited an anecdote about a young man who was a great admirer of beautiful women. When the man remembered the good-looking wet nurse who had suckled him when he was a baby, he remarked, "I'm sorry that I didn't make a better use of my opportunity."[8] Obviously the man had confounded the adult mind with the child's mind, expecting the boy to have treated the woman's body the way he would if he were already a man.

In Freud's last major work, *An Outline of Psychoanalysis,* he returned to the breast as "the child's first erotic object" and "the prototype of all later love-relations—for both sexes."[9] He insisted that the infant does not distinguish between the breast and its own body—a theory that has been turned into dogma by certain latter-day Freudians, although, like all other suppositions about the infant's experiential world, it can never be proved. Freud went further than ever in presenting suckling as the archetypal human experience. Indeed, he argued that "it makes no difference whether a child has really sucked at the breast or has been brought up on the bottle and never enjoyed the tenderness of a mother's care. In both cases the child's development takes the same path; it may be that in the second case its later longing grows all the greater." Whether one sucked at a real breast or not, and regardless of the length of time, Freud was convinced that a person "will always be left with a conviction after it has been weaned that its feeding was too short and too little."[10]

The breast, then, offers a psychoanalytic paradigm for the Garden of Eden. Once we were all sated in Paradise. Later, we were all ejected from the maternal breast (or bottle) and forced to wander in a nonmammary wilderness. As adults, we endlessly seek the comfort of the original bosom, finding it occasionally in sexual union, which Freud considers something of a grown-up substitute for the earlier pleasure. "No one," he remarks, "who has seen a baby sinking back satiated from the breast and falling asleep with flushed cheeks and a blissful smile can escape the reflection that this picture persists as a prototype of the expression of sexual satisfaction in later life."[11]

It cannot escape our notice that these two similar-looking phenomena are not necessarily identical. Just because babies often fall asleep after nursing and adults often fall asleep after sex does not mean that the later experience has somehow developed out of the earlier one. But even if we grant Freud his hypothesis that the baby's satisfaction from the breast provides the prototype for later pleasures, and especially sexual ones, a fundamental question remains concerning differences in the development of males and females. Freud says unequivocally that the breast is the first erotic object for both sexes. He then takes the boy through the Oedipal period, during which—in order to preserve his sexual organ, threatened with castration by the father—he renounces possession of the mother; thereafter he spends much of his life looking for substitute breasts. This theory, however convoluted, is at least credible on a symbolic level.

The girl, however, according to Freudian theory, does not renounce the mother's breast in the same way. She follows an even more bizarre trajectory determined early in life by her "envy for the penis." She "cannot forgive her mother for having sent her into the world so insufficiently equipped. In her resentment over this she gives up her mother and puts someone else in her place as the object of her love—her father."[12] The penis-envy hypothesis is the least defensible part of Freudian developmental theory, credible only as a parable for all the social advantages that accrue to males in patriarchal societies. Moreover, it offers no explanation for the reasons why girls abandon the maternal breast as an erotic object. Freud was, I believe, closer to the truth when he wrote, "Identification with her mother can take the place of attachment to her mother."[13] This identification does not result from resentment of the mother for having sent her daughter into the world lacking a penis, but from a growing sense of shared femaleness that includes their similar bodies. When the daughter develops breasts and begins to menstruate, she becomes, like her mother, an adult capable of sexuality and maternity.

In a few pages of notes left from the very last months of his life, Freud tried to rethink his penis-envy theory. First he turned to the idea of a girl's "identification" with her clitoris, still associating it with a sense of female inferiority vis-à-vis the penis. But then, in a series of hurried phrases, he began to reconsider the place of the breast in a child's mental life. "Children like expressing an object-relation by an identification: 'I am the object.' . . . Example: the breast. 'The breast is a part of me, I am the breast.' Only later: 'I have it' that is, 'I am not it' . . ."[14]

What do these cryptic notes, penned with the urgency of a man approaching death, mean? If, as Freud claimed, neither boy nor girl babies distinguish between the mother's breast and their own bodies, they eventually come to the realization that the breast belongs to someone else, who has the power to give it or withhold it. Both males and females move from an initial "I am it" (if we accept the premise that they first experience the breast as indistinguishable from themselves) to "I am not it." But girls have an opportunity to reclaim the breast as their own in a new way. At the moment of puberty, they can say something that boys can never say. They can say, "I have it."

If we carry Freud's elliptical insights to their fullest consequences, acquiring breasts as parts of one's body can be seen as a psychological advantage for women. The breasts they craved in infancy are given back to them in adulthood, as a source of pleasure for themselves, their lovers, and their babies. Because he was locked into a male-centered mind-frame, Freud conceived of the breast only from the outside point of view. He never fully valued the significance of the breast from the point of view of the person who begins life by nursing at the breast of another female, and subsequently, in maturity, becomes a breast-bearer herself.

Had Freud been a woman, he might have developed a breast-envy theory, instead of his penis-envy theory. It might have sounded something like this:

> A boy's mother is the first object of his love, and she remains so in essence all through his life. From the moment that he is attached to the mother's breast, he cannot get enough of it. If a new baby comes to replace him at the maternal breast, he will greet his younger sibling as an intruder and reproach his mother for withholding the breast from him — the earlier, rightful possessor. Hence, the feelings of ambivalence toward the mother and the sibling rivalry that festers within so many families.
>
> As the little boy advances toward puberty, he harbors the fantasy that the breast will someday be restored to him. Unconsciously, he believes that he, too, like his sisters, will develop breasts in adolescence. When this does not happen, he feels seriously wronged. He holds his mother responsible for his defective chest and does not forgive her for having put him at such a disadvantage. He feels hollow and inferior to his sisters, with their bulging breasts, and he never gets over this sense of deficiency. The hopeless wish for his own breasts leaves ineradicable traces on the boy's development and on the formation of his character. He desires throughout his life to avenge himself on women for possessing something which he lacks. Till the end of his days, the female breast will inspire in him both a desire for ownership and a rage at his own shortcomings in not developing breasts himself. The first sentiment usually translates into a need to touch or suck women's breasts, and the bigger the better. The second sentiment results in self-contempt, which is sometimes displaced into acts of violence against women, with breasts specifically targeted for retaliation.
>
> Even as a father, the adult male will be jealous of the baby at his wife's breast. He will always see that child as an interloper in the place that was originally his. Hence, the murderous wish he uncon-

sciously holds toward his own offspring, and the inevitability of conflict between the generations. The desire for the breast must be seen as the foundation on which all of civilization lies, with both Eros and Thanatos warring for its possession.

This spoof of Freud's three essays on female sexuality is intended to suggest that men's erotic craving for women's breasts *is* tied up with longing for the mother, with sibling rivalry, and possibly even with jealousy toward one's progeny.[15] When one sees a man strutting around with a busty woman on his arm as if she were a symbol of his masculinity, a breast-envy theory does not seem so outlandish.

By now, thousands of patients in thousands of offices have been asked about their memories of the maternal breast: "Did your mother breast-feed you?" was long a standard analytic question. The experiences of suckling and being weaned have not been considered beyond the reach of memory, as revived with the tools of the therapist.

A common reproach against the mother, reported by Freud and by subsequent generations of Freudians, is that the mother gave the child too little milk, which can be construed as lack of love. Worse yet, the fear of being poisoned by the mother's milk feeds into the fantasy of the "bad" or "poisonous breast."[16] This malevolent view of the breast subsequently became just one more feature added to the profile of the "castrating" or "schizophrenogenic" mother, which was popularized by American psychiatrists in the 1940s and '50s.

One of Freud's followers identified what has been called the "Isakower phenomenon." In dreamlike states, some adults have imagined a soft, doughy mass moving toward the face. Isakower interpreted this image as a revival of the infant's experience of being at the breast.[17] Analysts reporting cases of the Isakower phenomenon have used it to examine other memories from early childhood and to support highly conjectural theories about castration anxiety, incest fantasies, and other forms of regression in adulthood.[18]

Whatever reservations we may have about Freudian breast theories, we must give them credit for uniting the two major strands of breast history into a powerful psychological paradigm: the maternal breast and the erotic breast have become one. The mother and the lover will forever share a mysterious mammary incandescence, casting its glow into the present even as we move further and further away from its original warmth. Freud understood the lifelong psychic power of the breast as no one ever had before.

In Britain—where Freud spent the last year of his life, after the Nazi takeover of Austria forced him to flee Vienna—his legacy was carried further by several prominent analysts, most notably Melanie Klein, Ronald Fairbairn, and D. W. Winnicott. Often grouped together as "object-relations" theorists, they elaborated the Freudian belief that the baby takes in the qualities of the primary object—i.e., the mother's breast—and that this first object resides permanently in one's unconscious, like a kaleidoscopic image subject to limitless configurations. Klein, in particular, concluded that fantasies about the breast, begun in the first months of life, become part of an individual's unconscious, and affect all subsequent mental processes. To the Freudian discovery of sexuality at the breast, Klein added her conviction that sadistic-oral (aggressive) feelings fuel the baby's love-hate relationship with the breast, and hence with the mother.

Klein proposed an inborn polarity of instincts similar to Freud's life and death instincts. In her view, the death instinct is the original source of an infant's anxiety, which he or she deflects onto the original external object—i.e., the breast. This becomes the "bad" breast. Conversely, the gratifying breast associated with the life instinct becomes the "good" breast. In her words: ". . . the breast, inasmuch as it is gratifying, is loved and felt to be 'good'; in so far as it is a source of frustration, it is hated and felt to be 'bad.' "[19] This opposition between the good breast and the bad breast expresses itself in certain psychological mechanisms known as "introjection" and "projection." "The infant projects his love impulses and attributes them to the gratifying (good) breast, just as he projects his destructive impulses outwards and attributes them to the frustrating (bad) breast." His aim is to acquire and introject the ideal object, and to keep out the bad object. In this way, both a good breast and a bad breast are established inside the baby's mind.

Based upon her analysis and playroom observations of children in the 1920s, Klein believed she could see into the baby's mind: to the extent that the breast frustrated the baby's desires, it was a "terrifying persecutor." In the infant's destructive fantasies, "he bites and tears up the breast, devours it, annihilates it; and he feels that the breast will attack him in the same way." He fears retaliation from his "vampire-like sucking" or from fantasies of "scooping out the breast," emptying it of everything good, and then filling it with bad substances, such as his own excrement. When it comes to inventive descriptions of the infant's mental landscape (remember, we're talking about an infant of three or four months!), Klein can make even Freud look timid.

In time, the healthy baby moves from viewing his mother as either all good or all bad, to a fuller relationship with the mother as a complete person. The good and the bad breast, now the good and the bad mother, move closer together and become integrated. Conversely, in its pathological developmental form, the breast, and by extension the mother, continue to exist in the child's mind as one-dimensional, either as idealized or devalued forms.

Whereas Freud shocked his contemporaries with the discovery of infantile sexuality, Klein added the unsettling vision of demonic suckling. Today's mothers who have read Klein may find themselves musing, like the American poet Minerva Neiditz:

> Melanie Klein said
> that little children
> are envious of their mother's breasts
> and imagine that they can enter them
> and scoop out all their goodness.
> If what she says is true
> few of us would ever
> suckle such savages. . . .[20]

By now, the breast has been the combat zone for several generations of psychoanalysts and psychologists. Jung, for example, was mostly silent about the breast, but this has not prevented his followers from appropriating the breast for Jungian ends. The main Jungian addition has been to transform the Freudian view that associates mothers with libidinal orality into the "anima"—the unconscious female image in men. ("Animus" is the twin term, denoting the male image in women.)

According to Jungian analyst John Beebe, oral incestuous desire for the mother is not the only psychological meaning breasts can have.[21] Children pass through various archetypal stages, with the meaning of the breast changing at each stage. First there is the positive-mother stage, then the negative-mother stage, then the father stage. At the positive-mother stage, the breast is experienced as nurturing and comforting; at the negative-mother stage, the breast becomes persecuting, smothering, or devouring; and at the father stage, breasts or breast substitutes are associated with creative and spiritual possibilities.

Jungians believe that the man who develops the anima in himself will not be caught in the snare of breast envy, just as the woman who develops the animus in herself will not envy men their penises. She will have her own "phallic creativity." In contradistinction to Freudian theory, Jungians deny the assumption that breasts always imply regression to an oral stage of life. Yet, however much they protest their difference from Freudians, there is nonetheless a similar masculinist bias: the mature person is always the one who rises above the maternal stage (or stages) to embrace the realm of the father—whether it be called the "superego" in Freudian terms, or "anima" and "animus" in Jungian terms, or the "name of the father" in the language of the French psychoanalyst Jacques Lacan. The mother is always the person you have to get away from. These twentieth-century theorists could not conceive of maturity without replicating the patriarchal hierarchy of their times.

A representative example of how Freudian, Jungian, and Kleinian ideas are stitched together to fit the breast can be found in the writing of British analyst James Astor. Astor reconsiders the much-discussed subject of how the infant views the breast: "Immediately after birth and in the first few weeks of life the breast is experienced by the baby as his whole world, that is, not part of the whole, but as the whole. Only later, when the infant begins to explore the geography of his own and his mother's body, does the breast begin to be experienced as part of the whole."[22]

Astor extends the breast discourse beyond the mother-child interaction into the encounter between the analyst and the analysand. By analogy with the nursing pair, he asserts that "the mind of the analyst is in effect the breast, providing the food for thought that is part of the analytic upbringing of our patients." This "analytic breast" cannot be fully appreciated by the patient "until the weaning towards the end of an analysis." Metaphorically speaking, the comparison of the analyst to a nursing mother has its charms, though it adds little to our understanding of the therapeutic process.

Psychoanalysis can at least be credited with clarifying the way breasts function in the human psyche as overdetermined symbols, even if their interpretations have been limited to the nexus of maternal and sexual associations. What they have usually failed to recognize are other meanings unrelated to suckling and sex. Consider, for example, the subject of anorexia nervosa—a psychological illness characterized by an obsession to lose weight. For approximately one hundred years after the descriptions of this eating disorder by French and English physicians Charles Lasegue and William Gull in 1873, anorexia nervosa was considered a rare condition.[23] But in the past twenty-five years, it has grown from an isolated phenomenon to near-epidemic proportions among young females, who constitute around 90 percent of the anorectic population in the United States.

Psychoanalysis has traditionally interpreted anorexia as a "flight from womanhood"—that is, from adult heterosexuality. In the early 1970s, when anorexia began to appear in greater numbers, the prevailing psychiatric view was that it derived from deep neurotic conflict around sexuality, originating in the patient's family dynamics, and that it could be treated with a medical model of forced feeding and family therapy. But a number of feminist critics began to maintain that the anorectic's self-starvation derived equally, and perhaps more importantly, from such cultural imperatives as the "tyranny of slenderness" and the need to appear "boyish" in a world that privileges maleness.[24] They pointed out that many anorectics unconsciously, and rightly, fear that fat on their breasts and hips will make them appear stupid or vulnerable to boys and men. Rejecting their breasts is not only a rejection of sexuality and maternity, but a rejection of the entire panorama of social, economic, and intellectual inferiority which young girls see before them, often from having observed at close hand their mothers' lives. Anorectics know they cannot control the surrounding world—either that created by their families, or by culture at large—but they believe they can at least control their body weight. In fact, what happens is that, after a certain point of weight loss, they often can no longer control their food intake and slip into dangerous, and even fatal, weight levels. Today, with increased attention to anorexia and other eating disorders, psychiatry has expanded its view of the causative factors and developed more complex treatment models, which take into account the fuller range of meanings that culture reads into the female shape and inscribes upon the minds of young women.

Beyond the professional arena, the psychological breast has become a staple of popular culture. Think of the countless cartoons that depict an association between inanimate physical objects—apples, eggs, mountains—and a primordial breast image in the human mind. Think of the monster breast in the 1972 film *Everything You Always Wanted to Know About Sex but Were Afraid to Ask*, which escapes from a mad scientist's laboratory, ravages the countryside, and is defeated by a mock-heroic Woody Allen bravely brandishing a crucifix.

Think of Philip Roth's novella *The Breast*, whose protagonist turns into a huge mammary gland. When the hero of this fable (*pace* Kafka) tries to understand his predicament, the language he spouts is pure East Coast psychobabble: "Why this primitive identification with *the* object of infantile veneration? What unfulfilled appetites, what cradle confusions, what fragments out of my remotest past could have collided to spark a delusion of such classical simplicity?"[25] The transformation of an adult man into a humongous breast is presented as a form of wish fulfillment spoofing the obsession of an entire generation.

It is still so common to think in Freudian terms that Americans speak in shorthand of "oral" types and the French view the American mammary obsession as a form of arrested babyhood (forgetting their own age-old fascination with the bosom). When we recall the breast discourse popularized by psychoanalysis, we are able to laugh at much that was once considered gospel. Few take literally Freud's sacrosanct belief that "the child never gets over the pain of losing its mother's breast."[26] Nor do we call a mother unable to breast-feed a pathological "hysteric" and treat her with sessions of hypnosis, as Freud did in one memorable case.[27] Though we are sensitive to the many unconscious determinants involved in a person's life choices, we are no longer bound by dogmatic, flimsily founded interpretations masquerading as science. Sometimes a breast is just a breast.

Six

THE COMMERCIALIZED BREAST:
FROM CORSETS TO CYBER-SEX

I N O U R B R E A S T - O B S E S S E D society, breasts have almost endless commercial possibilities. They not only generate relevant products, such as brassieres and body lotions, but also, when pictured beside cars and beverages, promote the sales of those items as well. "You can sell anything you want with a breast," a French doctor recently opined.[1]

Women are both buyers and sellers in the breast market.

As buyers, they are bombarded by a barrage of products to clothe, support, protect, beautify, and enlarge their breasts. Ever since the late Middle Ages, when the corset was invented, fashion has profited from a continual progression of undergarments that correspond to changing visions of the ideal female form. Attempts to mold the body, to cover it up, squeeze it, pad it, shape or "train" or even mutilate it, are by now writ so deep in the collective unconscious that it is hard to speak of a "natural" body. The idea of the social construction of the body has become a given for most gender historians, one of whom summed up the visual interconnectedness of fashion and flesh in her ingenious book title, *Seeing Through Clothes*.[2] Clothes that come in direct contact with the naked body are often seen as sex objects in their own right, fetishes from the fantasy side of public dress.

Today breast products and services—bras and corsets, bust ointments and exercise classes, surgical augmentation and reduction—constitute a mammoth international industry. Throughout the Western world, women are willing to spend billions of dollars to create the breast illusion that will raise their sexual and professional stock. Taken in by feminine images which they themselves rarely create, some women become walking advertisements for push-up bras or silicone implants or other products geared to a standardized bust.

Yet it is all too easy to portray women exclusively as "docile bodies," in the words of Michel Foucault, all too easy to portray them as victims of commercial exploitation or collaborators in their own oppression.³ Women are now, and have always been, more than brainwashed victims of external pressures. Though we have reason to rail against the tyranny of the male gaze and the dicta of fashion, which affect women more generally than men, it is foolish to deny personal choice in these matters. Sometimes we choose blindly, it is true, and often we choose to please others, without even knowing that our choices mirror desires that are not our own; at best, our choices correspond to an inner aesthetic ideal (however socially constructed!) which contributes to a general sense of well-being, and to the admittedly pleasurable sense of feeling sexy.

As sellers, women have marketed their breasts since the beginning of recorded history. When wet nursing was a viable profession, countless women were able to earn a living through their lactating breasts. Those at the very highest levels, such as the wet nurses attached to the family of the pharaohs, were the equivalent of great court ladies presiding over significant networks of power. The wet nurses to the queens of France were entitled to any number of perks, including the name "Madame Poitrine" (Mrs. Breast), which was worn like a badge of honor in certain French families long after the monarchy had disappeared.

Many English wet nurses, as discussed earlier, earned at least as much as their working-class husbands—a rare parity given the age-old gap between male and female wages. This is not to suggest that the lot of the average wet nurse was enviable; most were probably treated little better than cows. If they lived in the nursling's home, some had to tolerate blows and grant sexual favors, and if they took babies into their own homes, they were subject to lapsed payments and even abandonment. When the body parts of an underprivileged class of women are purchased by members of a more affluent class, the chances for exploitation are very great indeed.

Selling one's breasts for erotic purposes is another, even more problematic, matter. Bare-breasted women in entertainment and the media, not to mention outright pornography and prostitution, have, throughout history, been subject to controversy and censure. Nonetheless, women exchanging the sight and touch of their breasts for money have never been in short supply. The hetairai of ancient Greece, the courtesans of ancient Rome and Renaissance Europe; renowned actresses, kings' mistresses, and demi-mondaines; the starlets, models, and striptease performers of our own era—

all perfected and continue to perfect an art of dishabille that reaps substantial material rewards.

Yet it is hard to tell whether women are the exploiters or the exploited when they exhibit their breasts for money. Are they exercising freedom of choice, or are they driven by irresistible economic rewards? Where is the line between the empowerment of an individual woman paid for showing her breasts, and the victimization of numerous other women all lumped together as sex objects? In the United States, where one rarely sees a breast-feeding mother in public, where topless bathing is generally illegal, and where even the sight of European topless bathers is censored on television, uncovered breasts are all the more precious because they are scarce. Many men will pay to see women's naked breasts in commercial enterprises because they don't see them anywhere else.

To illustrate the commercial history of the breast, this chapter will focus, first, on the evolution of products for the bosom; and, second, on breast exposure in the arts, media, and entertainment, including pornography.

CHRISTIAN DIOR's oft-quoted statement that "without foundations there can be no fashion" has been meaningful for the past seven hundred years. Foundations (namely, corsets, brassieres, and girdles) provide a "second skin" or a "second skeleton" aimed at constructing the preferred form of one's time, place, and class.[4] When, in the early fourteenth century, women definitively abandoned the loose tunics that had previously been worn by both sexes in favor of tighter-fitting clothes, undergarments began their fashionable assent. The stiff, clinging underbodice known as a *cotte* defined the new thin ideal. Large-busted women bound strips of cloth around their chests to acquire the small-breasted look then in favor. Women with droopy breasts sewed pouches into the top of their dresses to lift them as high as possible. Henceforth some kind of breast support was considered essential to the wardrobe of any self-respecting lady.

From that time until the beginning of our own century, breasts were supported mainly by corsets. One finds references to corsets in the late Middle Ages, as in the English royal-household accounts of 1299 listing two corsets lined with fur and the French royal-household accounts of 1387 listing six corsets belonging to Madame the Queen, but it is by no means certain that these early "corsets" resembled those that subsequently developed. Whatever it was that women were wearing on their chests in the early fourteenth century, it propped breasts up to new heights and made them visible above the new-fashioned low neckline. These stylistic changes, which emphasized gender differences, did not go unnoticed by clerical and civic authorities. In Germany, for example, around 1350, the Limburg *Chronicle* expressed concern that the new necklines allowed for the shocking sight of half the breast, which could only imply sexual lasciviousness.

Corsets became truly formidable in the fifteenth century with the invention of the "body" or "pair of bodys" in Spain. This armorlike structure, consisting of two pieces hinged together at the sides, made its way from the trendsetting Spanish court into French and English high society during the sixteenth century. Strengthened with slats of wood and whalebone, and sometimes made of leather or even metal, the "body" was worn as an undergarment or, in some versions, as an outer garment. It is possible that the metal versions (which have survived in a few museums) were used only for orthopedic cases, but there is no doubt that upper-class women subjected themselves to the agony of being encased in "bodys" stiffened by paste, leather, wood, and whalebone. English satirists did not spare those women who "Shut up their Wasts in a Whale-bone prison," and "reduce their Breasts into such streights, that they soone purchase a stinking breath" and open the door to consumption.[5]

The French version, alternately called a *corset* or a *corps* (body), was a kind of girdle that fit tightly across the chest from beneath the breasts to beneath the ribs and ended in a point on the stomach. Montaigne, always alert to human vanity, wrote of the pain women willingly and foolishly accepted in putting on their *corps*. "To get a slim body, Spanish style, what torture do they not endure, tight-laced and braced, until they suffer great gashes in their sides, right to the live flesh—yes, sometimes even until they die of it?"[6]

In most French and English versions, a single bone, wood, ivory, horn, or metal busk was placed in the middle of the corset to maintain its rigidity. This was the origin of all the boning and similar devices designed to support the figure that developed in corsetry over the next four hundred years. Made by specialist craftsmen and often engraved with amorous verses, the busk itself became an erotic object, the subject of boudoir poems and public gestures. It was considered daring to pull the central busk out from the bodice and to gesture with it as a form of flirtation.[7]

Between 1500 and the mid-seventeenth century, it was sometimes fashionable for women to appear flat-chested and sometimes fashionable for them to maximize the size of their breasts. When fashion called for thrusting one's breasts upward and baring them to the nipple, it was always a momentous sight for some male eyes. The poet and medical writer John Hall (born 1529) never forgot what he had seen as a boy during the reign of Henry VIII: "That women theyr breastes dyd shew & lay out." Thomas Nashe, author of *The Unfortunate Traveller* (1594), was distinctly disturbed by the brazen women who did likewise a half-century later: "Theyr breasts they embuske [place in ambush] . . . and theyr round Roseate buds immodestly lay foorth." And the anonymous author of *Quippes for Vpstart Newfangled Gentlewomen* (1595) condemned "These naked paps" as the work of the devil.[8]

Whenever the visible bosom was fashionable, men rushed into the breach with verbal and even physical assault. The French King Louis XIII (1601–43) — a far cry from his womanizing father, Henri IV — would not tolerate low-necked dresses at his court. One day, so the story goes, he spit a mouthful of wine onto the chest of a woman whom he considered too generously exposed.[9] During the reign of his son, Louis XIV (1638–1715) — who certainly had no quarrel with a womanly bosom — semiprofessional mammophobes continued to track down and denounce *les nudités de gorge* (nude throats and chests). To this day, French students chortle at the words uttered by Molière's hypocritical Tartuffe at the sight of Dorine's buxom charms: "*Couvrez ce sein que je ne saurais voir*" ("Cover that breast which I should not see").

A Flemish cleric, in a very nasty pamphlet entitled *Cancer or the Female Breast-Covering* (1635), tried to make a connection between breast cancer and breast exposure. A German pamphlet of 1686 alerted susceptible men to the dangers of "Young ladies with their naked busts, a tinder to all evil lusts" ("*Des Frauenzimmers blosse Brüste / Ein Zünder aller bösen Lüste*").[10] Pope Innocent XI, during his reign from 1676–89, went so far as to threaten women with excommunication if they did not cover their chests, shoulders, and arms with nontransparent materials.

When flat chests were the rage, women had recourse to various products and recipes dreamed up by apothecaries to keep the breasts small and firm. But when larger bosoms were in style, as during the kingship of Charles I in England (reigned 1625–49), traveling vendors went armed with a different set of lotions, ointments, and creams to make the breasts bigger. One treatment was surely as ineffectual as the next.

The cultivation of the breast as a fashion icon took on new commercial dimensions around 1670, when staymaking became a distinct branch of tailoring. Male staymakers established in small shops throughout Europe had a virtual monopoly on shaping the female body. If we are to believe the many eighteenth-century engravings that show women at their fittings, corset-makers took full advantage of the opportunity to ogle and prod their clients' bosoms.[11]

Corsets were a must for bourgeois and noble ladies, marking their distinction from the popular classes. Some even wore their lightly boned *corps de nuit* or *corsets de nuit* in bed. Wage-earning women and peasants could hardly afford the financial outlay that such garments entailed, and even if they could, corsets would have inhibited their labor. They wore only a *corselet* (little corset), which laced up the front, rather than the back, and did not require the aid of a servant.

From the mid-eighteenth century, a campaign against the corset raged through much of Europe. Under the banners of science and reason, and in step with the campaign against wet nursing, doctors in every country militated against the corset on the grounds that it deformed women's bodies. Like those who inveigh against the deadly effects of tobacco in our own time, the health crusaders of the past attacked the pernicious undergarment that women refused to give up. The Frenchman Jacques Bonnaud conceptualized the problem in a famous brochure, whose lengthy title encapsulates the entire debate: *The Degradation of the Human Race Through the Use of the Whalebone Corset: A Work in Which One Demonstrates That It Is to Go Against the Laws of Nature, to Increase Depopulation and Bastardize Man, So to Speak, When One Submits Him to Torture from the First Moments of His Existence, Under the Pretext of Forming Him.*[12] (Today we cannot help noticing how inappropriate the generalized form "man" sounds when applied to a specifically female person.)

These attacks did not go unanswered. Corset-makers, fearful for their commercial interests, sprang to the defense of their trade with the traditional argument that corsets "form" the body. A dressmaker from Lyons, for example, published an *Essay on the [Use of the] Whalebone Corset to Form and Preserve the Figure of Young Women.*[13] In it he asserted that corset-wearing city girls had better bodies than country girls, the latter developing round shoulders, narrow chests, and big stomachs in the absence of a corset. This was a direct reversal of the medical view that country girls, in a natural state, developed larger chests with protruding, well-rounded breasts as compared with the atrophied bosoms characteristic of corset-wearing city girls and aristocrats.

In the short run, women heeded the medical and moral critics: one of the first fashion changes of the French Revolution was the exile of the corset.

The height of the new mode was reached when Madame Tallien, wife of one of the Directors of the Republic, appeared at a 1795 ball at the Opéra in a silk tunic without sleeves and without any underwear at all.

In France and England, this near-nudity was much mocked by satirists and cartoonists, though it probably corresponded to the dress of only a small number of women. Another target of satire was the woman who augmented her chest with artificial breasts, as noted in *The Times* of 1799: "The fashion of *false bosoms* has at least this utility, that it compels our fashionable fair to wear *something*."[14]

Before long, the corset reappeared in both long and short models (figs. 64 and 65). The "Empire waist," fashionable throughout Europe during the reign of Napoleon (1804–15), broke with all previous conventions by raising the waist to the area immediately under the breasts. In this manner the breasts became the undisputed center of attention. With the Restoration of the French monarchy in 1815 and the triumph of political conservatism throughout Europe, the waist descended back to its natural level.

Around 1816, it was fashionable for breasts to be far apart from one another. The "Divorce Corset," invented and patented by the French corsetier Leroy, separated the breasts by means of a padded triangle of iron or steel which was inserted into the center front of the corset with its point upward. It became the rage in both France and England, although the English quickly reverted to the unified, shelflike bust.

At this time, in both France and England, corsets were still beyond the reach of the working class. When the Swiss industrialist Jean Werly installed the first corset factory at Bar-le-Duc in France, cheaper mass-produced models became available. His 1839 patent for machine-made corsets woven on a loom introduced a form of reasonably priced corsetry that could be bought by almost everyone.

By the 1830s, corsets began to be advertised extensively in European fashion magazines with line drawings and watercolor plates. Expensive American magazines like *Godey's Lady's Book* and *Graham's* were slower to introduce pictures of corsets—the highly respectable *Godey's* does not show them until the late 1860s. American manufacturers advertised "French corsets" that were produced on home soil in places like Detroit, Michigan; Worcester, Massachusetts; and New Haven, Connecticut.

The mid-nineteenth century was a time of major innovation in undergarment production. Eyelet holes began to be strengthened with metal rings. India rubber and elastic began to vie with whalebone to produce the desired

64. Short corset. Early nineteenth century.
After a brief period when corsets were abandoned, the French brought back a "mini-corset" that descended only to the waist.

compression and support. Waistlines moved up and down, dropping below the normal waist around 1840 and rising again in the late 1850s with the advent of the crinoline (a stiffened petticoat or "hoop"). The exaggerated hourglass figure required that waists be laced in so tightly that some women

65. James Gillray. *Progress of the Toilet*—THE STAYS. Long corset. Early nineteenth century.

The English preferred a longer version, reaching down over the hips.

reputedly died from the strain. A waist measurement of seventeen to twenty-one inches represented the ideal, but most young women, proud of the eighteen- or nineteen-inch corsets they had bought, were probably obliged to leave the laces open by several inches.[15] Stays with front fastenings were introduced in England in the 1850s, and gradually all but replaced the back-laced model.

By midcentury, women corset-makers outnumbered the men in both England and France. The French corset trade was firmly in the hands of women owners, managers, and laborers, though the latter were poorly paid. In Germany, where machine-made corsetry was introduced around 1850, the workers remained overwhelmingly men, with women limited to washing and ironing the products in the factory, or working at home on a piecemeal basis.

The English corset industry developed into a huge concern that received orders from the Continent and the United States as well as home territory. Fashion historian Rosemary Hawthorne, who has collected British undergarments and written lovingly about them, describes a corset she owns dating from 1860–70 "made of dull black satin lined with cotton," "close-stitched in a most complicated design," and containing "one hundred and four cased lengths of cording as well as twenty whalebones." Its superb craftsmanship resulted from a "peerless pedigree" that reached back through the centuries.[16]

The French, too, remember their corset history with national pride. They point to an astonishing variety of specialized models in a wide array of materials and colors. A turn-of-the-century French corset specialist called Violette laid out the following corset career: Around ten, a girl puts on her first brassiere—a light underbodice reaching down to the waist. At eighteen, for her debut in the world, she dons a batiste corset with supple stays. As soon as she marries, it is time for the "nuptial corset" with very firm stays.

To judge from the ads, a Frenchwoman had nothing better to do than spend her time changing between leisure corsets, sleeping corsets, pregnancy corsets, nursing corsets, and corsets for horseback riding, bathing, and bicycling. Ballerinas were obliged to have their breasts immobilized by tightly clasped whalebone gussets, which permitted an exaggerated décolletage in the back. And for the less fortunate, there was always the orthopedic corset. By the end of the century, French corsetry was at the pinnacle of its commercial heights.

And, not to be outdone by their French neighbors, German manufacturers made available "the right corset for every situation." These included medical and pregnancy corsets, nursing corsets with easy openings, sport and bathing-suit corsets, corsets for the thin and the fat, for the old and the young—even for girls between the ages of seven and twelve. "There are only a few women," one German writer noted in 1882, "who in the long run do not have the need of such a Stützbrust [corset, or more literally, bust supporter]."[17]

Falsies or "bust improvers" were commonly used throughout this period. Made from cup-shaped wire structures or flexible celluloid, or pieces of material with circular pockets into which a pad could be inserted, English models promised to "give roundness to those that are too slim."[18] French falsies were fashioned out of *peau de chamois*, padded satin, or, most frequently, rubber. American "bust pads" could be bought in exclusive foundation stores or ordered cheaply through the Sears, Roebuck catalogue (fig. 66).

For those who did not want their busts to disappear when they took off their corsets, there were numerous treatments to enlarge the breasts themselves. A ten-dollar "Bust Beauty Home Course" promised flat-chested

66. Bust pads. Sears, Roebuck & Co. Catalogue. 1897.

For as little as twenty-five cents a pair, "falsies" could be obtained to plump up the bosom.

women that they would be able to trade in their high-necked apparel for the most revealing décolletage. But surely one of the weirdest breast-augmenting gimmicks was "The Bust Developer"—a three-part program including a jar of cream, a bottle of lotion, and a metal object resembling a bathroom plunger (fig. 67). The bust developer was made of nickel and aluminum, and came in two sizes, either a four- or five-inch diameter.

French newspapers ran ongoing advertisements for miraculous lotions intended to "develop or maintain an opulent chest."

> SHOULD ONE COMPLAIN IF ONE'S WIFE IS TOO
> BEAUTIFUL!!! That is, however, the case of people who
> overuse LAIT MAMILLA. . . . To those imprudent ones
> whose chest becomes too ample, we suggest simply mixing
> LAIT MAMILLA with a little water. . . .

> THE VIRTUES OF CIRCASSIAN ALBATRINE. Albatrinc
> preserves the firmness of the breasts, while giving them the
> whiteness of alabaster. . . . Albatrine permits the

67. The Princess Bust Developer. Sears, Roebuck & Co. Catalogue. 1897.

The Bust Developer promised to make the bust "round, firm and beautiful."

abandonment of the corset, whose usage, always ungainly,
is often harmful to one's health. . . .[19]

The second advertisement was meant to take advantage of the revolt against the corset that had become increasingly vocal on both sides of the Atlantic. Both women and men, physicians and lay persons, began to speak out once more against the crippling effects corsets had on women's bodies. French, English, and American doctors targeted the corset as responsible for constricting respiration, deforming the ribs, compressing the abdominal organs, and causing a general "physical decadence" in women.[20]

A series of lectures delivered in Boston during the spring of 1874 featured five women speakers, of whom four were doctors, all passionately devoted to dress reform. Mary J. Safford-Blake, M.D., denounced the "six to ten thicknesses" of clothing which habitually encased the female torso, with special invective directed at the "immovable bondage" of the corset.[21] Caroline E. Hastings, M.D., blamed the corset for the deterioration of the thoracic muscles, so that a girl of sixteen or eighteen, who has been wearing "this instrument of human torture" since childhood thinks she cannot live without it. Mercy B.

Jackson, M.D., judged the deleterious effects of corsets to be even "more fatal" to Western women than the Chinese deformation of women's feet.

Arvilla B. Haynes, M.D., offered this sensible advice: "The corset should be discarded; but if it must be retained . . . , it should be made without whale-bone or steel springs, and should be held up by a band over the shoulder. . . . Nothing ought to interfere with the action of the abdominal muscles and the diaphragm."

The final lecturer in the series, the teacher and essayist Abba Goold Woolson, broadened these health critiques into a political manifesto that pre-figures the great wave of American feminism a century later. She spoke of the new "educated, enterprising, ambitious" woman, who was "made to work, to be looked at, but also to enjoy her own life; living not only for others, but for herself, and most helpful when most true to her own needs." She articulated an existential doctrine that many will still find radical: "I exist . . . not as wife, not as mother, not as teacher, but first of all, as woman, with a right to exis-tence for my own sake." And among the new women's claims was the right to be "strong and comfortable and happy" in her clothing. Alas, this doctrine went unheeded by the vast majority of American women.

The ideal form for American women fluctuated significantly during the nineteenth century. Before the Civil War, the frail, willowy type was fashion-able. After the Civil War, it was the voluptuous, buxomy model, and, in the last decade of the century, the natural-looking, athletic type.[22] Sears, Roebuck catalogues from the 1890s featured corsets for all these figures in at least twenty different models (fig. 68). Its most popular model, Dr. Warner's Health Corset, featuring straps over the shoulders and light boning, sold over six million units in seventeen years.

Corsets were everywhere in the late nineteenth century, not just on the bodies of women and girls, or on the shelves in lingerie shops and department stores, or pictured in catalogues and magazines. They were in the fantasies of poets and lovers, and on the tongues of orators and reformers. The latter saw in the corset a symbol of all that was wrong with the modern world, and some tried to legislate their extinction by proposing a special corset tax.

The American economist Thorstein Veblen, in his 1899 *Theory of the Leisure Class*, attacked the corset for rendering women weak and unfit for work, and increasingly dependent on their husbands, who could count their sickly wives as emblems of prosperity. In Veblen's words: "The corset is, in economic theory, substantially a mutilation, undergone for the purpose of lowering the subject's vitality and rendering her permanently and obviously

No. 23658 Yonng Ladies' Corset, with soft expanding bust; made of fine sateen with shoulder straps; clasp front; tape fastened buttons for skirt. Colors: white, drab or black; sizes, 19 to 28 waist measure; just the corset for growing girls **75c**

No. 23658.

No. 23659 Corset waist for girls from 8 to 12 years of age; button front; lace back; made of fine quality silesia; well corded; shoulder straps; tape fastened buttons for skirts. Colors: white or drab; size 19 to 28..................**69c**

No. 23659.

68. Sears, Roebuck & Co. Catalogue. 1897.

Standard adult corsets fit waist sizes of eighteen to thirty inches, weighed about a pound, cost between forty cents and a dollar, and were commonly made out of a twilled cotton cloth known as "jean." Special models for girls as young as eight were also available.

unfit for work," all of which contributed to "her visibly increased expensiveness."[23] It was time for the corset to disappear.

The transition from the corset to the brassiere that took place in the first decades of the twentieth century represented a major breakthrough for women. For the first time, a separate garment was designed exclusively for the breasts. From now on they would no longer be supported by the corset raising them from below, but by shoulder straps lifting them from above.

A French department store advertising its 1899–90 corset collection introduced the *soutien-gorge* (literally, "throat support") to designate what we would today call a brassiere, or at least the mother of today's brassiere (fig. 69). By 1907, a truly modern-looking brassiere, made from batiste without busks or whalebone, and owing its uplift to a special cut, was being sold under the label of "Mme Seurre's new *soutien-gorge*."

The first patented U.S. brassiere was the chance invention of a New York debutante, Mary Phelps Jacobs. Dressing for a dance, she abandoned the heavy evening corset laid out before her and, with the help of her French maid, fitted herself out with two handkerchiefs and pink ribbon. Afterward,

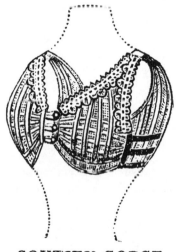

SOUTIEN-GORGE
(breveté), rose, ciel ou écru,
ne touchant pas la taille,
indispensable pour robes
d'intérieur et repos.
11·75
Nous donner le contour de la
poitrine en passant sous les bras.

69. *Comptoir des corsets* at the Galerie Rivoli, Paris. 1899–1900.

The first patented *soutien gorge* (brassicrc) was considered appropriate only for leisure clothes worn at home. Described as "not touching the waist," it was available in rose, blue, or ecru.

she made a few copies for her friends, and patented the design in 1914 under the name of Caresse Crosby, calling it the "Backless Brassiere." Eventually she sold her rights to the Warner Brothers Corset Company for fifteen hundred dollars. The patent was later valued at fifteen million.

It took time for the word "brassiere" to supersede all the other English terms. *Vogue* magazine first used it in 1907, and the *Oxford English Dictio-*

70. The Junon Reducing Brassiere. From the Ballets Russes program. 1912. The Junon Reducing Bra prefigures the postwar vogue for flat chests. Its caption reads: "Current Fashion requires very little breast. THE JUNON REDUCING BRASSIERE is . . . indispensable for heavyset women. It 'gloves' the chest to perfection and reduces it to the right proportions. . . ."

nary in 1912. The French alternately employed *brassière* and *soutien-gorge*. These first brassieres were very dainty and gave little support to the breasts. Like prisoners newly released from jail, breasts went through a period of non-support and indecision before finding a home in a truly functional brassiere.

During the period surrounding World War I, the kinds of corsets and brassieres that were available to women varied greatly. Already in 1912, the French were beginning to show signs of favoring the flat-chested look that would become fashionable after the war. An advertisement in the May–June 1912 program for the Ballets Russes showed a picture of the skimpy, stretchy, strapless "Junon Reducing Brassiere" intended to diminish the bosom (fig. 70). The Germans, on the other hand, were determined to resist nefarious French ways and to perpetuate the ample-breasted look propped up by heavy corsetry. A 1914 German advertisement that appeared in the *Leipziger Zeitung* shortly after the outbreak of World War I specifically targeted Parisian underwear as *Undeutsch und gefährlich* ("Un-German and dangerous"). Instead, it promoted the *Echt deutsch* ("Truly German") Thalysia Brassiere, which provided armorlike support and buckled at the waist.[24] Ultimately in fashion, as in the Great War, the French were destined to win the contest.

71. Scanties advertisement. 1928.

This "scant eight-ounce figure-moulding garment combining the brassiere, the vest, the girdle, the panties" promised to "banish all bulges" and reduce underwear to "A single garment of silken nothingness."

The twenties represent one of those historical anomalies when women sought to minimize their chests. Flappers strove for plank figures that would allow their long pearls to fall perfectly straight over their tuniclike dresses. Industry responded with bandeau bras that flattened the breasts and made them disappear into a boyish silhouette. Young girls took to wearing brassieres later and later, and some women dispensed with them altogether. Insubstantial fabrics like tulle and chiffon were very much in vogue; this was a far cry from the hefty upholstered look preferred by *fin-de-siècle* coquettes and Edwardian matrons. Rayon, developed around 1900, began to be used more and more frequently in the production of less expensive lingerie. For the first time, women with limited means were able to have the appearance of luxury by wearing rayon brassieres that resembled silk or satin. The accent was on simplicity, freedom, and stylish abandon, as can be seen in a 1928 ad that pictured a woman in a tubular one-piece undergarment joyfully throwing away her old brassiere, girdle, bloomers, and slip (fig. 71).

Yet not all women wanted to look like boys. Two young women, Ida Rosenthal and Enid Bissett, who were partners in a New York dress firm, found the flattened look unattractive and downright uncomfortable. Instead, in the early twenties, they built into each of their dresses an undergarment that emphasized the more natural contours of the bust. Clients soon returned asking for separate brassieres, and by 1925 the partners were producing and selling nothing but brassieres. With the help of designer husband William Rosenthal, a patent was filed in 1926 for a brassiere "to support the bust in a natural position." Such were the beginnings of the Maiden Form Brassiere Company.[25]

The women of the thirties adopted the simple formula that would be with us for the rest of the century: bra and underpants. (By this time the word "bra," instead of "brassiere," had become current.) Full slips and half-slips, girdles and garter belts, corsets and one-piece "combinations" vied for shelf space in the department stores, but the bra and underpants became every woman's staples. The new brassieres were becoming more and more functional, especially after the invention of Lastex, the yarn with the "two-way stretch." The Warner's company—which had bought Mary Jacobs's design for fifteen hundred dollars—was one of the first manufacturers to popularize elastic bras, and in 1935 it also created the system of cups in variable sizes, from A to D, which became the model for brassiere sizing throughout the world.

In 1938, Du Pont announced its discovery of nylon—a highly resistant synthetic thread that would once again revolutionize the fashion industry.

Nylon stockings and underwear were already in the marketplace by 1939, but two years later, when the United States entered World War II, nylon was mobilized for the war effort. Women would have to wait until the war was over for their nylon bras.

The war represented a major blow to the undergarment industry. In Britain and the U.S., many factories were taken over to make goods for the armed services. Silk and nylon went into parachute-making. Cotton, broadcloth, satin, fine net, and lace were in short supply. Steel and rubber were very scarce.

Maiden Form kept its latest models alive with substitute fabrics, while it simultaneously concentrated on products for the armed forces, including vests for carrier pigeons! It continued to advertise extensively, even when the bra supply was uncertain, as in the following ad from the March 1944 *Ladies' Home Journal:* "War-limited production makes Maiden Form's brassieres scarce but dealers receive regular shipments, so if you don't find your style at first, try again." No-nonsense brassieres in patriotic colors became the order of the day.

In England, lingerie companies tried to stay alive despite shortages and rationing. Berlei produced a series of eye-catching advertisements to remind its customers of its existence, and to call attention to its own war efforts. Posters of women in their undies were sent to men in the military to bolster their morale.

When the war ended, American companies were ready to launch a whole new line of underwear using the parachute silk, rayon, and nylon tricot that rapidly became available. New techniques of crisscross or "whirlpool" stitching were employed to create cone-shaped bra cups. These "torpedo" brassieres made each breast look like a projectile about to be launched. Maiden Form's circle-stitched Chansonette, introduced in 1949 and quickly dubbed the "bullet bra," would become its most popular model, selling almost ninety million units in over a hundred countries during the next thirty years. Women with small breasts looked to padded bras and "gay deceivers" for the appearance of a larger bust. The medical author of *The Hygiene of the Breasts* noted in 1948 that everyone wanted "to comply with the present Hollywood rule which requires that the bust measurement be one inch greater than that of the hips"—an impossible requirement for most women, even with the help of specially designed bras.[26] If we are to believe comic author Nora Ephron, even preteeners were not immune: in a famous article on her life as a flat-chested eleven-year-old in the 1950s, she recalled how she had bought a Mark Eden Bust Developer, a 28AA training bra, and three padded bras in three different sizes, which produced "one week nice perky but not too obtrusive breasts, the next medium-sized slightly pointy ones, the next week knockers, true knockers."[27]

In the immediate postwar years, English and French companies took longer to return to full production than their American ally. Yet, by 1947, the French had introduced the New Look, with its hourglass figure, pinched-in waist, and fully emphasized bust—a silhouette that was to dominate Western fashions for most of the 1950s.

New advertising possibilities opened up in the media. In 1949, Maiden Form ran the first of its legendary "Dream" ads with the picture of a woman in a satin bra and the words "I dreamed I went shopping in my Maiden Form bra." The "Dream" campaign ran for over twenty years, to be parodied in cartoons, greeting cards, and other expressions of American popular culture. A 1961 *Harvard Lampoon*, for example, spoofed the Maidenform Dream ads with the picture of a proper lady wearing hat, gloves, shoes, skirt, and nothing on top but her bra, taken into custody by two angry policemen. The caption read: "I dreamed I was arrested for indecent exposure in my Maidenform bra." The Dream ads spoke for an American culture on the verge of a sexual revolution. Breasts themselves were still carefully covered and packaged, but the very fact that women were shown in their brassieres in a number of unlikely public settings inched the fantasy of sexual freedom closer to reality (fig. 72).

As prewar radio gave way to postwar television, brassieres began to appear on the home screen. In 1955, Playtex was the first to advertise bras and girdles on American television, and in 1957, Berlei followed suit in Britain. A burgeoning supply of women's magazines, such as *Vogue, Vanity Fair, Harper's Bazaar, Cosmopolitan, Ladies' Home Journal, Seventeen*, and *Mademoiselle*, catered to American women of every age and income. Teenagers were identified as a distinct market to be lured by "training bras" and youthful styles. It was the golden age of postwar surplus capital, and packaged breasts.

In the early sixties, brassieres began to move away from the stiff forms of the fifties. Warner's 1963 elastic Stretch-bra was a veritable innovation, quickly imitated by other manufacturers. Rudi Gernreich, best known for the invention of the topless swimsuit, designed the "no-bra bra" in 1965, which gave support despite the transparent effect that one was wearing nothing underneath.

The sexual revolution of the late sixties and early seventies cast off the bra as an oppressive yoke. Feminists accused lingerie designers of packaging

72. Maidenform bra ad, 1962. "I dreamed I took the bull by the horns in my maidenform bra."

With her gloved hand on the bull's phallus-like horn, the woman in the Maidenform bra exuded sexual innuendos.

breasts according to men's—rather than women's—specifications. They asked why women were obliged to play into men's fantasies with rigid torpedo shells, rather than comfortable bras suitable for a living person. In response to the new unisexual ideal, manufacturers created brassieres that were as light and as discreet as possible. Warner's 1969 Invisible bra came close to the political wish for no bra at all.

The new look was distinctly androgynous—a far cry from the twin peaks of the forties and fifties. The waiflike form made popular by models Twiggy in England and Penelope Tree in America required only the barest of underwear—that is, if one was skinny and flat-chested to begin with. Though such fashion models were by no means politically radical, they joined frankly feminist women in popularizing an asexual look.

The 1960s, like the 1920s, were times of change for women. The "modern" women of the twenties had cut their hair short, minimized their breasts, and constituted the highest percentage of academically employed women in U.S. history. The sixties cohort resembled their grandmothers not only in their desire to look "boyish," but also in their aspiration toward greater social and political freedom. Their desire to "burn the bra" became a symbolic cry to banish all forms of external oppression. Even those women who rejected the word "feminist" would, in time, enjoy the benefits of women's liberation.

The French counterpart to the American "bra-burning" phenomenon was the removal of the top of the bathing suit. Although a few pioneers had been going topless on the beaches of Saint-Tropez since the early sixties, it wasn't until the late sixties that this became a widespread phenomenon. Following the "events" of May 1968, when French students and workers staged a minor political revolution, all of France underwent dramatic upheavals. For women, the desire to attain a new measure of equality with men and to exercise autonomy over their bodies began with the removal of the tops of their bathing suits. In a nation eternally split between the right and the left, uncovered breasts won a surprisingly easy victory: a quarter-century later, on the beaches of France, Italy, and Spain, women lie topless in the sun with little thought for those who might find such a sight provocative—or for the dangers of the ozone layer on their bare skin. Every year, in the spring, European entrepreneurs unleash a gigantic publicity campaign to sell special creams, suntan lotions, and tanning sessions to protect and enhance women's breasts.[28]

In the late seventies, another market was discovered in athletic-support undergarments, initially inspired by the jogging craze that had overtaken America. Women runners demanded underwear that could "go the distance."[29] In 1977, two running enthusiasts stitched two male jockstraps together to form the prototype for the Jogbra. The equation of breasts and balls—indeed, the female appropriation of a common symbol of maleness—undoubtedly made some people very squeamish. Very quickly, sport bras offering "motion control" became a major subcategory of the underwear business.

From the late seventies to the mid-eighties, more traditional forms of lingerie slowly crept back into the marketplace. Victoria's Secret, bringing sexy, affordable underwear to the masses, opened its first stores in 1982, and spread like wildflowers through America's shopping centers. Other manufacturers developed new models of highly feminine brassieres in a dazzling array of cotton, lace, satin, nylon, and Lycra models that rivaled the old corset industry at its best.

In December 1988, *The Wall Street Journal* announced that "Breasts are back in style."[30] It pointed to the foundation garment of the moment: the push-up bra, with its multimillion-dollar sales. It took note of new cosmetic treatments for the bust, and the growing demand for more bosomy high-fashion models. Though it raised some interesting psychological and even political questions (could the bosomy trend be linked to the macho conservatism ushered in during the Reagan years?), the *Journal* limited itself to the economic evidence: breasts were not only back in style, they were enormously profitable.

Self magazine of the same month featured an article titled "Breast Frenzy: America's New Obsession That's a $300 Million Business."[31] The specific business in question was breast-enlargement surgery. With the new focus on buxom figures, after two decades of fashionable flatness, some models who had been small-chested were now sporting more prominent busts. The late eighties were the heyday of what *Self* called "the new Amazons," with their "amazingly firm, round, *perfect* breasts." A female psychologist referred to implanted breasts as a "status symbol," implying that a woman can buy a perfect body, "the same way she can buy anything else." The American belief in purchasable perfectibility had come home to the bosom.

Other observers echoed this position, insisting that the breast craze reflected women's new managerial power and was not driven by men, as in the past. Still others, such as the feminist writer Susan Brownmiller, disagreed: The breast fixation was part of a backlash against women. It would send them and their enlarged chests out of the workplace and back to the home space, as in the fifties. Even the suspicion that they might be dangerous did not slow down the flow of breast implants. From 1988 it would take another six years for the Food and Drug Administration to put an end to the silicone boom.

But nothing stopped the fashion industry's promotion of aggressive brassieres. By 1992, women's magazines were clearly on the offensive in marketing the sexy bosom. Cleavage-producing bras were deemed to be at "The Cutting Edge" of the new femininity (*Vogue* editorial, January 1992). Women were told: "Don't be shy—it's fashion! and you want to show some cleavage!" ("The Bra . . . Meant to be Seen!," *Cosmopolitan*, February 1992). After two decades of playing down breasts, it was no longer considered bad taste to display them ostentatiously. By now males were supposed to be able to work alongside women with obvious female chests. By now women should not have to veil their breasts for fear of the jealousy of other women. By 1994, bras had become a three-billion-dollar U.S. industry.

That year was to mark one of the most heralded episodes in underwear history—the invasion of the Wonderbra. Created thirty years earlier, the Wonderbra languished in obscurity until 1991, when supermodels started showing up for photo shoots in New York wearing the Wonderbras they had found in London. When the American company Sara Lee Intimates took up the Wonderbra license, they began marketing it aggressively, with ten million dollars' worth of publicity and a carefully orchestrated sales program in stores throughout the nation.

In May 1994, when the bra first went on sale in New York, it sold three thousand units in ten days. Factories across the U.S. worked around the clock to try to catch up with the demand. In August, when the Wonderbra invaded San Francisco, cleavage reached new levels of hype. Outside Macy's, trumpets heralded its arrival and opera tenors sang its praises. It was delivered to Macy's by a cable car full of football cheerleaders, and to the Emporium in an armored car. At both stores, people lined up before the doors were opened. Buyers who showed up after the stock was depleted were delivered rain checks. "I can't think of any product that's had this kind of drama associated with it," said the manager of the Emporium.[32]

Hard on the heels of the Wonderbra phenomenon, other lingerie companies rushed production of their own versions, but the fashion surprise of the Paris 1994 fall collection was the return of the corset. *Harper's Bazaar* (October 1994) featured on its cover "Couture Curves & Corsets" as part of a series of articles telling its readership how to "Dress Like A Woman." Inside the magazine one learned that corsets had returned to the Paris runways after an absence of forty years. When asked what place corsets can have in the 1990s, after three decades of women's liberation, fashion designer Donna Karan retorted: "You always get to the point where one part of the body is being played up—and now it's the bust."

The waist-length corset that quickly made its way into department stores has the advantages of plastic bones and streamlined design, and is undoubtedly more comfortable than those of earlier centuries. Yet the "new corset" is hardly suitable for regular wear; at best, it may liven up a one-night sexual encounter, and then find itself tossed into the drawer with other discarded items. The appeal of the corset and the push-up bra continues to spark heated debate—and wild-fire sales—as we edge toward the millennium.

For the moment, the waif look is out and cleavage is in. The spring-1995 fashion issue of *The New York Times Magazine* (part 2) noted, almost wearily, that "Fashion aficionados are already acclimated to the return of the bosom, since big breasts have been a prominent style point for several seasons." If the prominent breast bears some relationship to national politics, Americans are probably reaping the dubious benefits of their conservative shift toward the right and the backlash against women. It may be that the current emphasis on breasts is an unconscious attempt to resuscitate the fifties' nonworking, maternal bosom. We shall probably have to wait another decade for a reappearance of the androgynous figure so popular in the "liberated" twenties and the liberal sixties. With the flat-chested cycle occurring every forty years, according to our twentieth-century sample of two cycles, we should expect to see the return of androgyny sometime after the year 2000. Manufacturers, take note.

MEN HAVE ALWAYS ENJOYED looking at women's nude bodies, and countless women have turned a profit from this pastime. Sight, Brantôme argued in the sixteenth century, constituted men's primary erotic pleasure; our latest U.S. sex survey indicates that this has scarcely changed.[33] During the Renaissance, Titian sold his bare-breasted beauties to the crowned heads of Europe, and his Italian contemporary the poet Pietro Aretino made a fortune out of less costly pornographic drawings and texts. Seventeenth- and eighteenth-century artists flooded the market with images of breasts spilling over from tightly laced corsets. Nineteenth-century painters situated female nudes in contemporary landscapes that shocked the bourgeois world and quietly found their way into private collections. None of these works, as art historian Linda Nochlin aptly notes, is "based upon women's erotic needs. . . . Whether the erotic object be breast or buttocks, shoes or corsets . . . the imagery of sexual delight or provocation has always been created *about* women for men's enjoyment, by men."[34]

What do we know about the models who posed for these works? How much did they profit from the commercial success of their portraits? One nineteenth-century model's story has come down to us through the efforts of a determined biographer. It is the story of Victorine Meurent, the model for Manet's celebrated *Déjeuner sur l'Herbe* (*Luncheon on the Grass*) and

Olympia. In both paintings, a nude woman stares out of the canvas with un-usual self-assurance, her breasts as pert as her face. Meurent was a model in the 1860s and '70s, and a painter for the next thirty years. In the early eighties, when she was deeply impoverished and severely alcoholic, Manet's stepson found her unrecognizable: "Only her breasts seemed unchanged."[35]

Around this time, new opportunities arose for nude models in advertis-ing. Profiting from recent technological advances, colored posters were cheaply produced and plastered across the walls of European cities. What was being sold was not the breast per se, or undergarments for the breast, but other, totally unrelated, products. Somehow the sight of a woman's naked torso, as in one notable British poster, was supposed to induce people to buy Root's Cuca Cocoa. Noting how a proper English lady was forced to turn her eyes away from that shocking sight, a literary gentleman wrote that, "even in England, the home of the proprieties," a woman drinking cocoa seemed to "require very little else." The gentleman's British understatement was an ob-vious allusion to the lack of covering for the model's breasts.[36]

Among those items promoted by pictures of the breast was the newly in-vented bicycle. Americans associate turn-of-the-century bicycle posters with proper Gibson girls in bloomer pants and high-necked shirtwaists, but Euro-pean publicity sometimes featured bare-breasted cyclists. Dainty English fairies and sturdy Gallic women rode into the new century with their chests uncovered, in ads for the Spinner Linton shipping agents and Liberator Cy-cles. The accent was on freedom, motion, and sexuality. The Czechoslova-kian artist Alfons Mucha's 1898 poster for Waverly Cycles showed a woman with breasts escaping from loose shoulder straps; one had to look hard to find the bicycle hidden in the foliage, which—along with the unruly breasts—suggested amorous opportunities in the countryside.

Mucha (1860–1939) was known for his many Art Nouveau posters de-ploying women's bodies to pitch a product. The one he did for Heidsieck Champagne shows a woman carrying a magnificent bouquet of fruit that seems to grow out of her bosom like a cornucopia. Another poster portrays a mother carrying three white cups of steaming hot chocolate at the level of her chest, while three children raise their happy faces like babies anticipating the breast. Images of women with cups of cocoa, glasses of milk, apples, grapes, or mangoes placed near their bosoms present an archetypal breast-food equation.

A particularly striking example of this is found in a turn-of-the-century Italian poster showing a woman leaning over to drink a glass of Liquore

Strega (fig. 73). One of her breasts is propped up on the table, while the other—a white ball of flesh—hangs down and threatens to fall out of her blouse. From such early beginnings, advertisers have continually exploited the juxtaposition of breasts and beverages to suggest that both women and drinks will satisfy your "thirst."

From the 1920s to the 1950s, the sale of American fruit was also promoted through a subliminal identification with breasts. Fruit-crate labels often contained pictures of buxom pin-ups, with or without images of the fruit in question (fig. 74). The label for Yankee Doll Apples pictured the upper half of a woman in a red blouse with round breasts that look good enough to eat (fig. 75). Many Americans in the forties and fifties formed their idea of womanhood according to these "apple-pie" pictures exuding sweetness, wholesomeness, and health.

73. Poster for Liquore Strega. Ca. 1900.

The precarious state of the woman's breast and the drink mirror each other: both could easily spill over the edge of their containers. Together the large breast and the small liqueur glass establish a sense of tension that is palpably erotic.

74. Fruit Crate Label. Ca. 1950. "BUXOM MELONS."
Fruit-crate labels for such companies as "Sweet Patootie," "Woo Woo," and "Buxom Melons" suggested sexual as well as gustatory satisfaction.

75. Fruit Crate Label. Ca. 1950. "YANKEE DOLL APPLES."
It is no accident that the word "APPLES" is set apart, like a label, alongside the woman's breasts.

Bosomy models also found an outlet in erotic postcards, which, like the brassiere, have been around for about a hundred years. "Naughty" postcards were already a big industry in France during the first decade of the twentieth century.[37] Women were shown in various stages of undress, often at the hands of their lovers, with breasts peeping out of mounds of lace and linen, or coyly exposed over the edge of the bathtub. Sometimes nude or near-nude women were fancifully posed in groups of twos and threes, with subtle and not-so-subtle lesbian overtones. In contrast to the "dirty" postcards of the late twentieth century, there is something sentimental and almost endearing about some of these cards. Many show women and men together in affectionate and playful poses, she as often as he in command of the situation. Designed

76. Postcard. Ca. 1950. "Will I measure up?"

A woman's worth is judged according to the size of her bosom.

to titillate to be sure, they are nonetheless bathed in a soft erotic glow that leaves something to the imagination.

These early picture postcards eventually evolved into the more explicit images of the mid- and late twentieth century. The importance of breasts in the postcard industry, as well as in the culture at large, was clearly stated in one 1950s card showing a blonde American sweetheart wearing the lower half of a two-piece bathing suit and holding a measuring tape across her nude chest, strategically positioned to cover the nipples. The caption on the other side of the card—"Will I measure up?"—sums up the measure of self-worth imposed upon an entire generation of American women (fig. 76).

Beach beauties bursting out of bathing suits now promote the attractions of Hawaii or Hamburg or any number of tourist destinations. Many of these cards reflect the cheap sexual humor that has always been present in lowbrow culture. Breasts transformed into cartoonlike animals, with captions that read "All the Breast from London" and "We're a couple of Swells in London" will get a laugh from all but the most straitlaced.

The use of breasts in tourism is but one example of how advertising appropriates women's bodies. This practice, with its underlying sexual message, has become so ubiquitous that today almost anything is permissible, as long as the sexual images "are considered artistic or are used to sell something."[38] Contemporary ads have even discarded the "no-nipples rule" that was still standard ten years ago.

Today's nude models, working almost exclusively with photographers, have opportunities in glossy magazines that were unknown to the likes of Victorine Meurent, but one thing has remained constant—they have to have the kind of breasts that our society considers sexy. Both male-oriented publications like *Penthouse, Playboy,* and *Hustler,* and general-interest magazines like *Vanity Fair* and *Rolling Stone,* consistently feature bare-breasted women on their covers. These covers are subject to faddish poses that jump from

77. (Right) Reid S. Yalom. Magazine covers. 1993–94.
Rolling Stone (September 16, 1993) with singer Janet Jackson on the front and *Esquire* (January 1994) with Los Angeles madam Heidi Fleiss featured male hands on female breasts. Other American and European magazines showed women holding up their own breasts. Note, in particular, the tiny-breasted German model whose hands were carefully placed so one could see her nipples (*Der Stern,* July 7–13, 1994) and the soccer-ball breasts held up with carefully manicured fingers on the Czech edition of *Penthouse* (August 1994).

magazine to magazine and from country to country, so that one ends up staring at the same globular breasts in Honolulu or Prague. Covers in 1993, 1994, and 1995 were characterized by "hands on the breasts" (fig. 77). Some of these covers showed male arms reaching around from behind the model to cup her breasts; others posed the model alone holding up her own breasts. As we have seen, the woman holding up her own breasts is a long-standing iconographic trope that can be traced back to the sacred breast offerings of ancient Mesopotamian figures. Today, however, the breast "offering" is a distinctly secular phenomenon intended to stimulate sexual arousal.

A nude model known only as "Gail" offered these insights into the sexy effects her breasts were expected to produce when she was a cover girl in the late seventies: "Hard nipples are definitely considered a turn-on. That's what photographers think looks best. So the one thing I do to them is make them hard by putting ice on them or somehow getting them cold, and that's a bitch! Either my nipples get really sensitive or frozen or numb!"[39] Would it dampen the male fantasy of female arousal to know that those erect nipples are merely ice-cold?

Like other nude models and entertainers, Gail was fully aware of the negative effects of the breast fetish on the female population. "There's such an emphasis on breasts as the almighty symbol of womanhood . . . and it's really too bad because there are a lot of flat women that think they're not even women!" She recognized that magazines "give people a false idea of what a woman's body really is," since they feature only one kind of body: young, thin, and large-breasted. Yet, predicting a continued increase in nude photos—a prediction that has proved correct since the late 1970s—Gail linked her financial future to them: "I use magazines for my own ends. . . . I make money from them, but for other women who don't look like young playmates they do a lot of damage. . . . If I thought I could single-handedly stop them, then I might consider it. But I'm not gonna lose out on money and be the one girl who's so selfless."

Gail seems to be speaking for a whole generation of women who have decided to run with the money, despite the suspicion that their work contributes to widespread psychological damage. The narrow range of perfect bodies shown in magazines—or placed in the hands of little girls in the form of the Barbie Doll with her pencil-thin legs, nonexistent hips, and protruding bosom—is destined to make many women feel dissatisfied with their own less than doll-like figures. Already in 1973, a national poll of sixty-two thousand readers discovered that 26 percent of the women responding to questions about their "Body Image" reported being "dissatisfied" with their breasts, and 49 percent were "dissatisfied" with their hips.[40] More recently, a startling April 1996 "20/20" television show revealed the extent to which some women truly *hate* their breasts. Social science studies seeking to understand this phenomenon suggest that women are unhappy with their bodies because they do not conform to the slim, full-breasted figures they sense men admire; in fact, women often tend to overestimate the importance of breast size in appraising their overall attractiveness.[41] There is good reason to believe that society pays a price over and above the monetary when it feeds the fantasy of perfect bodies and perfect breasts, without acknowledging any other kind.

Helen Gurley Brown, the editor of *Cosmopolitan* for thirty years, took this feminist position in the late 1960s "Women," she said in defense of the use of nude women in advertising, "don't get to see nearly as many naked women as they would like to." Especially in this country, American women have so little opportunity to see other bare-breasted women that they have an "idealized idea of how other people's bosoms are. . . . My God, isn't it ridiculous to be an emancipated woman and not really know what a woman's body looks like except your own?"[42] Of course, Gurley Brown's pronouncements did not open up fashion photography to a wider range of old as well as young, flabby as well as firm, and other departures from conventionally beautiful breasts: *Cosmopolitan* and all the other women's fashion magazines continued to display only youthful cleavage.

LIKE MODELS, actresses are also expected to have perfect bodies, whatever else they may possess in the way of dramatic talents. In the 1920s and '30s, women stars were sleek and sexy, their breasts scantily covered by loose-fitting slips and brassieres. Such was the image of Marlene Dietrich in *The Blue Angel* (1930), when she incarnated the ultimate femme fatale. At the other physical extreme, Mae West paraded her prodigious bust across the screen with a brazenness that enchanted several generations of onlookers. The hyperbolic breasts of Jane Russell in the 1943 film *The Outlaw* were raised to new heights by a metallic uplift bra, so impressive that the film was kept off the screens for six years for reasons of immorality! The American war and postwar years were dominated by the bosomy idol "the sweater girl," incarnated in Lana Turner and a succession of buxom film stars.

The unwritten law in much movie casting during the fifties was that "Only big busts need apply." The careers of starlets Jayne Mansfield and

Diana Dors, for example, "were built on their busts' pneumatic proportions."[43] Mansfield's 42DD bosom was reported to have been insured for a
million dollars. Another unstated law was that "Only blondes need apply."
The combination of big breasts and blond hair (albeit dyed) was best embod-
ied by Marilyn Monroe in the 1959 box office hit *Some Like It Hot* (fig. 78).
Here, as in many other American films, big breasts were identified with lower
class, the busty woman using every ounce of mammary flesh to attract an affluent husband and move up the socioeconomic ladder.

The French actress Brigitte Bardot, another artificial blonde with notable breasts, rivaled Monroe with her "sex-kitten" allure. Italians Anna
Magnani, Gina Lollobrigida, and Sophia Loren offered an alternate vision
of passionate and even vengeful sexuality smoldering beneath their dark

78. Marilyn
Monroe. From
the film *Some
Like It Hot*,
1959.

hair and heaving bosoms. All of these women gave the impression that sexuality was centered in the bosom. Or, in the 1947 words of John Steinbeck observing the "bust development" featured on calendars and posters, "a visitor of another species might judge . . . that the seat of procreation lay in the mammaries."[44]

If big breasts were the markers of sexuality and fertility, what was left for small-breasted women? Actresses like Katharine Hepburn and Audrey Hepburn, whose chests were hardly their defining features, represented something quite different. They were not symbols of sex, but of upper-class elegance. It was as if they were above the exigencies of the body. Even when they starred in love stories, as they almost always did, their absence of flesh signaled sophistication and wit, rather than passionate physicality.

79. Josephine Baker.

She was an American dancer and singer, and a Paris sensation in seminude music-hall shows during the 1920s and '30s.

Steamy sex, as dreamed up by Hollywood moguls, could be associated only with generous protuberances. A full-breasted woman was thought to be more passionate than her flat-chested sister; it did not matter to Hollywood that the size of one's breasts has more to do with male fantasy than with an individual woman's sexual appetite. It also seemed to matter little if the breasts were fully or partially covered, as long as they were selected and packaged for maximum size: one certainly did not expect to see them nude in fifties movies.

As compared with the cinema, live entertainment could be more daring, especially in Europe. Berlin in the twenties and Paris before and after World War II were known for lavish spectacles featuring virtually naked women (fig. 79). Uncovered breasts and buttocks, bodies adorned with plumes, sequins, lace, and small nipple-coverings known as pasties (often with fringe tassels that could be spun in different directions) paraded before the unbelieving eyes of locals and foreigners willing to pay handsomely for the ultimate night on the town. The *Folies Bergères* became synonymous with staged female nudity fit for a king, or at least an Arabian prince.

Back in the U.S.A., nudity was generally kept under cover by pervasive blankets of puritanism—that is, until the permissive sixties. Then, on June 19, 1964, in San Francisco, topless dancing was born. Carol Doda, at that time a go-go dancer at the Condor nightclub on Broadway, was asked by her boss to put on one of Rudi Gernreich's new topless swimsuits and perform her regular act on top of a piano lowered from the ceiling.[45] The next night, the Condor's line was halfway around the block, and within days, breasts were being bared up and down Broadway.

One nightclub featured a French-Persian star with a forty-four-inch bust. Another offered a "Topless Mother of Eight." Someone even opened up a topless shoeshine stand. At the Condor, the crowds grew larger and larger, as Carol Doda's breasts simultaneously increased, presumably through a series of silicone injections. By 1966, the San Francisco Chamber of Commerce noted that nearly a third of the city's 101 nightclubs were topless. Some topless clubs eventually gave way to full nudity, and even to X-rated peep shows. Throughout the sixties and seventies, San Francisco was the topless hub of the new morality—or immorality, as its critics charged.

A topless dancer from the seventies known only as "Susan" recorded an account of her experience.[46] At first she thought: "It just seemed so very weird! I mean there were people coming into a place to have few drinks, but mainly to watch my breasts being exposed. This was a form of entertainment? To watch them?" Then her attitude changed. "Once the shyness left I felt fine about it. It was like—'You guys wanta sit here and pay money to see 'em? Great! Cause I need the money!' "

Susan was surprised to discover, from talking to men at the bars, that some of them really believed the fantasy she was creating onstage: "... they think it's reality," and tended to put down their wives who did not correspond to a staged performance. This insight gave Susan pause. She began to wonder what effect dancing topless was having on society at large. But in the end, she continued dancing to satisfy her financial needs and, in her own words, her "narcissism and freedom."

Susan's appraisal was, on the whole, extremely upbeat: "topless dancing was an incredibly liberating experience for me.... There's so much camaraderie between the women, and not because we were all banding together as 'victims.' It's that we just keep being amazed that these guys pay to see our breasts."

And pay they will! The red-light districts of London and Amsterdam, New York and Los Angeles are magnets for millions of men willing to unload their pounds, marks, and dollars for the five-minute glimpse or hour-long perusal of "tits and ass." In glass-enclosed cubicles, women fondling their breasts converse through telephones with excited male clients, or they perform self-caressing dances on miniature platforms, goaded on by men on the other side of the barriers. In seedy peep shows or gala striptease spectacles, bosoms are often the feature attraction. "Showgirls" in Las Vegas, who perform topless—as opposed to "dancers," who keep their breasts covered—get flashier costumes and an extra fifty dollars a week—which doesn't add very much to a weekly salary of between five and eight hundred dollars.

Today one does not have to step out of one's home to view the flesh of female entertainers. Cable TV and the video cassette have brought breasts and butts right into the living room. The peep show now occurs on thirteen-to-sixty-inch screens where they can be ogled by the entire family.

No woman has been more successful in exploiting this market than Madonna. Singer, dancer, actress, superstar, Madonna projected herself into the homes and minds of millions of fans, including teenaged girls, gay men and lesbian women, and straight adults, who turned her into a cultural icon worth an estimated $125 million.[47] In her first and best film, *Desperately Seeking Susan* (1985), Madonna flaunted her full breasts and stomach with an impudence that became her trademark. Yet, within a few years, she had slimmed down considerably and developed, through a rigorous exercise program, a slender, muscular body that corresponded more closely to the national ideal.

Madonna has been credited with redefining underwear as outerwear.[48] This was accomplished largely through the conical bras designed for her by Jean-Paul Gaultier. In her colossally hyped film *Truth or Dare* (1991), she appears in one number in a pin-striped business suit with her oversized pink satin bra cups peeking through slits in the jacket, and garters dangling down over her trousers. This combination of classical business suit and sexy underwear makes a mockery of traditional gender roles. In another sequence, Madonna's pointed bras are themselves parodied by two dark-skinned male dancers who wear, strapped to their chests, grotesque phallic breasts, each about a foot long. The men energetically stroke their false breasts, and sometimes Madonna's as well, while she caresses her own body and simulates masturbation. It's a lewd scene that came close to being shut down by the police when it was performed in public.

Whether it takes the enticing form of Madonna or Marilyn Monroe, or any anonymous pair of breasts on a magazine cover, sex sells. Sex sells because it taps into subterranean networks linking our earliest memories of the maternal breast with later memories of our own bodies. Like Pavlov's dogs salivating at the sound of the bell even when food no longer appears, we still anticipate some sort of satisfaction from the breast long after it has ceased to provide milk. Overlaying our earliest unconscious memories are subsequent experiences of our own breasts in an adult state of arousal, the nipple exquisitely sensitive for most women, and for some men, at the touch of a knowing hand. For both sexes, the sight, and certainly the touch, of breasts can draw us into the whirlpool of desire.

Through the visual association of apples and breasts, men are made to believe that, when they buy apples, they are also buying women and sexual pleasure. By conflating bras and sex, women are made to believe that, when they purchase a Wonderbra, they are also purchasing an option on an ideal lover, or a least the potential to change their present mate into a more sensual and romantic partner. Of course, the consumer is not always so easily manipulated. He may recognize the simplistic intent in an ad and ask himself: What does a bicycle have to do with a bare-breasted woman? And the female consumer may respond with skepticism to the blissful face of a woman wearing a Victoria's Secret Miracle Bra. But there are enough unpsychologically-minded people who do respond to such strategies because they offer a vision of sexual happiness contingent only on buying a certain product.

After all, sex in the late twentieth century has been hyped into the greatest human good. Before then, and notably before Freud, sex had its place within a whole range of human experiences; for many women and some men, it was less a pleasure than a marital duty. After Freud, in the popularized (and vulgarized) version of his libido theory, sex became not only a force that shapes one's adult personality, but the royal road to life satisfaction. Increasingly, the pursuit of happiness became, for many Americans, the pursuit of sexual happiness *tout court*.

According to historians John d'Emilio and Estelle Freedman, American sexuality has changed over the last three and a half centuries from a family-based system in the colonial period, to a romantic-maternal ideology in the nineteenth century, to a commercialized industry in the modern period.[49] This last transition was accelerated in the 1920s by the introduction of many products catering to erotic desire.[50] Advertising was enlisted to sell the American woman a new self-image: she had to be sexy, as well as domestic. Commercial products began to promise that they alone could lead her to sexual fulfillment. The equation that commerce equals sex equals happiness is by now so commonplace that many adults have come to believe that purchasable items are the key to the good (read: sexy) life.

Americans have come to rely on consumer products to attract and keep sexual partners, to avoid venereal diseases and unwanted pregnancies, and to inform us when we have become pregnant. We also depend on a vast popular literature to tell us how to perform sexually and how to enjoy it fully (Alex Comfort's *Joy of Sex*, first published in 1972, has sold over ten million copies). Dating services and advertisements in the personal columns stimulate dreams of an "ideal mate"—sometimes for a very small fee.

The London tabloid *Sunday Sport* publishes "Play Mate" ads complete with photos for only three pounds for three issues. Although nude pictures are not accepted, many of the photos show women with their faces covered and their breasts uncovered! Here is a sample of the texts accompanying some of the bosomy photos from the issue of January 16, 1994.

BUXOM, very busty, married lady, 30, seeks mature generous gent, any age/status for adult fun, games. Hubby approves.

BUSTY blonde, attractive 40DD-26-36, lives in South London, wishes to entertain gent.

MATURE lady, late-40s, 48DD-bust, full figure, seeks gent, 30–60, for fun times together. You may have tried the rest, now try the best! Scotland.

These faceless, bare-breasted advertisements tell us something that is less obvious in the personal columns of *The New York Review of Books* and other highbrow publications. They speak for a sexuality featuring the body, or just the body parts. The face with its expressive mouth and eyes (the "windows of the soul," in Dante's lovely language) is no longer relevant. After all, who even has a soul nowadays? All that remains are the breasts, and for some people that's apparently good enough.

Lately, when I despair of this commodification and see people as victims of a marketplace run wild, I think of this letter found in the "Dear Abby" column (San Francisco *Chronicle*, December 22, 1993).

> Ten years ago, after 18 years of marriage, my husband left me for a silicone princess. My college-age son said, "Fight fire with fire," so I went to a plastic surgeon and had a "UTES"—upper torso enhancement surgery. I went from a 32B to a 36DD. You cannot believe how it changed my life.
>
> I needed a job, and was hired on the first interview. My first day on the job, I was asked to dinner by three single men. A year later, I married a man 10 years my junior. He adores me. I am in heaven!

The letter writer wonders whether she should tell her second husband that her breasts have been surgically fashioned, to which Abby replies with an emphatic "no."

In this vein, it is also worth considering the male counterpart to breast augmentation—penile enlargement. Drawn in by newspaper advertisements, radio talk shows, and aggressive marketing directors, some men in the United States and Europe are now undergoing operations that add length and girth to their penises. One San Francisco diplomate of the American Board of Urology invites prospective clients to join the thirty-five hundred satisfied men he has already operated on. Not surprisingly, other members of the medical profession have been highly critical of this procedure. At the

1995 American Urological Association meetings, a team of doctors from the University of California at San Francisco called such operations unnecessary and potentially dangerous, and concluded that surgeons who perform them are taking advantage of their patients.

Is laughter, rage, or disgust the appropriate reaction? Women may take perverse pleasure in seeing the tables turned, but on deeper reflection, the making of enlarged body parts—men's or women's—is cause for concern. Setting aside health issues, breast and penile augmentations are sad admissions of our failure to relate to one another as full human beings. If we are nothing more than breasts and penises, why not simply purchase, for the male, one of those life-sized rubber dolls like "Milky Maid" and "Lastex Lass," offered by so-called adult stores, or, for the female, a dildo of the desired length? These can be found in any porno shop, where the range of "sexual aids" is quite staggering: rubber body parts, nipple rings, leather underwear, whips, chains, and other bondage items.

Men who look to the latest technology for their kicks can purchase interactive sex through virtual-reality programs. A German version allows a player to don goggles and a tactile glove (*Tasthandschuh*), and then manipulate the breast that appears on the computer screen (fig. 80). The promotion material for this model predicts that two-person sensual pleasure, already on the wane, will soon be replaced by the wonders of Cyber-Sex.[51]

Those who prefer real-life women can satisfy their appetites—however bizarre—with X-rated movies and videos. Women acting in these films range from the upbeat Annie Sprinkle, who has become a successful photographer, to the hard-core porn star Savannah, who took her life in 1994. Savannah's story raises many disturbing questions about the negative effects of pornography on the women who star in it.

For five years before her death, Savannah earned hundreds of thousands of dollars by performing sex acts that featured her girlish body and twice-augmented breasts. After a decline in her career, an increase in her use of alcohol and drugs, and mounting financial troubles, she shot and killed herself. Although we can never say that the pornography itself caused her suicide, it certainly must have played a role in Savannah's confused sense of identity and in her decision to take her life. A fitting epitaph for Savannah would be her own words, uttered months before her death: "Too much pressure."[52]

Since its earliest beginnings, pornography has united sex to money, as implied by its linguistic origins in the Greek words *pornē* (prostitute) and *graphō* (write)—literally, the writing of prostitutes. In time, pornography came to refer to all literature concerning prostitutes and their clients, and, according to the *Oxford English Dictionary*, any "obscene writing or pictorial illustration." Of course, the difficulty lies in determining exactly what is obscene. For most of history, obscenity meant anything that offended acceptable sexual morality. But "acceptable" sexual behavior has always varied deeply from one era to the next, from one country to the next, from one community to the next, from one individual to the next, from one life stage to the next.

Like other people who consider themselves tolerant, I am not generally offended by sexually explicit material. Neither the writing of D. H. Lawrence, which occasioned the most famous pornography trial of our century, nor the pictures of women holding up their giant breasts on the covers of men's magazines are, to my mind, pornographic. To commodify body parts as sexual objects may be repugnant, but it is not, in and of itself, pornographic.

What makes a work pornographic—in my view—is the combination of sex and violence inflicted on a person, who is usually female, by another person, who is usually male. Sociologist Diana Russell offers a carefully worded

80. Cover. *Der Spiegel*.
November 15, 1993.
Now virtual reality offers
men the pleasures of the
breast, in computerized
solitude.

definition of pornography as "material that combines sex and/or the exposure of genitals with abuse or degradation in a manner that appears to endorse, condone, or encourage such behavior."[53]

This kind of material can usually be distinguished from erotica, which is sexually suggestive, even explicit, and certainly arousing, but not essentially harmful to the persons involved. I say "usually" because people do not necessarily agree on the point where harm begins. Some see it beginning in the Renaissance portraiture of nude women alongside fully dressed men, their dissimilar attire bespeaking a gendered power gap that has certainly not disappeared in our time. Others see it in any objectification of women's body parts displayed like purchasable commodities.[54]

There is, indeed, a gray area between erotica and pornography, but when a woman is represented in a sexual act that appears to have been forced upon her—when she is stripped nude, handcuffed, whipped, or raped—the face of pornography is unmistakable. When the rap lyrics of Ice-T describe the gang rape of a woman, with a flashlight to "make her tits light up"—that is pornography. When *Hustler* magazine shows a man placing clamps on an African American woman's nipple and claims that a penis will become "¾ erect" if its owner sees the film from which this clip was taken—that is pornography.[55] When bondage photos show men sticking needles into a woman's breasts or cutting them with scissors or pinching a woman's nipple with kitchen tongs or pliers, that is pornography.

The magazine *Tit and Body Torture Photos* contains pornographic pictures devoted almost exclusively to breast mutilation. Why the breast receives preferential treatment from sadists is not too difficult to understand: disturbed people often assault what they fear the most. Lorena Bobbitt, whose husband had repeatedly raped and abused her, cut off his penis while he was sleeping. (Mr. Bobbitt has gone on to act in violent pornographic videos.) Men who get sadistic pleasure from butchering female breasts—or seeing them butchered— attack the locus of what is perceived to be women's greatest power. It takes a lot of hate to mutilate a woman's most seductive and most maternal flesh.

Walk into the local porn store and take a look around. Open up some of the magazines lined up on the racks. And then ask yourself if you want such material in your neighborhood—or your city, for that matter. It's easy to defend pornography on the grounds of free speech when one has not really looked at it.

One defender of pornography, Nadine Strossen, believes that censorship and antiobscenity laws are actually harmful to women by limiting their opportunities for self-expression.[56] She notes the growing market for pornography among women themselves, including feminists, heterosexuals, and lesbians. Her enemies are the antipornography feminists, like Catherine MacKinnon and Andrea Dworkin, who drafted a model law defining pornography as a form of sex discrimination. That law, passed in Indianapolis but struck down by the Supreme Court in 1986, has subsequently been adopted in Canada.

The current national battle over pornography reflects the underlying opposition between two dearly held American concepts of freedom: freedom of speech and freedom from fear. In the climate of violence that prevails in the United States, many people, including this author, are convinced that uncontrolled pornography, like uncontrolled arms, undermines that second freedom. Freedom from the fear of being violated—from being sexually abused, shot, battered, and raped—is for many women a constant concern, and one that merits thoughtful legal restraints. To my mind, pornography, which links sex and violence and thus contributes to women's realistic fear of being violated, should not be able to flourish under the banner of free speech.

The emphasis on women's breasts in pornography, as in less offensive consumer products, leaves many women very ambivalent about their breasts. Large-busted women are constantly harassed by men's wolfish comments and unsolicited attempts to "cop a feel." If the women themselves succumb to fetishistic consumerism, they may find themselves paying large sums for products that enhance their bosoms, and bring on unwelcome as well as welcome advances.

THERE IS NO DOUBT that breasts in the late twentieth century have become fully commodified. They are dollar signs for the publishers of the magazines *Titanic Tits* and *Bra Busters*, dollar signs for the model willing to harden her nipples with ice, dollar signs for the plastic surgeon performing breast augmentations, dollar signs for the brassiere industry that creates the illusion of fullness, dollar signs for the cosmetic industry that promises whiteness, smoothness, and firmness, dollar signs for the British woman advertising for a "generous gent." If this exploitation of the bosom continues—and so far there is no sign of a letup—the next millennium will see even more outlandish permutations of the Western breast fetish.

Already it is impossible to ignore the phenomenon of nipple rings (fig. 81). They have become popular among some adventuresome youth of both sexes, especially in big cities like London and Los Angeles, where professional body-piercers ply their trade. Although the process of acquiring a nipple ring is reported to involve relatively little time, pain, or money, still one asks why anyone would want to subject her/himself to such a procedure. What is the meaning of the nipple ring?

Like everything else connected to the breast, the symbolic meaning of the nipple ring draws from both conscious and unconscious motivations. Women with nipple rings speak of "marking a transition" in their lives or "creating a new sexual identity" or making their breasts "more exciting" or simply wanting to distinguish themselves from more conventional folk. Perhaps they also want to signal to prospective partners that they are not breeders or nurses, at least temporarily. Many observers, however, see the nipple ring (like the Victorian corset) less as the sign of a stage of life or an erotic adornment than as a form of bodily mutilation.

Body piercing—of ears, nostrils, navels, and nipples—constitutes just one more attempt to improve upon nature. The long, worldwide history of

81. Reid S. Yalom.
Nipple ring. U.S.A.
1995.
A new form of
liberation or an old
form of bondage?

pierced body parts has intriguing cultural variations. The piercing of earlobes for rings of every conceivable form, shape, and material—so common in much of the world—has been traditionally frowned upon by the Japanese, for whom pierced ears represent bodily harm and an invitation to bad luck. The jewel in the nostril of Indian women, once considered barbaric by Americans, may now come home on one of our daughters or granddaughters. However we try to improve upon our bodies, those "improvements" run the risk of appearing barbaric to someone. And however strange the latest bodily fad, however bizarre the latest breast fashion, someone is out there ready to commercialize it. The products that find their way to female chests—falsies and wired bras, creams and lotions, breast implants and nipple rings (why not rouge or tattoos?)—keep the wheels of business rolling and feed the fantasies of countless women and men, for whom the breast merits all the enhancement and attention it can get.

Seven

THE MEDICAL BREAST: LIFE-GIVER AND LIFE-DESTROYER

N O C O N S I D E R A T I O N of the breast would be complete without a look at its medical history. Of course, a truly comprehensive study would have to cover thirty-five hundred years of recorded medicine, scores of civilizations, and innumerable sources ranging from ancient scrolls to sophisticated mammography. It would have to encompass numerous subspecialties of medicine, such as anatomy, gynecology, pediatrics, oncology, plastic surgery, and psychiatry. Ideally, it would also touch upon the ongoing relationship between official medicine and popular healing. This chapter can only suggest the contours of such a vast enterprise, with emphasis on those moments when some new understanding of the breast's physiology and pathology entered into medical lore.

Breasts have commanded the interest of medical doctors in two primary areas, one centered on lactation, the other on disease. (Cosmetic breast surgery is still too new to have had much of a history.) Physicians from antiquity through the nineteenth century paid considerable attention to both the life-sustaining and the death-related aspects of the breast, with the focus shifting from the former to the latter, and especially to breast cancer, in our own century. Lactation and disease—matters of life and death—these will be the two poles of our inquiry into the treatment of the breast by the medical profession since ancient times, with some attention to cosmetic surgery.

Among the earliest extant medical documents concerning breasts are Egyptian papyri from the eighteenth dynasty (1587 to 1328 B.C.E.). These describe methods of stimulating a nursing woman's milk flow: she was advised to "warm the bones of a *Xra*-fish in oil" and have her back rubbed with this odorous concoction, or to "sit cross-legged and eat fragrant bread of soured Dourra," while rubbing her breasts with a poppy plant.[1] Both treatments at least had the merit of relaxing the nursing mother. Other magico-medical papyri also included tests to help determine whether the mother's milk was good or bad.

Ancient Egyptians seem to have prized breast milk for its healing powers for people of all ages. In one papyrus, the prescription for a sleeping potion included the milk of a woman who has borne a boy. This prejudice in favor of the male baby, with its belief that he conveyed long-term benefits to the milk of the mother who had borne him, was to remain current in medicine for the next three thousand years! Generally speaking, human milk was used for a variety of medicinal purposes, as can be inferred from extant pottery vessels, believed to be milk containers, that were made in the form of a kneeling woman holding her breast in one hand and a baby in the other.[2]

The most informative Egyptian papyrus regarding diseases of the breast contains a description of forty-eight cases treated by surgery. Case forty-five—perhaps the earliest recording of breast cancer—tells us that a breast with bulging tumors which is cool to the touch is an ailment for which there is no cure.[3] Egyptian remedies for diseased breasts often involved fanciful ingredients. One recommended applying a plaster made from calamine, cow's brain, and wasp dung to the afflicted breast for a period of four days.[4] An accompanying incantation to the god Iser was also advised. Since the gods and goddesses were generally seen as responsible for both the onset of illnesses and for their cures, such magical formulas were a standard part of the medical repertoire.

European medicine had its origins a thousand years later in classical Greece (430–136 B.C.E.). There the medical profession tended to support the philosophical view that women's physical nature was basically inferior to men's. Both scientists and philosophers used the presence of breasts, womb, and menstruation to demonstrate that women were unfit to perform male tasks.[5] The writings of the physician Hippocrates (460–377 B.C.E.) upheld this position by arguing that women's bodies were spongy and porous, in contrast to the muscular, more perfect bodies of men.

The most influential and long-lasting Hippocratic theory was that a person's health depended on a perfect equilibrium of the four bodily humors—blood, phlegm, yellow bile, and black bile, linked to the four universal elements—earth, air, water, and fire. If one humor became excessive, the body's equilibrium could be restored through bleeding, purging, sweating, or ejaculation. What makes even less sense to us today was the theory that these fluids were interconvertible. Thus, menstrual blood somehow made its way to the breasts and emerged, at the right moment, as milk for the newborn. This belief remained in the medical literature until the seventeenth century! In this vein, Hippocrates associated the origin of breast cancer with the cessation of menses; he assumed that menopause led to engorgement of the breasts and to the presence of nodules which ultimately degenerated into hidden cancers. His position was that a breast tumor should be cut out only if it moved around easily. Otherwise breast cancer was incurable. In one of his characteristic short case-histories he wrote: "A woman of Abdera had a carcinoma of the breast and there was a bloody discharge from the nipple. When the discharge was brought to a stand-still she died."[6]

Gynecology and obstetrics were highly speculative subjects among the Greeks, of interest not only to practitioners but also to philosophers. Aristotle (384–22 B.C.E.)—a philosopher and a naturalist—considered breasts and menstruation as biological markers of female inferiority throughout the animal kingdom. In his *Historia Animalium,* he paid special attention to problems of lactation and to methods for determining whether the mother or wet nurse's milk was suitable for consumption. Aristotle believed, mistakenly, that the thin milk produced in the first days following childbirth was unsuitable for infants. Of course, we now know that this milk, called "colostrum," is eminently suitable, since it transmits much-needed antibodies from the mother to the baby. Aristotle also wrote a good deal of nonsense about swarthy women giving healthier milk than fair women, and nurses with warm milk inducing earlier dentition in the infants they suckled than women with colder milk.

The best-known gynecologist of antiquity, Soranus of Ephesus (early second century C.E.) was more favorably disposed to the use of a wet nurse than most medical thinkers of his time. Although he agreed that the mother who nursed her child might feel more affection for it, he recognized the wear and tear produced by parturition and successive nursing, and advised the use of a wet nurse "lest the mother grow prematurely old, having spent herself through the daily suckling."[7] Soranus dismissed certain popular superstitions, such as the belief that a wet nurse hired to feed a male should already have given birth to a male. He laid that myth to rest by reflecting that, in the case of twins of different sexes who are nursed at the same breast, the boy does not become more feminine, nor does the girl become more masculine.

Like other Greco-Roman doctors, he established extremely precise crite-
ria for the selection of a wet nurse. She should be between twenty and forty
years old, already the mother of two or three children, in good physical condition, and preferably large and swarthy. Her breasts should be medium-
sized, elastic, and unwrinkled, with nipples that are neither too large nor too
small, neither too compact nor too porous. She should be affectionate, clean,
temperate in disposition, and Greek by birth. Himself a Greek, though he
practiced in Rome, Soranus maintained a prejudice in favor of Greek wet
nurses that was shared by many of his contemporaries.

As for the milk produced by the ideal nurse, that, too, was subjected to severe scrutiny. It should be white with no red or greenish tinge, with a pleas-
ant odor, sweet taste, and medium consistency. The last quality could be
tested by squeezing a drop of milk on a fingernail or a laurel leaf and observing whether it held together without dispersing too rapidly.

Soranus counseled strict supervision of the wet nurse's conduct. She
should be encouraged to exercise, so as to avoid producing thick and indi-
gestible milk, with special exercises recommended for the arms and shoulders. This could be accomplished by throwing a ball, drawing water in a
bucket from a well, grinding grain, or kneading bread. Such movements reputedly activated the breasts to produce better milk.

As for the wet nurse's diet, she should abstain from foods that cause the
milk to taste bitter, such as leeks, onions, garlic, and radishes; meat that is
hard to digest, such as lamb and beef; and all foods that are highly seasoned.
Instead, she should eat hard bread made from fresh wheat, the yellow of eggs,
brains, partridges, pigeons, chicken, freshwater fish, and occasionally a suckling pig. She should drink only water during the first forty days of the infant's
life, after which she could add a little white wine.

In the best of circumstances, Soranus counseled two wet nurses rather
than one, and in the worst of circumstances, animal milk—preferably that of
a goat. If the wet nurse fell sick or if her milk dried up, various remedies were
suggested, ranging from breast massage to self-induced vomiting. He sensibly
rejected more bizarre remedies, such as drinks mixed with the ashes of burnt
owls and bats.

With the authority of a seasoned practitioner, and one who wrote for
midwives as well as for physicians, Soranus offers a lengthy guide to every aspect of breast-feeding. He tells the nurse exactly how to hold the baby in her
arms, and exactly when and when not to feed it. It doesn't hurt, he says, for
the baby to cry a little before being put to the breast—that's good for its respi-

ratory organs. But it's bad for the baby to sleep with the nurse's nipple in its mouth. Above all, it should not spend the night in her bed, for fear of being crushed if she should roll over in her sleep.

Although Soranus had a tremendous reputation during his lifetime, his writings had little posthumous influence; instead, it was Galen of Pergamon (129–99) whose authority dominated medical thinking for centuries to come. Like Plato and Aristotle, Galen believed that the male was more nearly perfect than the female, and that the female body needed special adaptations to make up for its insufficiencies. Thus he wrote of the breasts that they were placed where they were, over the heart, to give added warmth and protection to that organ. He also believed that melancholy women had a greater tendency to suffer from breast cancer than cheerful ones—a notion that would not be out of keeping with some of the psychosomatic speculations of our own time, although today's studies have failed to find an association between breast cancer and depression.[8]

To the Byzantine compilator Aetius, we owe an early description of breast-cancer surgery. Aetius considered tumors at the end of the breast and occupying less than half the organ the only ones suitable for surgery. Before resorting to the knife, the practitioner was advised to detoxify the body, either by purging or by administering theriac, an antidote composed of numerous odd ingredients. Crawfish boiled in ass's milk were also thought to have a cleansing effect. The use of crawfish was based on the belief that the appearance of an object, or even its name, was indicative of its therapeutic utility. Thus "cancer," the crab or crawfish, cures "cancer," the tumor. The medical use of the word "cancer"—*karkinos* in Greek—may have occurred because the crab or crawfish walks backward and attaches itself firmly to anything it touches, or simply because many malignant tumors look like crabs.

Aetius copied this description of breast-cancer surgery from Leonides, a physician of the first-century Alexandrian school:

> I make the patient lie on her back. Then I make an incision into the sound part of the breast above the cancer and I apply cauteries until an eschar [scar] is produced that stops the bleeding. I then make another incision and cut into the deep of the breast and again sear the several parts. This I repeat often, alternately cutting and burning in order to arrest the bleeding. For in this way the danger of haemorrhage is avoided. When the amputation is completed, I burn once again all parts until they are dry. The first cauterisations are

made for the purpose of arresting haemorrhage. The rest however
with the intention of eradicating all remnants of the disease . . .[9]

This form of breast-cancer surgery, with its use of cauterization to control the
bleeding, would be standard practice for centuries to come.

By the seventh century C.E., a substantial body of medical literature on
the breast, derived largely from Greek and Roman sources, had accumu-
lated. This information on breast-feeding, wet nursing, and the treatment of
breast diseases would survive practically unchanged until the nineteenth century, side by side with indigenous folk remedies.

During the early Middle Ages, the first medical school in Christian Europe was founded at Salerno, in southern Italy. Here both male and female
practitioners dealt with obstetrics and gynecology as well as general medicine. One of the women—a certain Trotula, who flourished around 1050—is
credited with having written an early textbook on the diseases of women that
was known under various titles and in various languages. In one version, an
early-fifteenth-century Middle English text, the author gives this advice to the
woman with a tumor of the breast: "Let this be warded off by 1 drachm of Ar-
menian bole, 3 ounces of oil of roses, applied with vinegar and juice of
morel. . . . Also man's excrement when burnt cures cancerous ulcers that
seem incurable." Excrement of all kinds seems to have been prized in the
cure of breast cancer, whether "the dung of a goat mixed with honey" or "the
dung of mice smeared on with water."[10] Such advice suggests that the treatment of breast afflictions had advanced very little beyond the wasp dung of
the ancient Egyptians and the burnt bats of the ancient Greeks.

Other Latin and vernacular manuscripts also suggest the role that folk
healing played in medieval medicine. Peyre de Serras, for example, living
near Avignon around 1350, counseled women who had problems in childbirth, difficult menses, or pain in the breast that might have been caused by
cysts, abscesses, cancer, or monthly hormonal changes to drink an infusion
made from elderberry roots pickled in vinegar for nine days. Another popular
treatment for a painful breast was to apply a plaster prepared from pork
blood.[11] Plasters could at least immobilize the affected area and were generally deemed successful if the symptoms were relieved—even if the patient
eventually died. With such remedies counseled by medical practitioners, it is
no wonder that medieval women clung to their beliefs in religious cures.
Praying in the churches before the Virgin Mary and protective saints or
under effigies hung above their beds could at least do no harm. As noted ear-

lier, the many stories of miraculous cures effected by priests and saints suggest how closely religious beliefs were intertwined with medical practices.

In the thirteenth century, the Italian surgeons Bruno da Longoburgo, Theodoric Borgognone, and Guglielmo da Saliceto wrote medical treatises that contained everything known about breast cancer at that time. Guglielmo recognized that treatments consisting of diet and local applications were generally worthless and that breast cancer could not be truly cured except by surgery. This was done by cutting away the entire affected part with "a very sharp knife," followed by cauterization with a hot iron and the application of soothing substances.[12] Theodoric's *Cyrurgia* included an illustration of a breast examination performed by a doctor on a seated woman, and another of a woman being taught to examine herself for breast abscesses.[13] Given the heavy emphasis placed today on breast examinations, these images seem way ahead of their time.

The most important French surgeon of this period, Henri de Mondeville (1260?–1320), also had his say on the subject of breasts. Surgeon to the king of France, Philippe le Bel, and professor of surgery at Montpellier and Paris, he believed that one should operate on breast cancer only when the growth could be totally eradicated; otherwise the intervention would just make matters worse. Empirically he had observed that cutting through a tumor generally produces a nonhealing wound, though he had no understanding of why this should be the case. There was not yet any awareness that cancer could be spread by such surgery and become a systemic disease.

De Mondeville also elaborated on Galen's statement about the placement of the breasts: "The reasons why the breasts of women are on the chest, whereas other animals more often have them elsewhere, are of three kinds. First, the chest is a noble, notable and chaste place and thus they can be decently shown. Secondly, warmed by the heart, they return their warmth to it so that this organ strengthens itself. The third reason applies only to big breasts which, by covering the chest, warm, cover, and strengthen the stomach."[14] What de Mondeville lacked in anatomical knowledge he made up for in gallant language.

Medical descriptions of the human body often relied on very flimsy evidence—sometimes no evidence at all. This was the case for the long-standing view, stretching back to Hippocrates, that breast milk was a form of menstrual blood. Commenting on this "poetics of milk and blood," historian Thomas Laqueur sees it as a part of a medical epistemology that relied more heavily on clinical and folk wisdom than on actual observation.[15] Renaissance

anatomical artists sometimes went so far as to draw in a connection between
the vessels of the uterus and the female breasts, as in a famous drawing by
Leonardo da Vinci.[16]

It was not until the work of Andreas Vesalius (1514–64) that the study of
anatomy developed into a real science. From his dissection of cadavers in
Padua, where he was professor of surgery, Vesalius was able to bring new understanding to the functions of the human body. Yet his groundbreaking
anatomical treatise, first published in 1543, was still informed by Aristotelian
and Hippocratic ideas about women. He believed, for example, that the substances from which the embryo was formed were "genital semen" and "menstrual blood." Breast milk was still a mystery, miraculously transformed from
blood as it passed to the breasts. Vesalius's interest in the breast centered on
its relation to the needs of the newborn, as is apparent in this description:

> When the fetus is given forth into the light of day, it sucks the
> milk as its own nourishment from the breasts, untaught by anyone.
> The breasts have their location in the chest and are furnished with
> nipples; they are built up of a glandulous material which, by an in-
> nate force, converts the blood brought to them by the veins into
> milk.[17]

Other Renaissance physicians discussed all aspects of nursing in texts that
were undoubtedly read more by other doctors than by women, given that
many of these works were written in Latin. Even for those written in the vernacular, the readers were predominantly other humanists and professionals,
since the lettered population contained relatively few men and even fewer
women.

The most famous French medical figure of the sixteenth century, Ambroise Paré (1510–90), wrote copiously on the subject of breast-feeding. Influ-
enced by his Greco-Roman predecessors, he concentrated heavily on the
subject of wet nursing. In one chapter titled "On the Breasts and the Chest of
the Wet Nurse," he states that "She should have a large chest and rather big
breasts that are not flaccid and hanging, but midway between hard and soft."
This "medium firmness" was the sign of good milk which would flow easily
when the baby suckled. As for the hard breast, its milk was considered too
concentrated, and the baby, "finding it too hard, gets angry, and does not
want to suck."[18] Such a breast also had the disadvantage, according to Paré, of
rendering the baby pug-nosed!

Paré's work is full of such questionable assumptions. Dark-haired nurses are better than light-haired ones, and above all, he warned, do not hire a red-head. If the nurse's last child was a male, she has special advantages: her blood will be "less excremental," and her milk better "because the male child, being in the belly of his mother, warms her with his natural heat more than a female." Yet despite such unfounded biases in favor of dark haired nurses, the male child, and so on, Paré also brought to the subject of breast-feeding useful practical advice and a good deal of common sense.

He was sensitive to the state of exhaustion many women experience after childbirth, showing unusual concern for the mother's health as well as that of her offspring. For the mother who chose not to nurse, he devoted a long chapter to various ways of drying up her breasts. These include massage, plasters, lotions, suction cups applied to the thighs and stomach, and suckling by another adult or little dogs! And if the mother could not find such assistance, Paré counseled her to use a glass pump, which she should place at the tip of her breast while sucking on the other end of the instrument with her mouth.

Like other medico-moralists of his time, Paré had reason to believe that maternal breast-feeding was better for the infant's health than wet nursing. By the second half of the sixteenth century, it was known that the mortality rate for infants put in the charge of wet nurses was extremely high. One of the causes for this high incidence may have been that wet nurses, who had been suckling for months and even years, lacked the "first milk," containing colostrum, which transfers maternal antibodies to the baby. The babes of poor women, suckled by their mothers from the day of their birth, may have had lower neonatal mortality rates. An early observer of this phenomenon, the Welsh physician John Jones, noted in 1579 the "relatively robust condition of the infants of poorer mothers."[19] Even if an upper-class mother had chosen to breast-feed, she would not have done so during the first few days of her infant's life, since it was mistakenly believed, following Aristotle and others, that the "first milk" was bad for the babe.

While Renaissance doctors were creating a new body of obstetrical literature, the actual care of most mothers during pregnancy, childbirth, and nursing was the province of midwives. For the most part, midwives were trained by other midwives without the benefit of institutional instruction or municipal surveillance. In Paris, however, by the late sixteenth century, the midwife profession was carefully controlled by civil, medical, and religious authorities. The official list of midwives for 1601 contains sixty names classed according to seniority, and among them that of Madame Louyse Bourgeoyse.

Louise Bourgeois (to use the modern spelling) has come down in history as the midwife who brought into the world the French King Louis XIII and the five other children of Marie de Médicis and Henri IV. She is also known for having published, in 1609, the first French obstetrical book written by a midwife. Bourgeois repeats much that could already be found in the work of Ambroise Paré (with whom her surgeon husband had studied), but she also brings to the care of women her personal experience and a distinctive voice—which smacks more of the kitchen than the consulting room. For instance, one of her many recipes for drying up a mother's milk is an ointment made from beeswax, honey, an ounce of oil of roses, an ounce of fresh butter, and the juice of sage and chervil, to be spread on fine hemp and placed upon the breasts, after they have been rubbed with oil of roses and vinegar, all of which should be covered over with hot linens and left for a period of eight days. For nursing mothers who, for one reason or another (fear, anger, sickness, bad food, or melancholy), lose their milk and want to bring it back, she counsels a good soup made of fennel, chicory, sorrel, and lettuce, to be eaten morning and evening. Women with a swollen or tumorous breast are told: "Take a half-pound of lard and dissolve it, a small amount of new wax, two ounces of pitch [tar], and from all of this make an ointment, with which you will plaster the breast once it has been lanced."[20] Bourgeois's homey style probably accounts for her popularity among generations of midwives, mothers, and wet nurses who would have been unable to pore through more formal medical treatises.

Her advice on the choice of a wet nurse, lacking the moralistic tone found among many male writers, indicates that this practice was becoming increasingly acceptable among the bourgeoisie as well as the aristocracy. There are, of course, old caveats to be taken into consideration: check out the prospective wet nurse's teeth, hair color, medical history, and especially her character (those with an amorous nature are to be studiously avoided). Considering that a baby spends nine months in its mother's womb and two years at a wet nurse's breast, Bourgeois was not surprised to discover that some children have more of the tendencies of the latter than the former. In the seventeenth century, wet nursing—like midwifery—was becoming a more regulated profession, one that offered women an opportunity to earn a decent wage and occasionally to rise in the social hierarchy (fig. 82). The midwife and the wet nurse were part of a network of women healers that was only beginning to be challenged by male physicians.

Both medical doctors and women healers continued to understand illness along humoralist lines. They repeated the views of Hippocrates and

82. Louis XIV as an infant and his wet nurse. Anonymous painter.

Wet nurses to the French royal family were carefully chosen according to strict standards laid out in medical treatises.

Galen, prescribing emetics, blood-letting, and certain foods that would ostensibly restore balance to the system. Insofar as the breast was concerned,
they believed that cancer was caused by a fluxion of a sluggish, thick humor
and that the degree of malignancy was determined by the humor in question. They were generally conservative in treating breast cancer, preferring
restorative diets and local applications to mastectomy, except in the case of
ulceration.

The most outstanding German surgeon of this period, Wilhelm Fabry
(1560–1634), believed that breast cancer began with a drop of milk curdling
and hardening within the breast. He became known for his removal of breast
tumors, including the swellings under the armpit. This is how he described
one of his cases:

> After five years (if I remember correctly) of such suffering, when
> the hard cancerous swelling had approached its gravest point, I was
> approached. I found in the right breast a hidden cancer, far larger
> than a fist, hard and pale. In the axilla there were also hidden three
> hard swellings, one of which was as big as an egg; . . . After her body
> was sufficiently prepared, by a suitable regimen of food and drink,
> and also by purging and bleeding, . . . I cut out all these hard
> swellings and she became well again.[21]

If the results were as successful as Fabry claims, it was partially because
he followed a policy of removing not only the tumor but every bit of mem-
brane surrounding it. He was aware that, if a part of the tumor or surrounding
tissue, however small, remains behind, "it flares up again and becomes worse
than ever before."

Another famous German surgeon, Johannes Schultetus (1595–1645),
placed illustrations of the sequential steps of a mastectomy in his posthu-
mously published book, *Armamentarium Chirurgicum* (1653). Translations of
this work into German, French, and English, and the use of his illustrations
in other surgical books, account for its widespread influence over the suc-
ceeding centuries.[22]

With the discovery of blood circulation by William Harvey in 1628 and
the discovery of the lymphatic system, designated as *vasa lymphatica* by
Thomas Bartholin of Copenhagen in 1652, science entered a transitional
stage between the gradual abandonment of humoral pathology and the acceptance of cellular pathology in the nineteenth century. For the next two

hundred years, medicine and quackery, superstition and science, unfounded prejudice and empirical observation coexisted willy-nilly, as they still do, if less flagrantly, in our own time.

Some doctors believed that cancer was contagious, especially the ulcerating kind. The Amsterdam physician and anatomist Nicolaes Tulp (1593–1674) — known to later generations through Rembrandt's famous painting *The Anatomy Lesson* — cited the case of a patient suffering from open breast cancer who was reputed to have conveyed it to her housemaid.[23] The belief in the contagiousness of cancer persisted well into the nineteenth century, and even today the relatives and friends of cancer patients sometimes harbor this scientifically baseless fear.

Among physicians consulted for breast cancer, surgery was usually considered the treatment of last resort. This was the case in 1663 when Anne of Austria, mother of King Louis XIV of France, discovered a small nodule in her left breast. It was treated with bleed-letting, emetics, enemas, compresses, ointments, and later, after it had ulcerated, with belladonna and burnt lime. A slew of French and foreign doctors, healers, and quacks examined the queen, and proposed every manner of remedy. Observing all these interventions in a series of letters, Gui Patin, the former dean of the Paris Medical Faculty, stated in exasperation, "Cancer cannot be cured and will never be cured; but the world wants to be fooled" (May 22, 1665).

By August 1665, Anne had been so weakened that twice she had been pronounced near death. At this time, she placed herself in the hands of a doctor from Lorraine, whose special remedy was an arsenic paste; its effect was to mortify the diseased tissue, which was then progressively cut away. She underwent these operations from August 1665 to January 1666, showing little signs of recovery. Finally, the Oorschot surgeon, Arnoldus Fey, was brought in to operate. Since the situation was clearly beyond help, he issued a legal document declaring that he could not be held liable for the results. The queen suffered agonizing pain from the operation Fey performed upon her, and died in January 1666, in her sixty-fifth year.[24]

The honor of performing successful breast-cancer surgery for the first time in France was claimed by Adrian Helvétius (1661–1741), a Dutch physician practicing in Paris. His 1697 "Letter on the Nature and Cure of Cancer" relied heavily on the case of a woman who underwent what we would today call a lumpectomy.[25]

Marguerite Perpointe, aged forty-six, born in England twenty-five leagues from London, discovered she had breast cancer in April 1690. Crossing the

Channel, she experienced a pain in her right breast and felt a small, hard growth about the size of a walnut. She consulted Helvétius as soon as she arrived in Paris, telling him that several months earlier she had bumped against a key sticking out of a door. Helvétius sent her to two surgeons, explaining that the only remedy was to operate according to his instructions. Because she was too frightened, she tried other remedies—plasters, cataplasms—all of which proved useless. Six months later, the tumor had grown to the size of a fist, and her pain had increased accordingly.

Fearing the cancer would burst open, she returned to Helvétius, who decided it was still operable. In his words: "I helped the patient resolve to suffer its extirpation." The operation, performed by two surgeons chosen by Helvétius, took place in the presence of more than twenty distinguished members of the medical profession, notables, and scientists "brought there by curiosity to witness something that had been unknown in France until that moment." All expected the worst, "a spectacle of cruelty, a long and painful operation, with dolorous cries, a great effusion of blood from the patient, and to see her exposed to mortal danger." Instead, the operation took place "without great pain, without cries, without the appearance of weakness, without the slightest danger, without spilling more than two palettes of blood, with ease, facility, and promptness." Everyone present examined the enormous mass that was removed, which had become "hard like a horn," and all agreed with Helvétius that "extirpation had been the only possible remedy." Helvétius was proud to report several years later: "Since that time, the patient has been entirely restored. Her pain has completed ceased, the scar has perfectly healed, and she is enjoying a state of health such as she had before the cancer."

Helvétius distinguished between amputation, necessary when the cancer had spread throughout the breast, and extirpation (lumpectomy), when the cancer was restricted to a single "gland." In the latter case, it was sufficient to remove only the diseased tissue, without cutting off the entire breast. Helvétius assured his readers, "Each of these two operations is easy." He was also proud of having invented a kind of iron instrument, called *la tenette Helvétius* (the Helvétius pliers), which had been used to lift the tumor out of the breast after it had been opened with a razor and a scalpel.

The operation itself clearly had the nature of a performance played before a choice audience. Helvétius noted in particular the presence of the bishop of Perpignan, who served as a "witness" to the event, and the "general applause" that greeted the surgeons at the end of the spectacle.

To confirm the soundness of the procedure he had orchestrated, Helvétius pointed to the cases of two other breast-cancer operations performed in France by the surgeon Le Dran, and to numerous mastectomies performed in Holland. Elsewhere he boasted that his own father had extirpated more than two thousand breast cancers in The Hague. But in this particular treatise he cast the spotlight on himself as the leading player in a new chapter of medical history. It was characteristic of medical writing at this time to pay little attention to the subjective state of the patient. From the vantage point of our own era, we would like to know more about the women named in the treatise—Madame Marguerite Perpointe, Mademoiselle de Courcelles, and "a certain Poitiers, the wife of a tailor"—three courageous heroines in the early drama of breast-cancer surgery.

Although physicians had been writing about mastectomy since antiquity, the operation itself was always performed by a "surgeon"—that is to say, someone whose expertise was limited to the knife. Physicians looked down upon surgeons, and surgeons themselves had their own hierarchy, at the bottom of which were the "barber surgeons."

The link between barber surgeons and physicians can be seen in the case of a peasant woman whose story was recorded by the German physician Johann Storch in his voluminous *Diseases of Women*. The woman appeared in Storch's house in March 1737 and asked him to examine her left breast. She wanted advice on what should be done with the lump inside it, which had grown to the size of a "small chicken egg." Storch recommended that she come back after her next monthly period and have an excision performed in his presence. The next time, she appeared with a barber surgeon from her neighborhood, who wanted to know how to perform the procedure. Subsequently, the woman had the lump cut out in her own dwelling by this man in order to "lower the costs." Obviously Storch, the physician, had been consulted as an authority, but the dirty work was performed by the less learned and less well-paid barber surgeon.[26]

Storch's peasant woman was definitely more willing to be examined than many of his patients. Among them, a bashful twenty-year-old "had to force herself" to show him her painful left breast, and a court lady uncovered her breast "with great embarrassment" despite the pain she had felt there for three years. All these women seem to have experienced what the medical historian Barbara Duden has called "a taboo" against touching and showing.[27] Typically, a woman remained fully clothed before the doctor while she de-

83. Jan Steen. *Doctor and Patient.* Seventeenth century.

A fully dressed woman sits across the table from her doctor. While she points to her breast, he fixes his eyes on his copious notes. It would have been unseemly for the physician actually to touch his female patient.

scribed her symptoms to him, whether she was seen in his consulting room or in her own bedroom (fig. 83).

Since most patients waited as long as possible before consulting a doctor, and thus presented with advanced stages of disease, the victims of breast cancer rarely lived long after the operation. Not that early detection would have yielded significantly better results in those preantiseptic days, since they were likely to die from infection and blood poisoning resulting from the surgery itself! The case of the English writer Mary Astell is probably a representative example of the fate one could expect from breast cancer at that time.[28] Astell discovered her tumor in 1731, when she was sixty-three. She waited until it had grown quite large and ulcerated before seeking the hand of the famous Scottish surgeon Dr. Johnson and entreating him to remove her breast in as private a manner as was possible. According to an early account of her life, she underwent a mastectomy "without the least struggling or resistance or even so much as giving a groan or a sigh."[29] But her bravery was of little avail. Within two months, she died of a disease that was already too advanced to have been arrested by surgical intervention.

In the seventeenth and eighteenth centuries, breast cancer was still understood along Galenic lines as a stagnation or coagulation of one of the bodily humors. As such, it was often treated with dietary regimes aimed at restoring proper circulation; these included mineral water, milk, and broths prepared from chicken, frogs, or toads, as well as laxatives and starvation cures. Blood-letting was also believed to be able to drain off excessive humors and restore the proper balance. External remedies included poultices and plasters; the juice of deadly nightshade, plantain, and tobacco plants; arsenic, lead, and mercury ointments; and even rotten apples, compresses saturated with urine, and a pigeon cut up alive.[30]

A mounting number of physicians began to favor more aggressive surgery, following procedures described in Dutch, French, English, and German treatises. One of the most influential was Lorenz Heister's three-volume *General System of Surgery*, which was quickly translated from Latin into German and English.[31] Heister claimed to have extirpated numerous breast cancers "bigger than one's Fist" and even one that weighed twelve pounds (fig. 84)! The surgery was performed without the benefit of anesthesia, as were all operations performed before the mid-nineteenth century. Only wine or occasionally opium was given against pain.

The English writer Fanny Burney recorded the agony of the mastectomy she endured in October 1811. From the journal letter she wrote to her sister in

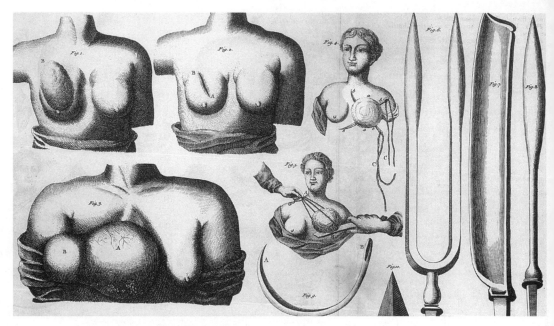

84. Lorenz Heister. *A General System of Surgery*. London. 1748. Mastectomy and relevant surgical instruments.

This plate shows the method by which the German doctor Lorenz Heister performed lumpectomies and mastectomies, as well as the instruments he used.

England, we have the benefit of a first-person account written, not from the perspective of the surgeon or a later biographer, but from the subjective stance of the breast-cancer patient herself.

Burney had married the Frenchman Monsieur d'Arblay during his exile in England. After the revolution, she had returned with him to France, where they were received in the highest circles. It was to Napoleon's famous army surgeon, Baron Larrey, that she appealed when she began to have frequent violent pains in her breast. In consultation with two of his associates, Larrey decided upon surgery. In Burney's words: "I was formally condemned to an operation by all Three. I was as much astonished as disappointed—for the poor breast was no where discoloured, & not much larger than its healthy neighbour."[32] Fearing "the evil to be deep" and her life at stake, Burney consented to surgery.

She extracted one promise from the surgeons: that they give her only four hours' notice before the procedure. In this way, she felt she could assume the best spirits in her power "to meet the coming blow." Three weeks later, she was informed while she was still in bed that the surgeons would be there at ten o'clock. Burney insisted they delay the procedure until the afternoon to give her time to prepare herself for the surgery, which was to take place in her own home. As she remembers:

> I strolled to the Sallon—I saw it fitted with preparations, & I re-coiled—But I soon returned: to what effect disguise from myself what I must so soon know?—yet the sight of the immense quantity of bandages, compresses, spunges, Lint—made me a little sick:—I walked backwards & forwards till I quieted all emotion, & became, by degrees, nearly stupid—torpid, without sentiment or conscious-ness;—& thus I remained till the Clock struck three. A sudden spirit of exertion then returned,—I banished pen to write a few words to M. d'A—and a few more for Alex [her son], in case of a fatal result.

This description was written at a time when breast cancer was a highly private matter, to be confided only to one's nearest and dearest, and then with carefully chosen words. Yet, as the author of the novel *Evelina* and other well-known works, Burney knew that the letter she sent to her sister would be shared with other family members and friends, and that it would not be thrown away. What follows bears the mark of the seasoned novelist.

> Dr. Moreau instantly entered my room, to see if I were alive. He gave me a wine cordial, & went to the Sallon. I rang for my Maid & Nurses,—but before I could speak to them, my room without previ-ous message, was entered by 7 Men in black, Dr. Larrey, M. Dubois, Dr. Moreau, Dr. Aumont, Dr. Ribe, & a pupil of Dr. Larrey, & an-other of M. Dubois. I was now awakened from my stupor—& by a sort of indignation—Why so many & without leave?

Burney's reactions range from indignation to terror. Told to mount the bed which has been placed in the salon, she found herself "suspended for a moment" and even contemplating escape. But when she heard the doctors ordering her maid and two nurses to leave the room, she recovered her voice. "No, I cried, let them stay! . . . This occasioned a little dispute, that re-animated me—The maid, however, & one of the nurses ran off—I charged the other to approach, & she obeyed. M. Dubois now tried to issue his commands en militaire, but I resisted all that were resistible." In a last-ditch act of rebellion against her fate, Burney pitted the female forces against the male. Alas, two-thirds of her female entourage defected, and she was left to face the male onslaught alone, with the aid of only one nurse. Against the male barrage, she wistfully thought of her sisters in England as a form of would-be protection.

Burney's description of the surgery itself remains one of the landmark moments in the literature of breast cancer. Her story is told with such lucidity that one marvels at the author's courage, both during the harrowing procedure and afterward, when she forced herself to relive it in writing.

There she was stretched out upon the bed, with nothing more than a cambric handkerchief placed upon her face, and a transparent one at that, through which she could see everything. As she closed her eyes to shut out "the glitter of polished Steel," she heard the melancholy voice of Dr. Larrey asking "Qui me tiendra ce sein?" ("Who will hold this breast for me?") Whereupon Burney answered that she would hold up her breast herself. It was then that she realized, from the doctor's finger drawing "a straight line from top to bottom of the breast, secondly a Cross, & thirdly a Circle," that the entire breast would have to be removed. At this point, Burney closed her eyes once more, "relinquishing all watching, all resistance, all interference, and sadly resolute to be wholly resigned."

Now began "the most torturing pain."

When the dreadful steel was plunged into the breast—cutting through veins—arteries—flesh—nerves—I needed no injunctions not to restrain my cries. I began a scream that lasted unintermittingly during the whole time of the incision—& I almost marvel that it rings not in my Ears still! so excruciating was the agony. When the wound was made, & the instrument was withdrawn, the pain seemed undiminished, for the air that suddenly rushed into those delicate parts felt like a mass of minute but sharp and forked poniards, that were tearing the edges of the wound.

Burney goes on to recall in excruciating detail "the terrible cutting" and the knife scraping against the breastbone. The operation lasted for twenty minutes—twenty minutes of "utterly speechless torture" performed on a fully conscious woman whose sole anesthesia had been a glass of wine. Little wonder that Burney had taken almost a year to be able to "speak of this terrible business" and to pen the letter that has come down to us as one of the earliest accounts of breast-cancer surgery as experienced by the patient.

Fanny Burney went on to live for almost thirty more years after her operation. Such was not the case for another breast-cancer victim, who underwent a mastectomy in America within days of Fanny Burney's and died less than two years later. The medical case of Abigail Adams Smith is brilliantly reconstructed in a recent biography of her mother, Abigail Adams, wife of the second president of the United States.[33] In it we find the letter that Abigail Smith wrote to the eminent Dr. Benjamin Rush (a signer of the Constitution, as well as a physician and social reformer) with a description of her symptoms:

> I first perceived a hardness in my right Breast just above the nipple which occasioned me an uneasy sensation—like a burning sometimes an itching—& at times a deep darting pain through the Breast—but without any dis-colouration at all. it has continued to Contract and the Breast has become much smaller than it was.—the tumour appears now about the size of a [Cap] and does not appear to adhere but to be loose—

Rush replied, not to Abigail Smith but to her father, John Adams, that he considered her tumor ready for "the knife." Smith bowed to Rush's experience of fifty years and within weeks submitted to surgery. A month later, Abigail Adams wrote to her son John Quincy Adams that his sister "is doing as well as could be expected after an operation in which the whole Breast was taken off." During the first year postsurgery, Abigail Smith believed she had put the cancer behind her, but the following winter her health began to decline, and in August she died peacefully with her mother at her side. Abigail senior was inconsolable at the loss of her only daughter. She poured out her grief in numerous letters, unusual for their lack of restraint about a subject that was conventionally shrouded in secrecy. "The wound which has lacerated my Bosom cannot be healed," she wrote, in metaphoric identification with her daughter.

During this period, it became increasingly common for operations to be performed in an amphitheater for teaching purposes. Dr. John Brown never forgot the mastectomy he saw as a student in a crowded operating theater in Edinburgh in 1830. Twenty-eight years later, in *Rab and His Friends*, Brown told the story of a Scottish peasant woman named Alie, who entered the theater dressed in her regular clothes, accompanied by her husband, James, and her dog, Rab. While the master surgeon performed his work as quickly as possible and Rab growled at the sight of his mistress's blood, Alie bore her unanesthetized pain with remarkable courage. When it was over, she stepped "gently and decently down from the table, looks for James: then, turning to the surgeon and the students, she curtsies, and in a low, clear voice, begs their pardon if she has behaved ill."[34] This self-effacing and apologetic manner was characteristic of cancer patients, especially among the poor, who expressed concern for the surgeon's discomfort rather than their own well-being. Unfortunately, this brave woman succumbed from sepsis a few days later.

Although the treatment of breast cancer was still crude by our standards, early-nineteenth-century science was beginning to make progress in understanding the fundamental structure of the disease. In Germany, Matthias Schleiden and Theodor Schwann described the cell as the basic element of both plants and animals, Johannes Müller established that pathologic growth consists of cells just like any other tissues, and Hermann Lebert confirmed the existence of a characteristic cancer cell, described as small and round, with a distinctive oval nucleus.[35] Alfred Velpeau, in his 1854 *Traité des Maladies du Sein*, gave a voluminous overview of existing medical research on the breast, which had profited during the first half of the century from extensive use of the microscope. Belief in the wonders of science gave birth to a new era of medical positivism that would increasingly shape women's lives.

By the eighteenth century, medical spokesmen had assumed the stance of societal guardians in regard to women's bodies. Remember Dr. William Cadogan's highly influential *Essay upon Nursing*, addressed to the medical community, which was followed by similar works in various European languages. The new trend in the nineteenth century was to appeal directly to women themselves. Before long, women became accustomed to consulting male experts for guidance and advice, rather than the midwives and other female healers who had sustained them in the past. The love affair with science that had begun in the eighteenth century was beginning to rival religion as a comprehensive guide to life.

Consider, for example, Dr. Napheys's highly popular *The Physical Life of Woman* (1869). In the section on motherhood, Napheys claims that his rules for nursing would benefit every mother. The child should be applied to the breast immediately after birth, since "there is always a secretion in the breast from the first, which it is desirable for the child to have."[36] Medical doctors had finally understood the value of the pre-milk liquid, colostrum.

They could also muster statistical evidence to support the benefits of maternal nursing over wet nursing or "dry-nursing," the term used for a semiliquid mixture. Thus Napheys wrote that in the European cities of Lyons and Parthenay, where foundlings were wet-nursed, their death rates were 33.7 and 35 percent. In Paris, Rheims, and Aix, where they were dry-nursed, the foundlings' death rate rose to 50.3, 63.9, and 80 per cent. In New York City, where foundlings were also dry-nursed, their mortality rate was nearly 100 percent. Grounded in the statistical science of his day, maternal nursing took on the aura of a medical command. From the mother's breast the infant "should receive its *only* nourishment during the first four or six months, and in many cases the first year of its life." The mother's "duties to her infant, instead of ceasing, augment in importance. The obligation is imposed upon her of nourishing it with her own milk." Physicians now commanded the "should" language of "duties" and "obligation" like ministers or priests.

With the gradual demise of the wet nurse at the turn of the century and the increased use of sterilized animal-milk, usually cow and sometimes goat, bottle-feeding became the major alternative to breast-feeding. The old quarrel between the mother and the wet nurse was replaced by the breast-bottle controversy. Though most people still believed that mother's milk was best, few considered it essential to an infant's survival. Medically speaking, most babies born in the West no longer ran the risk of death from the hazards of wet nursing or unsterilized animal-milk.

This was unfortunately not the case with breast cancer. Since the late nineteenth century, when people began to live long enough to acquire cancer in statistically significant numbers, cancers of all sorts have taken on the aspect of a modern malediction, like the plague in the Middle Ages, syphilis in the Renaissance, and tuberculosis in the nineteenth century.[37] And among these cancers, breast cancer alone "has achieved the proportions of an epidemic."[38] Why that should be true has baffled and preoccupied several generations of doctors and scientists, who are still uncertain as to what sets breast cancer in motion.

What we do know is that breast cancer begins with the development of abnormal cells in the lining of the milk ducts. These malignant cells then reproduce and grow, soon filling the ducts of the breast. Dr. Susan Love likens this buildup to "rust in a pipe."[39] Eventually, the wildly reproducing cells break through the walls of the ducts and invade the breast tissue. If untreated, the cancer continues to metastasize, often first invading the lymph nodes under the arm, then spreading to the bone, liver, lungs, and other lymph nodes.

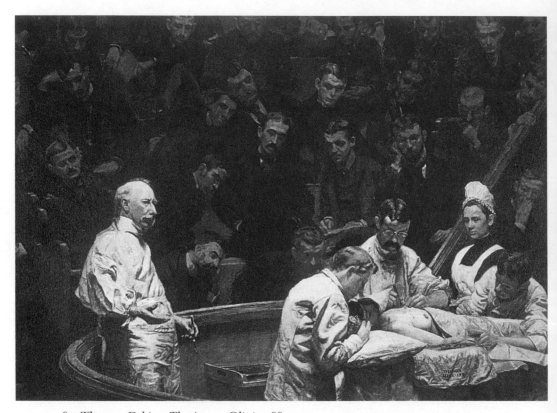

85. Thomas Eakins. *The Agnew Clinic*. 1889.

The master surgeon directs a breast operation performed in a Philadelphia amphitheater for the benefit of medical students.

To combat breast cancer, four major modes of treatment have been developed during the past 150 years: surgery, radiation, chemotherapy, and hormones.

In the second half of the nineteenth century, the ancient practice of surgery began to offer new hope derived from two revolutionary innovations—the introduction of anesthesia and the adoption of antiseptic principles. Anesthesia was developed by a dentist named William Morton, who used ether to kill pain during an operation in 1846 at Massachusetts General Hospital in Boston. The surgical use of antiseptics to eliminate bacteria, derived from Pasteur's 1864 germ theory, became widespread with the production of the compound called "antiseptic" developed by the English surgeon Joseph Lister.

By 1867, Charles Moore, another prominent British surgeon, formulated the general principles on which the surgical treatment of breast cancer would rest. Moore concluded that recurrences were always due to fragments of the principal tumor and that it was necessary to remove the whole breast, including the skin, lymphatics, fat, pectoral muscles, and diseased axillary (underarm) glands.

By the last decades of the nineteenth century, the radical mastectomy developed by William Halsted of Johns Hopkins University became the standard procedure for breast-cancer surgery in America (fig. 85). Halsted and his followers routinely removed the entire breast, the lymph nodes, and the large pectoral muscle with its connecting ligaments and tendons. Retrospective studies proved that patients who had undergone the Halsted radical mastectomy had a significantly better survival rate than women who had undergone a nonradical operation. Halsted's radical mastectomy prevailed as the standard procedure for the next sixty years.

Yet, by the mid-twentieth century, the radical mastectomy was gradually replaced by the modified radical mastectomy. This involved removing the breast and axillary lymph nodes, but not the underlying pectoral muscles. Not until the late 1970s would both the Halsted radical mastectomy and the modified radical mastectomy be seriously challenged by vocal patients and doctors who believed that many women were being unnecessarily mutilated.

Among them, an articulate breast-cancer victim, Rose Kushner, took the controversial position that patients should decide for themselves aspects of their treatment that were usually determined solely by their doctors. In her vanguard book, *Breast Cancer*, Kushner became an outspoken critic of radical forms of surgery, and especially "one-step" breast surgery—the operation that allows a surgeon to amputate the breast at the time of the biopsy, if it proves to be malignant.[40] (In a biopsy, tissue is removed for diagnostic purposes, either by surgery or by a hollow needle inserted into the lump.) If breast cancer is diagnosed, the choice for the patient is usually between a mastectomy (the removal of the entire breast and some lymph nodes from under the arm) or a lumpectomy (the removal of the lump and a margin of surrounding tissue, as well as some lymph nodes). In the seventies and eighties, studies began to show that, when a tumor is small and detected at an early stage, lump removal plus radiation is as effective as removing the entire breast. In 1990, the National Institutes of Health recommended lumpectomy followed by radiation therapy as an effective alternative to mastectomy, and one that leaves fewer physical and emotional scars.

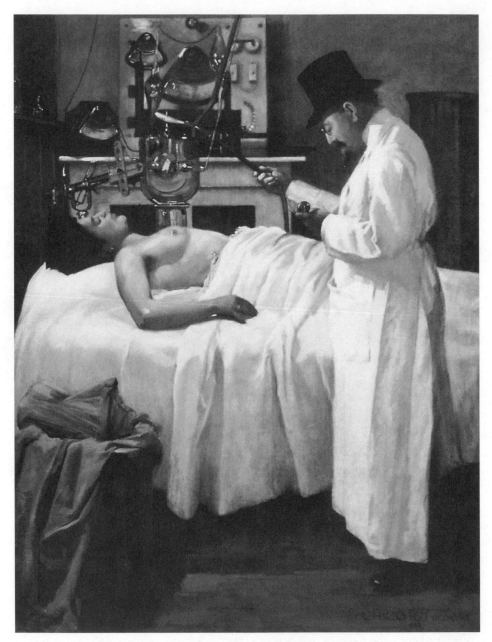

86. G. Chicotot. First X-ray treatments for breast cancer. 1908.
Stretched out upon the table in the classical pose of a reclining nude, a woman
patient exposes her chest to the X-rays that may save her life. Her horizontal
vulnerability contrasts with the doctor's vertical authority, accentuated by his
high hat.

Today, some form of surgery is almost always recommended for patients diagnosed with breast cancer. In the case of both lumpectomy and mastectomy, it is the evidence of cancer in the lymph nodes that helps determine a woman's chance of recurrence. The greater the number of positive nodes, the worse the prognosis. Surgery offers hope, but hope contingent upon a vast number of variables.

Though surgery is still the most common method for arresting breast cancer, other forms of treatment have also been making progress. Consider the use of X-rays, first discovered in 1895 by Wilhelm Roentgen. With the discovery that radiation inhibits cell division, X-rays were soon employed for inoperable cases of breast cancer, or after surgery to kill off any cancer cells that were left behind (fig. 86). In the 1930s, supervoltage X rays became available, and in the 1960s, radioactive cobalt beams. But X-rays administered in strong doses also have negative effects. A study of several thousand women who received radiation treatment from 1935 to 1971 discovered they had nearly twice the risk of developing lung cancer as did women who had received other treatments for breast cancer.[41] On a more positive note, however, it has been estimated that the combination of surgery and radiation reduces the recurrence of breast cancer by a third compared with surgery alone.[42]

In the 1960s, chemotherapy—the intravenous administration of a combination of drugs that interfere with the replication of cancer cells—was added to the oncologist's armamentarium. By now, it is routine treatment to start chemotherapy at the time of the initial diagnosis, especially for premenopausal women with positive nodes. There is some controversy as to how effective chemotherapy is with postmenopausal women, but, on the whole, it is safe to say that chemotherapy will prolong the patient's life by at least two to three years beyond what could otherwise be expected.[43]

A fourth form of treatment—hormonal—has been available to breast-cancer patients since the turn of the century. At that time the long-suspected link between breast cancer and the reproductive organs was pinpointed to the female hormone estrogen, which is produced in the ovaries and stimulates breast development. Since then, the removal of the ovaries to stop the production of estrogen has been performed on many young women with advanced cases of the disease.

Today it is believed that estrogen plays a role in promoting the growth of breast-tumor cells, and that estrogen levels are linked in complex ways to fatty diets and many other environmental factors. This relation between breast cancer and estrogen has led to the development of a synthetic hormone known as "tamoxifen." Tamoxifen is a weak estrogen that occupies and blocks estrogen-receptor cells, preventing the uptake of endogenous estrogen. Tamoxifen has proved to be as effective as chemotherapy with postmenopausal women, but it is still not clear that it works as well as chemotherapy in premenopausal women.

The four major treatments for women diagnosed with breast cancer—surgery, radiation, chemotherapy, and hormones—give patients more options than ever before. Yet, even with these sophisticated forms of treatment, women are still dying of breast cancer in increasing numbers: whereas over 560,000 died of the disease globally in 1980, it is predicted that the annual death toll will be one million women by the year 2000.[44] These statistics have led many researchers, practitioners, and activists to focus heavily on prevention, as well as treatment. Many have come to believe that the incidence of breast cancer, which is highest in the industrialized nations of the West, could be reduced significantly by changes in Western women's diet and lifestyles and the environment.

Advocates of prevention through diet cite the evidence of differential breast-cancer rates in the West and Asia. The United States and Great Britain, which have some of the world's richest diets, also have the highest breast-cancer rates, whereas countries such as Japan and China, which have low-fat diets, have one-fifth the incidence of white American or British women.[45] Epidemiologists point out that, when Asian women move to the U.S. and begin to eat a high-fat diet, their breast-cancer rate begins to rise—further proof that overnutrition, and especially high fat content, contribute to the high incidence of the disease in America.

Although fat in general has been identified as an enemy, olive oil—an unsaturated fat—continues to have its defenders. A Greek study of more than two thousand women found that the risk of breast cancer was 25 percent lower among women who had olive oil in their diet more than once a day.[46]

All this concern with diet has, not surprisingly, been picked up by the popular women's magazines, which often promise more than diet alone can possibly deliver. Consider the cover of the July 1994 *Ladies' Home Journal*, announcing: "You Can Prevent Breast Cancer—Here's How." Inside, couched in more conditional language, the hopeful reader finds "The Anti-Breast Cancer diet. A leading doctor's revolutionary plan that *might* save your life" (my italics).

Another preventive approach has to do with eliminating carcinogenic agents from the environment. This approach targets the use of pesticides and other toxic substances, which have chemical structures similar to estrogens produced by the body. It is believed that pesticide-originated xeno-estrogens can attach themselves to the estrogen receptors of the human breast and act in ways to induce breast cancer. This highly politicized issue has attracted a growing number of scientists and activists, whose aim is to establish the implications of a carcinogenic environment and to find ways of combatting it on a global level.

Some of the most dramatic evidence for an environmental connection to breast cancer comes from Long Island, New York, which, in 1990, had a 27-percent-higher incidence than the rest of the United States.[47] The residents of Long Island had a long list of suspects, including pesticide contaminants and radiation from nearby reactor plants. But research into the relationship between toxic substances and breast cancer has rarely provided conclusive results. Whereas some studies suggest a role for environmental carcinogens in the genesis of mammary carcinoma, others do not support that hypothesis. Nancy Krieger, for example, at the Kaiser Foundation Research Institute in Oakland, California, found no statistically significant links between the incidence of breast cancer and levels of DDT or PCBs—chemicals that persist in the environment and can become lodged in breast tissue, where they mimic the tumor-promoting hormone estrogen.[48]

Preventive measures for special groups of women must now take into account the 1994 discovery of the gene, known as BRCA 1, responsible for inherited forms of breast cancer. This type of cancer, which runs strongly in some families, accounts for some 5 percent of the approximately 180,000 cases of breast cancer diagnosed in the United States each year. Women who learn they are genetically predisposed to breast cancer are advised to intensify their efforts to detect the tumors as early as possible, to take tamoxifen as a preventive measure, or even to consider having their breasts removed.

Because early detection offers the best hope for survival, the medical profession recommends that *all* women perform regular breast self-examinations and be attentive to changes in their breasts, such as the appearance of lumps, tenderness, redness, or discharge. Another standard tool for early detection is the mammogram, a special X-ray that can pinpoint tiny tumors. Though it is generally agreed that women over fifty should have mammograms on an annual basis, the practice of mammography is by no means perfect.

For one thing, even mammograms miss some tumors. For another, the twelve-month intervals between mammograms allow some tumors the time to grow substantially before being detected. In addition, there is some evidence that mammography for women under fifty may actually increase a younger woman's risks, even though the radiation exposure of a mammogram is roughly the same as that of a dental X-ray. Also, since younger women's breasts are denser, it is easier to miss a real tumor or to diagnose a normal lump falsely, leading to unnecessary intervention. Still, most experts believe that women between ages forty and forty-nine should have the procedure every one to two years.

With the prevention of breast cancer in mind, young women are encouraged to have their children at an early age and to breast-feed. Both activities are believed to reduce the risks of breast cancer. Young women are also advised to be wary of contraceptive pills, especially before the age of twenty-five (which is, of course, when one often needs them the most).

Postmenopausal women are beset with similar uncertainties about the use of hormone-replacement therapy, which has been linked to a modest increase in breast-cancer risk. This risk seems to increase the longer one stays on the hormones. Doctors are now advising postmenopausal women to weigh the potential breast-cancer danger of hormone-replacement therapy against its potential benefits in combatting heart disease and osteoporosis.

The new emphasis on individual decision-making in the hope of preventing breast cancer has left many women with the feeling that they are in some way responsible if they contract the disease. Have I brought this upon myself by not eating a proper diet? Or by living in an area that is unhealthy? Or by deferring childbirth or not breast-feeding? Or by taking contraceptive pills or estrogen-replacement therapy? Whereas women in the past believed breast cancer was caused by a stagnation of the humors or an injury to the breast or the punishment of God, it is becoming increasingly common for women to assume a personal sense of blame for their illness. Past explanatory systems, be they religious or scientific, assumed that the cause of breast cancer was out of one's control; now we seem to believe that, if we change our behavior, we may be able to reduce the likelihood of developing the disease.

Today, after a century of research on cancer in general and a decade of increased attention to breast cancer in particular, scientists are still unsure about the exact causes of the disease. Heredity, estrogen, fat, and environmental agents have all been implicated, but no one knows for certain what actually triggers breast cancer. The newest research seems to suggest that the gene BRCA 1, initially believed to cause only a small proportion of breast cancers, may be responsible for nearly all of them.[49] In time, this discovery may lead to new ways of predicting and treating breast cancer. But for the present, we must live with the statistical knowledge that one in eight or nine American women can expect to be diagnosed with the disease.

Statistics tell us little about the inner experience of breast-cancer patients. To that end, psychiatry began to offer its resources in the mid-1970s. At that time, my husband, Dr. Irvin Yalom, professor of psychiatry at Stanford Medical School, inaugurated the first support group for patients with metastatic breast cancer.[50] He met weekly with groups of eight to twelve women, offering them a forum to discuss their fears and losses and, in many cases, their imminent deaths. At first, much of the group's cohesiveness resulted from a common bond of enmity toward the medical profession. The patients felt their oncologists were too impersonal and too authoritarian, and did not include them sufficiently in important decisions regarding their treatment. In the group, the women learned from one another what they could and could not expect from their doctors. It became apparent that the most basic anxiety for most of them was not so much the fear of dying but the loneliness that surrounded the road toward death—breast cancer was still a taboo subject in those days. The patients tended to isolate themselves from their families and friends, because they did not want to drag other people down with them; conversely, even their nearest and dearest tended to avoid them, because they did not know how to act or what to say. Over a four-year period, the women struggled together to help one another live as meaningfully as possible. As one of Yalom's coleaders, Stanford psychiatrist Dr. David Spiegel, later wrote: "This direct approach to the worst" somehow freed the patients "to enjoy the best."[51]

A follow-up study of these group patients demonstrated that they were less anxious and depressed than patients who had received only routine oncological care. More surprising were the results of a ten-year follow-up: Dr. Spiegel found not only an increase in the quality of their lives, but an increase in quantity as well. The women in the support group lived on average twice as long from the time they entered the study as the women in a control group. Although this one study cannot be seen as conclusive, it does point to the possibility that good psychotherapeutic treatment for women facing terminal illness can help them live better and even longer than previously expected. This and other forms of support have increasingly been made available to breast-cancer patients throughout the nation.

The American Cancer Society's volunteer organization, Reach to Recovery, founded in 1953, contacts women after a mastectomy with information about artificial breasts, known as prostheses. A well-fitting prosthesis worn in a bra can cover up the loss of a breast, or both breasts, as long as one has clothes on. Even bathing suits are now designed to hide surgical disfigurements.

If a woman wants to rebuild her body so that she looks similar to her former self even in the nude, she has the option of surgical reconstruction. The most common form of natural breast construction, known as the TRAM-flap operation, takes tissue from the abdomen to make a new breast. It can be performed either after the mastectomy has fully healed or at the very same time as the mastectomy itself. There is generally little difference in appearance between the old breast and the new one. Until recently, women with mastectomies could also choose a simpler surgical procedure involving silicone-gel breast implants. This process was used widely in the seventies and eighties not only for survivors of breast-cancer surgery but also for women who simply wanted to have bigger busts.

The use of silicone implants has by now become a hotbed of controversy. How chemical companies and plastic surgeons profited from silicone implants has been the subject of countless articles, books, and lawsuits. But it is well to remember that the United States is not the only country where implants have been popular. Western Europe and South America have also had their share of silicone breasts, adjusted to the ideals of each country. In France, for example, the ideal breast size seems to be smaller than in the U.S., to judge from statistics presented in 1988 at the twenty-first Annual Congress of Plastic Surgeons. In Argentina, the tendency has been for large breast implants. In Brazil, upper-class families go in for breast reduction—even to the point of offering such operations as presents to their daughters on their fifteenth birthdays! One plastic surgeon sees these practices as reflecting different national and class norms: whereas upwardly mobile Brazilians wish to distance themselves from the larger breasts associated with the low-status black population, Argentineans—many of Spanish origin, with highly macho men—want to accentuate sexual difference at all costs.[52]

One Swedish study of thirty-nine women who had chosen cosmetic breast augmentation found that most of them associated the size of their breasts with their degree of femininity. Their flat chests had made them ill-at-ease in heterosexual situations and even reluctant to appear nude before other women. After the surgery, most of the women reported positive changes in their self-image and sexual relations. The few patients who criticized the results usually wanted larger breasts, or were displeased because their breasts had become too hard and looked unnatural.[53]

The emotional and ethical issues surrounding breast enlargement were explored more fully in a study of forty-two women in the Netherlands, where breast augmentations are the single most frequently performed cosmetic surgery.[54] Conducted by a woman who identifies herself as a long-standing feminist, this study sought to understand why women choose to subject themselves to breast enlargement, even when they themselves are fully cognizant of its risks and critical of women who succumb to the social pressure for larger breasts. All of the women insisted that breast augmentation was something they had done for themselves, contrary to the popular belief that they had been pressured by their husbands, surgeons, or society, and, like the Swedish women, most expressed satisfaction with the outcome. Whatever reservations one may have about the product, it is hard to argue with a satisfied customer.

In the United States, breast augmentation is second only to liposuction as the most common form of cosmetic surgery. Since the early sixties, breast implants have enlarged the dimensions of between one and two million women, with an estimated 70 percent of them for purely cosmetic reasons. In 1992, when a moratorium was imposed by the United States Food and Drug Administration on their use, the implant controversy erupted into a media frenzy. The moratorium was the result of evidence collected by the FDA suggesting that implants might be unsafe—that they sometimes leaked or ruptured and bled silicone into the body, possibly causing such problems as chronic fatigue, arthritis, and damage to the immune system. Almost immediately, this decision was denounced by the major manufacturers, the American Medical Association, and the American Society of Plastic and Reconstructive Surgeons as unnecessary meddling. Though implant makers continued to deny that their products were unsafe, they nonetheless agreed in 1994 to the largest settlement ever negotiated in a class-action lawsuit. Dow Corning, Bristol Myers–Squibb Co., Baxter Healthcare Corp., and Minnesota Mining and Manufacturing agreed to pay more than four billion dollars to twenty-five thousand women with diseases attributed to the implants: rheumatoid arthritis, lupus, and scleroderma (a progressive hardening and thickening of the skin and internal organs).

Hard on the heels of this multibillion-dollar settlement came the surprising results of a large epidemiological study with the baffling finding that women who got implants to enlarge or reconstruct their breasts were no more likely than anyone else to develop those diseases. The study, conducted at the Mayo Clinic, had as its sample all the women given breast implants in one

Minnesota county from 1964 to 1991, as compared with women of the same age who did not get implants. Precisely the same proportion got the illnesses in both groups.[55]

This study, and subsequent reports which have been unable to prove a direct relationship between breast implants and connective tissue diseases and other disorders, brought little comfort to the silicone-implant manufacturers, who had already agreed to the huge settlement. It was of no use to Dow Corning, which was forced to declare bankruptcy because the number of litigants demanding a piece of the action had swollen to over four hundred thousand women. But it should provide some reassurance for the women who are terrified by the prospect of developing implant-related diseases. The final word in this matter has by no means been pronounced: it may be that silicone leakage from a ruptured implant does indeed adversely affect some women, whose symptoms do not fit standard disease descriptions and constitute a "new disease." One study-in-progress of 123 women who had their silicone gel implants removed reports that more than 60 percent of the women experienced a significant improvement in their symptoms after surgical removal of the implants. These data support the view that silicone implants contribute to a constellation of systemic complaints, and may represent an atypical connective disorder not previously described in the literature.[56] Experts now line up on both sides of the debate, with some continuing to support the FDA ban and others urging that it be dropped.

Because large breasts represent a deeply entrenched American ideal, breast reduction has not been sought out to the same extent as breast augmentation. Yet reduction mammoplasty is increasing in popularity—in 1992, nearly forty thousand people chose this form of surgery. Women with very large breasts often suffer a number of medical problems, most notably neck and back pain, stooped shoulders, and skin irritations. Some complain that their large breasts interfere with running or exercise, and others are simply embarrassed by the size of their breasts.

A more difficult operation than breast implantation, reduction mammoplasty requires in-hospital surgery, general anesthesia, and a convalescent period of around three weeks. Some publicity for this procedure, such as the 1994 and 1995 ads in *The New York Times Magazine* with drawings of a breast before, during, and after breast-reduction surgery, give the false impression that breasts can be altered with the same ease as taking tucks in a blouse. But despite the pain and inconveniences involved, women who undergo breast reduction are generally pleased with the results. Dr. Michael Carstens, a

Berkeley plastic surgeon who has performed many such operations, says that all his patients wished they had known about the surgery before and done it earlier.

Women who elect this surgery may have to do battle with their husbands and lovers. One woman whose very large breasts had given her chronic neck and back pain made up her mind to have her breasts reduced in size. The surgeon she selected told her he would be glad to perform the operation, but only if she secured her husband's permission. Although she protested that it was *her* body, the doctor was adamant: he had been hassled by too many men dissatisfied with the smaller size of their wives' chests!

Another woman, writing about her experience in *Women's Sports and Fitness* (April 1995), remembers that her 36DD breasts had become a "burdensome bundle" for her. Not only did she develop a habit of rounding her shoulders and wearing bulky sweaters to hide her chest, but she also avoided exercise classes so that others would not see her breasts "jiggling up and down." When she went jogging, she stuffed her ten-pound breasts into three jogging bras. Ultimately, she chose breast-reduction surgery that downsized her breasts to a C cup. Although her breasts still bear the scars of her operation, she "never imagined how completely liberating it would be." She says she has regained her self-confidence and her passion for sports.

Lactation, tumors, and, more recently, cosmetic surgery—these have been the major breast-related concerns of the medical profession. In the hands of doctors, breasts have been covered with every conceivable concoction, strapped to electric machines, bombarded with radium, squeezed between mammogram plates, injected with silicone, and, as a last resort, cut off from the rest of the body. Conventional breast-cancer treatment has been summed up by Dr. Susan Love as "slash, poison and burn."[57] But lest we ascribe to the medical profession more that its fair share of horrors, let us also remember the progress it has made. We now know why breast milk is beneficial to infants: the hormones and enzymes that promote growth and the antibodies that protect against common infections have been largely identified. Those who choose not to breast-feed no longer need worry about the health of bottle-fed babies, if the formula is properly prepared and administered. We also have a better understanding of some of the factors that trigger the onset and hasten the spread of breast cancer, and many reasons to be relatively optimistic even if we contract the disease. Some of us will live to see a cure for breast cancer in the next century. And for those of us who want larger or smaller breasts, well, there are always the plastic surgeons, and even hypnotists who promise changes in breast size through the power of the mind.[58] One hypnotist says he can plump up your chest in a twelve-week program costing $375; under hypnosis, he takes his clients back to puberty and asks them to "release the breast suppression" they had experienced as girls.[59] Yes, the charlatans are still around, as they have always been. But so are the true healers. To paraphrase Proust, it is a great folly to believe in medicine, were it not an even greater folly not to believe in it.

Eight

THE LIBERATED BREAST:
POLITICS, POETRY, AND PICTURES

F OR MOST OF WESTERN HISTORY, women's breasts have been controlled by men. This has been true whether the control was exercised individually by husbands and lovers, or collectively by male-dominated institutions like the church, the state, and medicine. Yet, however widespread these forms of control might have been, it is unlikely that people in the past were consciously aware of them. The long-standing belief that women "belonged" to men, that they were inferior to men, that they owed obedience to men, was woven so deeply into the fabric of Western society that most people probably accepted the situation without giving it much thought.

Certainly there were some women in the past, and even a few men, who questioned the unequal relationship between the sexes. We have only to listen to the exuberant speech of the Wife of Bath, penned by Chaucer in the fourteenth century, to know that a few bold Englishwomen took a mind to reversing traditional marital roles. A century later in France, the widowed writer Christine de Pisan exhorted women to transcend misogyny and provided in her person and books a concrete model of feminine power and force of character. The Renaissance reactivated the old debate in humanist terms, seeking, on the whole, to provide for the "new" man a suitable, albeit deferential, companion. Though most people held fast to strict Judeo-Christian notions of women's inferior nature and status, a few sought to free women from the ideological constraints that made them little more than lifelong servants. By the eighteenth century, at the heart of the Enlightenment, the seeds of women's liberation began to take root, so as to flower in Olympe de Gouges's *Declaration of the Rights of Women* and Mary Wollstonecraft's *Vindication of the Rights of Woman*. These are only the best-known of a series of manifestos written by women, who would continue to speak their rebellion on both sides of the Atlantic for the next two hundred years.

By the nineteenth century, women were expressing their concerns not only as individuals but, more important, as members of groups. Movements in favor of women's education, suffrage, dress reform, and financial independence slowly produced widespread sympathy for greater equality with men, despite the continual efforts of conservatives to turn back the tide.

The successive waves of women's liberation that have crested throughout history are only beginning to be fully documented, including the last great wave that began in the 1960s and '70s. What was perhaps new and different about this period was the link between the struggle for women's rights and the reclaiming of the female body. The revolutionary book *Our Bodies, Ourselves* became the battle cry for a whole new generation of women, who asserted that the destiny traditionally attributed to women was not God-given, but only man-made.[1] What happened when these women began to reappropriate their bodies, when they began to repossess their breasts? The following is a selective look at some of their strategies during the past thirty years.

Overheard in an American women's spa in 1993:
"I'm not going to wear a bra."
"What a liberal!"

Given the symbolic importance of the breast, it is not surprising that the women's liberation movement began with a form of protest subsequently called "bra-burning." Led by the poet Robin Morgan, members of the Women's Liberation Party picketed the 1968 Miss America Pageant in Atlantic City and urged women to throw away their bras, girdles, curlers, false eyelashes, and other "mindless boob girlie" symbols that they considered demeaning.[2] The organizers of the demonstration handed out a position paper condemning a cluster of negative forces in American society, including sexism, conformism, ageism, and racism, all of which found a receptive home at the annual beauty pageant.

The stories of women removing their bras on the boardwalk outside Convention Hall gave rise to the myth of bra-burning, although bras were initially not burned, but merely thrown into trash cans. The reporter who coined the term surely meant to associate it with other incendiary acts, such as burning draft cards or flags.[3] Though many women did not want to be thought of as "bra-burners" or "women's libbers," many others rallied around the shibboleth of the discarded bra.

One woman, remembering when bralessness symbolized freedom and rebellion, left this testimony: "Already I had given up girdles and now I gave up razors, make-up, high heels, and skirts. . . . My style was casual—no fitted blouses or jackets with darts which might have demanded a bra for a decent fit. I worried what some people thought when they noticed my bralessness. But eventually I stopped thinking about it."[4]

Two years after the first "bra-burning," the Australian writer Germaine Greer wrote *The Female Eunuch*, a feisty account of how patriarchal societies disempower women. In it, she reserved some of her most colorful language for the exaggerated attention men lavish on women's breasts. "A full bosom," Greer concluded, "is actually a millstone around a woman's neck. . . . Her breasts are only to be admired for as long as they show no sign of their function: once darkened, stretched or withered they are objects of revulsion. They are not parts of a person but lures slung around her neck, to be kneaded and twisted like magic putty." Like the American bra-burners, Greer responded to breast fetishism by refusing to wear the kind of underwear that perpetuates "the fantasy of pneumatic boobs, so that men must come to terms with the varieties of the real thing."[5]

The bra-burning demonstrations that took place during the late sixties and early seventies were intended to de-emphasize the overerotization of women in general, and breasts in particular, and to call attention to more pressing economic and social needs.[6] Ironically, the discarding of bras was turned against women by numerous detractors who saw in it an affront to public decency, good taste, and a man-made vision of physical beauty that required its breasts to be round, large, firm, and clearly delineated. Whereas the packaging of breasts as sexual objects had been the norm in the forties and fifties, the unbound bosom of the late sixties represented a form of lawlessness, a deregulation of breasts, which were now permitted to flop about without constraint, and a harbinger of greater license yet to come.

In the 1970s and '80s, women sometimes removed not only their bras but their blouses as well. Along with "streaking" and "flashing" and "mooning" (practiced by both men and women), female breast-baring became a way of thumbing one's nose at society. One woman persuaded several of her friends to expose their breasts as they were sitting by a fountain. "I said, 'One, two, three. Pull up your shirts!' And one, two, three, we pulled up our shirts. A male photographer came over and said, 'Would you do that again?' We said, 'Sure.' So one two three and the shirts came up and there we were. Then the police came over and began to hassle us."[7]

This kind of incident was clearly new and unsettling for law-enforcement agents. A U.S. Army Military Police school pamphlet titled *Keeping Your Cool in a Civil Disturbance* gave this advice to its trainees:

> SITUATION: You are in formation faced by a group of females about your age. They yell: "If you are on our side, smile" and then raise their blouses to expose their breasts. How do you handle this?
> SOLUTION: Concentrate on what you're there for. After all, you've seen breasts before. The girls are just teasing and want you to make a mistake so they can ridicule you. Stay sharp and alert![8]

On the whole, American police were up to the situation; at least there were no reported incidents of roughing up bare-breasted provocateurs.

Topless demonstrations became a means of calling attention to a wide range of women's issues, including pornography, sexism, health care, and safe sex (fig. 87). In 1984, for example, sixty bare-breasted women and men paraded through the streets of Santa Cruz, California. They came out to protest the abuse of women's bodies in advertising and pornography. This was articulated in a speech read by Ann Simonton, a radical feminist who had once been a New York model.

> If women's breasts weren't hidden in shame or seen as obscene and wicked, how could Madison Avenue, pornographers, movies and television continue to profit off their exposure? . . .
> We are saying 'no' to the assumption that our bodies belong to advertisers, beauty contests, pornographers, topless bars, peep shows . . . ad nauseam.
> We reclaim our inherent right to govern our own bodies.[9]

Some people held placards reading "Our breasts are for the newborn, not for men's porn," and "The myth of a perfect body oppresses us all." Afterward, some of the group congregated on the Santa Cruz beach, and one of the men went swimming nude in the Pacific waters. The lifeguard announced that they could go topless on city and county beaches, but that they all had to keep their bottoms on.

Throughout history, laws have been made to control what parts of the body men and women may exhibit in public. Currently in the United States, neither men nor women can appear publicly with their genitals exposed, but

87. Topless car wash. Santa Cruz, California. August 1993.

Students from the University of California at Santa Cruz raised $250 toward printing costs for a calendar promoting safe sex among lesbian and bisexual women. But as one of them admitted: "It's not just for the calendar. . . . We get to confront boob-phobia."

only women cannot show their breasts "at or below the areola." Should we see this as a form of discrimination against women? Should women have to sweat under the sun in parks and stadiums, while men have the liberty of removing their tops? Does the law simply reinforce stereotypes about the seductive nature of women's breasts and the idea that men cannot control themselves in the presence of an uncovered bosom? Are such laws made in the interest of preserving naked breasts for pornography, movies, television, and advertising, where they are more precious because they are hidden elsewhere? These questions point to some of the reasons breast coverage is legally enforced, beyond the vague notion of "propriety." But even if we accept the principle of mandatory breast coverage, exceptions should be made for breast-feeding in public and sunbathing on beaches.

Nursing in public, as we have noted, is acceptable in most nations (if not in all the United States), and topless sunbathing is permitted on many European beaches. It is true that both of these activities have certain informal codes of behavior attached to them. Nursing mothers are expected to be as discreet as possible, to uncover one breast at a time, and to cover up immediately as soon as the baby has finished its meal. To flaunt the breast itself would be considered in very bad taste. Similarly, on the European beaches where women may take off the tops of their bathing suits, the codes are equally rigid. A sociologist who has studied this phenomenon on French beaches points to two preconditions for the majority of topless sunbathers: that they be young (under forty-five) and that their breasts not be overly large or pendulous. Strict rules of conduct prevail: the topless woman is expected to remain prone, rather than standing; she should not call attention to herself in any obvious manner; and men can look only if they appear not to be looking.[10] (Italo Calvino's novel *Mr. Palomar* has some delicious pages on the art of not seeing a bared bosom on a beach.) Such are the rules of the game that have developed during the past twenty-five years.

In Europe during the 1970s, there were only a few isolated instances of women displaying their breasts for overtly political ends. A Frenchwoman turned up topless in 1974 before Jean Royer, the perennial mayor of Tours, to protest his conservative policies. Several female students danced bare-breasted around the rostrum of an unnamed "great German philosopher" (possibly Habermas), forcing him to leave the room speechless.[11] But these sporadic manifestations never took on the collective force of the American demonstrations.

One aspiring European politician derived enormous personal benefits from uncovering her breasts in public. In the spring of 1987, "La Cicciolina" (born under the name of Ilona Staller in Budapest thirty-five years earlier) occupied the forty-ninth place in a list of candidates proposed for Parliament by the Italian Radical Party. A well-known porno star, she became a political sensation overnight. Her election tactics were, to say the least, unusual (fig. 88). Note this press report: "A red convertible stops in front of the Italian Parliament, Place Montecitorio, in the middle of Rome. A young blonde woman, dressed all in pink, standing upright, generously uncovers her chest. Photo flashes. 'No to sexual repression!' she chants through her megaphone. A small crowd of enthusiastic onlookers warmly approve."[12]

In a country where women occupied only 6.5 percent of the parliamentary seats, Cicciolina's candidacy placed her among a small number of female hopefuls. But unlike her sister candidates, Cicciolina had no political or academic background behind her: she had only her breasts in front of her, and they were up to the task.

88. La Cicciolina. Rome. 1987.

With her breasts uncovered and her arm triumphantly raised high above her head, the Italian candidate Cicciolina appeared before the crowd like a sexy statue of liberty.

In the June elections, to the great surprise of most pundits, Cicciolina won a seat among the 630 *onorevoli* (honorable ones) destined to represent the nation. Her message of sexual liberation brought her to the inner sanctum of political power. During her four years as a deputy, she introduced seven propositions: the right of prisoners to engage in sex, sexual education in the schools, the creation of "love parks," the reform of obscenity standards in the cinema, an ecological tax on motorized vehicles, an interdiction on the sale of fur and experimentation on living animals, and the reopening of legal houses of prostitution.

But Cicciolina's role as a deputy was complicated by the fact that she continued to show her breasts, and often the rest of her body, outside the legislature. Witness this headline from October 1987: "Cicciolina's breasts sow scandal in the Holy Land."[13] Arriving in Israel, where she had been booked for two porno shows, she was greeted with protest by the Orthodox Jewish community and refused entry into the Knesset. Decidedly, the Israelis were not willing to accept the mixture of pornography and politics that was applauded in her homeland. Two legal charges were registered against her in Tel Aviv, and she beat a hasty retreat back to Italy, where her porno shows were protected by parliamentary immunity.

Cicciolina resigned from office in April 1991, during a period of parliamentary crisis. Whatever her motives, Cicciolina returned to her first love—pornography—and to a second husband, the American artist Jeff Koons, with whom, during their short-lived union, she made a series of sexually explicit photos.

In the meantime, back in America, women had gone from "bra-burning" to more substantive acts. The fights for women's reproductive rights, for legal, educational, and economic parity with men, for health care and child care, for an end to degrading forms of pornography, violence against women, and sexual harassment—these were all being pursued by millions of women, despite ongoing opposition and repeated pronouncements that feminism was dead. A revolution was taking place that encouraged women to unrail their bodies from the dual tracks of compulsory heterosexuality and reproduction. Many women were choosing, or being forced into, other options: sex without marriage, marriage without children, paid employment, single parenting, same-sex unions, and, most frequently, a combination of work, sexual partnerships, and parenting. And in this confusing maelstrom, the breast emerged as a powerful marker of women's new situation.

89. Hope Herman Wurmfeld. Women's Health Action Mobilization (WHAM) on
Fifth Avenue, New York City. 1992.
WHAM members march for Pro-Choice.

It figured prominently around 1990 in some of the demonstrations that
called attention to women's health issues (fig. 89). It became increasingly visible in the early nineties, as women—taking a lesson from AIDS activists—
began to agitate for more governmental support of breast-cancer research. By
1993, a high-profile *New York Times Magazine* article titled "The Anguished
Politics of Breast Cancer," with its arresting picture of a postmastectomy
woman on the cover, numbered 180 breast-cancer advocacy groups throughout the nation.[14] Fired by anger and unashamedly militant, these groups took
their cause to the legislature and the media, and into the streets.

In 1991 and 1992, demonstrations in Boston featured in-your-face signs
demanding "Ask Me About Cancer and Poverty" and "Ask Me About Breast
Cancer and the Environment." In May 1993, seven hundred activists gath-
ered near the Reflecting Pool in Washington, D.C., wearing buttons and
T-shirts with such catchy slogans as "Draw the Line at 1 in 9" and "The Wife
You Save May Be Your Own." In October 1993, one thousand people, mostly

90. Reid S. Yalom. Gay and Lesbian Parade. San Francisco. 1994.

A demonstrator, displaying her postmastectomy chest, carries signs reminding us that "Cancer Affects Every/Body" and "Invisibility Equals Death."

women, marched on the Ellipse, near the White House, wearing small pink ribbons and waving large signs. After meeting with some of the leaders, President Clinton and his wife pledged to draw up a national action plan for preventing, diagnosing, and treating breast cancer.[15] In a few short years, breast-cancer activists have accomplished remarkable results on the funding front. They have pressured national lawmakers, who had previously ignored or trivialized women's health issues, to increase funding for breast-cancer projects from $90 million in 1992 to $420 million in 1995.

But politically inspired government funding does not always make for the best research, according to some members of the scientific community.[16] They contend that progress toward the cure of cancer in general may suffer because resources are siphoned off for breast cancer in particular, leaving a smaller fund for basic cancer research, which may eventually discover the key to all cancers. Breast-cancer activists counter with the argument that, until recently, women's issues received far less than their share of research moneys. They note, with reason, that most medical studies in the past focused on the ills of men, or managed to bypass women as research subjects even when they shared the same ills (for example, heart disease or lung cancer). Breast cancer—a specifically female disease—demands the attention it has acquired, and the resources necessary to help stop its growth.

Breast cancer is an issue that cuts across the political spectrum, drawing together both Democrats and Republicans, feminists and nonfeminists, straight and lesbian women, the rich and the poor. Among those committed to the same goals are the feisty feminists of the Long Island Breast Cancer Action Coalition, the politically conservative women of the Komen Foundation for Breast Cancer in Dallas, and the lesbians who founded the Women's Cancer Resource Center in Berkeley. The latter make use of the huge annual Gay and Lesbian Parade in San Francisco to call attention to the disease. Marching bare-chested in the 1994 parade was Raven Light, a mastectomy survivor (fig. 90). She has also uncovered her chest at other demonstrations— for example, in a 1995 protest against a proposed power plant in the heavily industrialized Bayview–Hunters Point area of San Francisco, where breast-cancer rates are already considerably higher than in the rest of the nation.

From California to the New York islands, breast-cancer advocacy has taken on the character of a national movement. Patients and nonpatients, drawing strength from each other, have declared war against the disease with a fervor reminiscent of earlier abolitionists and prohibitionists. Consider the case of Laura Evans, who was diagnosed with breast cancer in 1989 and subsequently underwent extensive medical treatment. In January 1995, Evans led a group of seventeen breast-cancer survivors to Mount Aconcagua in Argentina, the highest peak in the Western Hemisphere. This "Expedition Inspiration," sponsored by the San Francisco–based Breast Cancer Fund, raised $1.5 million dollars for innovative projects in breast-cancer research.

Laura Evans's story, however dramatic, is similar to that of many others who have made near-religious commitments to wiping out breast cancer. As individuals and as group members, these women speak for themselves and for all women threatened with the disease—which is to say, all women. They write haunting testimonials in books, magazines, newspapers, and newsletters. Who would have thought even ten years ago that breast cancer would become a respectable subject for highly visible plays and gallery exhibitions?

Individually and collectively, with whatever means they can muster, breast-cancer survivors take on the enemy. Their fight against breast cancer has become the most prominent cause spearheaded by women in the late twentieth century, with the possible exception of the fight for access to legal abortion. By now, the concern with breast cancer has spilled over to invigorate the whole area of women's health.

Whereas earlier political ideologies surrounding the breast were largely invented and promoted by men, those of our era result primarily from women's assessment of their own needs. It is significant that women voters and legislators have crossed traditional party lines to become advocates of breast-cancer research, just as they have crossed party lines to protest sexual harassment. There is a new women's agenda in American politics, and the breast could very well be its cross-party symbol.

BREAST POLITICS have required women to bring a very private subject into a very public arena. Poetry, on the other hand, allows the personal to remain personal. It tunnels inward to thoughts and feelings that are not necessarily politically relevant. It leads backward to both painful and pleasurable memories, veers off into fantasy, twists into humor, or dead-ends in tragedy. When it concerns the body, such writing stirs up our most visceral feelings. After the early chapters of this book, it should come as no surprise to discover that poetry is still the home of the breast, with the major difference that such verse is now being written by women.

There has probably been more female-authored breast poetry in the past twenty-five years than in all the preceding centuries. Prior to the early seven-

ties, it was all but impossible to find women writing openly about their bodies, especially on the subjects of sex, reproduction, and disease. But as women
reclaimed their rights from doctors, religious authorities, and politicians, they
also gave voice to the truths of the flesh. For the first time in recorded history,
breast poetry expressed women's subjective thoughts, rather than men's fantasies about women's breasts.

Like women's art of the same period (which will be discussed afterward),
women's poetry offered radically new ways of seeing the female form. Looking in the mirror, women saw breasts that did not correspond to the male poetic ideal. They did not see ivory orbs tipped with strawberries or cherries.
Their breasts were not invariably firm, symmetrical, and perky.[17] Their chests
were just as likely to be flat or sagging, just as likely to inspire irony and
humor as reverence and desire. Women began to articulate the feelings
breasts evoked for them, from the pleasures of lovemaking to the nightmares
of breast cancer. With the tremulous daring of the newly enfranchised, they
claimed their literary rights to the breast.

It was finally possible to write about female flesh from the point of view
of the insider. Consider this exuberant poem by Alicia Ostriker on the acquisition of breasts.

> All the years of girlhood we wait for them,
> Impatient to catch up, to have power
> Inside our sweaters, to replace our mothers.
>
> O full identity, O shape, we figure,
> We are God's gift to the world
> And the world's gift to God, when we grow breasts,
>
> When the lovers lick them
> And bring us there, there, in the fragrant wet,
> When the babies nuzzle like bees.[18]

The view from inside the breast is radically different from the view of the
outsider. Not simply the object of male desire, the breast is now the marker
of the budding young woman's sense of identity and her newly discovered
eroticism.

The breast houses a welter of overlapping sensations, as seen in this stunning poem by Sharon Olds about new motherhood.

> A week after our child was born,
> you cornered me in the spare room
> and we sank down on the bed.
> You kissed me and kissed me, my milk undid its
> burning slip-knot through my nipples,
> soaking my shirt. All week I had smelled of milk,
> fresh milk, sour. I began to throb. . . .[19]

To speak of the smell of sour milk and surgical stitches and the tenderness of the husband-lover integrates the connections between childbirth, lactation, and lovemaking. Here breasts are not separate sex objects: they are parts of the mother's entire being-in-the-world, her physicality, her strength and pain, her sense of caretaking and of being cared for. Any woman—and not just women who have nursed—can identify with the feelings of pride and vulnerability that these breasts convey.

In the past, nursing and sexuality were often considered antithetical to each other. Remember how wet nursing became institutionalized during the Renaissance, with upper-class breasts reserved for sex and lower-class breasts reserved for suckling. But women know otherwise: nursing and sexual feelings are often entwined. Poet Alicia Ostriker was one of the first to speak openly about the fact that mothers can become sexually aroused by suckling.

> Greedy baby
> sucking the sweet tit
> your tongue tugging the nipple tickles your mama
> your round eyes open appear to possess understanding
> when you suckle I am slowly moved
> in my sensitive groove
> you in your mouth are alive, I in my womb

She asks why mothers must deny this pleasure. "Is it so horrible if we enjoy ourselves: another love that dare not tell its name?"[20]

Apparently, from at least one reported incident, it *is* horrible for a mother to admit that she becomes aroused while nursing. Denise Perrigo of Syracuse, New York, had her two-year-old child taken away from her after making such an admission. She was accused of sexually abusing her child, even after a judge found that no abuse had taken place. After eight months of foster care, the child was returned to the custody not of her mother but of her grandparents![21] Unfortunately for Perrigo, members of the social services, police, and the courts who judged her feelings abnormal were not familiar with writers like Ostriker, or the pronouncements of La Leche League or Dr. Susan Love, who recognize sexual arousal as "normal" when one suckles.

Rosanne Wasserman wrote a "Moon-Milk Sestina" in honor of breast-feeding and her suckling son's first words. "It must be true: babies drink language along with the breast-milk."[22] Deborah Abbott recalls the many pleasures caused by her milk-producing breasts when she was much younger: "Such fondness I have for these breasts, such pleasure they have known. Babies have choked on the milk of them, lovers have been finely sprayed and I, too, have tasted and touched. My breasts are those of a woman who has lived long and well. I call them lazy breasts now. They have done their work and lie on my chest like fruit upon the ground."[23] This could not have been written by a man. No lament for the loss of the firm young bosom, no thoughts of witchlike dugs. Only the sweet memories of past pleasures and the mature acceptance of her aged "lazy breasts."

At the same time that women poets were celebrating nursing and sexuality, they were also producing a less joyful body of poetry on breast cancer. This once-tabooed topic suddenly split open into unlikely poems dealing with mammograms, mastectomies, and prostheses. Linda Pastan's "Routine Mammogram" captures the vulnerability every woman feels when she undergoes this procedure: "We are looking for a worm / in the apple."[24] For Joan Halperin, the terrible moment was the "Diagnosis":

> On the third of May
> the blunt forefinger of a doctor
> pokes at a tumor
> he says is in my breast.[25]

Many of the poems deal with the aftermath of a mastectomy, as in Patricia Goedicke's "Now Only One of Us Remains," which shows the author looking in the mirror and asking, "Who is that lopsided stranger?"[26] Alice J. Davis's "Mastectomy" conveys the author's full measure of anguish in only eleven words.

> No cushion
> muffles

> my heartbeat—
> skin pulled tight as a drum.[27]

The subject of the prosthesis has inspired quite a number of wryly humorous lines, as in Sally Allen McNall's "Poem for the Woman Who Filled a Prosthesis with Birdseed, and Others":

> my mother's new breast
> cost more than $100 and the girl
> at I. Magnin's was so
> matter of fact "you'd
> think
> everyone was doing this."[28]

These poets confront the body's asymmetry, treat their loss with lucidity, and try to cherish what remains.

But poet Audre Lorde, in her passionately angry *Cancer Journals*, refuses any artificial solace. When a kindly woman from Reach for Recovery came to see her in the hospital, "with a very upbeat message and a little prepared packet containing a . . . pale pink breast-shaped pad," Lorde wondered "if there are any black lesbian feminists in Reach for Recovery" and ached to talk to someone more like herself. She suggests that the postmastectomy trauma and the ensuing decisions that have to be made may be different for a black lesbian from those of a white heterosexual. Before leaving the hospital, Lorde came to a tearful decision:

> I looked strange and uneven and peculiar to myself, but somehow,
> ever so much more myself, and therefore so much more acceptable,
> than I looked with that thing stuck inside my clothes. For not even
> the most skillful prosthesis in the world could undo that reality, or feel
> the way my breast had felt, and either I would love my body one-
> breasted now, or remain forever alien to myself.[29]

To love one's one-breasted body, to love one's body at all—this has been no easy matter for women. American women are notoriously unhappy with their bodies and continually seek remedies in diets, exercise programs, and cosmetic surgery. As Naomi Wolf convincingly argued in *The Beauty Myth*, facial and bodily alterations have virtually become a national religion.[30]

Women's writing and women's art often counter this unrealistic and unhealthy bent. The breast-cancer poems are, among other things, attempts to make us cherish our less than perfect bodies, such as they are.

When Adrienne Rich writes about breast cancer in "A Woman Dead in Her Forties," the poem's first words, "Your breasts /   sliced-off," leaves a space for the absent breasts, a gap more evocative than language. The author's rush of tenderness for the wounds of a double mastectomy goes far beyond conventional sympathy: "I want to touch my fingers / to where your breasts had been / but we never did such things."[31] This is a poem for everyone—lesbian and heterosexual women, straight and gay men—for it speaks to the transcendence that can occur when human beings see each other's wounds and caress each other's scars.

Clearly such poetry has little in common with traditional male eulogies to the bosom. It finds its truth in the magnifying glass, unmediated by an idealizing imagination. However painful, even when "the body tells the truth in its rush of cells" (Rich), this is the truth contemporary women are choosing to tell.

SINCE THE READERS of poetry are always relatively few, even the most powerful poems rarely have widespread political influence. Pictures, on the other hand, because they are so immediately accessible and so ubiquitous in our image-dominated world, are more likely to feed societal change. In our time, and for the first time in history, women have begun to exert a collective influence upon the visual arts. No longer mere objects of the male artist's gaze, they have seized the painter's brush, the photographer and filmmaker's camera, and presented startling new images of themselves.

The aim of many of these artists is "to construct a female body in the face of patriarchal convention."[32] Consciously turning their backs on male norms of female beauty, they look to women for the expression of a feminine sensibility. They have found ancestors in Mary Cassatt's paintings of sturdy nursing mothers, who look as if they are really nursing for the benefit of their children rather than for a prurient voyeur. And in the nude self-portraits of Paula Modersohn-Becker, who, in 1906, shocked her German contemporaries with realistic depictions of herself when she was pregnant. And in the bare-breasted self-portraits of the French artist Suzanne Valadon (1917, 1924, and 1931), which "constitute a unique documentation of a woman's aging."[33] Each of these artists, in her own way, defied centuries-old conventions by downplaying the traditional erotic message of female nudity. Some of today's artists have also been inspired by the vulvar/floral paintings of the American Georgia O'Keeffe and by the haunting allegories of the Mexican Frida Kahlo.

Frida Kahlo (1907–54) offered a revolutionary corpus inspired both by her personal life and by the art of her country. Her most representative works are self-portraits that document her strange facial beauty, her exuberant native costume, and the unflinching truths of her suffering body. Doubly crippled — first from polio, then from a bus accident — Kahlo paints herself as she wishes to be seen: as a proud and lonely martyr, unwilling or unable to resolve the basic contradictions stamped into the flesh of a handicapped, creative woman. In her paintings, her "trademark" winged eyebrows and visible mustache seem at war with her delicate cheekbones and long black hair; similarly, her passionate relationship with her artist husband, Diego Rivera, seemed to contradict the existential loneliness she assumed as her lot.

But what gives Kahlo's work its uniquely haunting quality are the surrealistic depths of her imagination. The isolated body becomes linked to friends and lovers, flora and fauna — indeed, the whole universe — by a dreamlike web of associations. In *My Nurse and I* (1937), breasts carry the symbolic burden of cosmic interconnections (fig. 91). Kahlo visualizes herself as a baby with an adult face, sucking at the breast of her Indian nurse. The nurse, wearing a pre-Columbian mask, is dark-skinned and massive; pearl-like drops of milk ooze from her nipples. The left breast, at the baby's mouth, is painted so as to show what is imagined to be under the skin: no anatomical network of ducts and veins, but the plant patterns used to decorate breasts in certain pre-Columbian sculptures.[34] The interconnectedness of this nurturing breast and the nurturing universe is suggested by the foliage surrounding the suckling pair, with one leaf enlarged so as to reveal its milky veins, and a background sky with milky raindrops.

My Nurse and I makes a dramatic break with the familiar religious paintings of *Maria lactans*. In the first place, the baby is no longer male. He has ceded his privileged position to a female, to a doll-like Frido Kahlo. Equally unusual, though the girl baby's frail body is that of an infant, her oversized head is that of an adult, indicating that it is Kahlo the mature artist who has envisioned this scene. Moreover, the suckling maternal figure is no longer a white-skinned queen, or even a domesticized wife: she has the brown skin, powerful chest, and dark mask associated with the mysterious rituals of pre-Hispanic Mexico. This nurse and this baby do not look at each other with in-

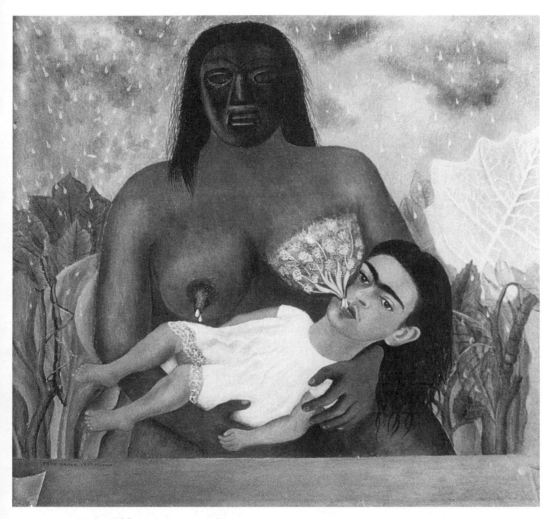

91. Frida Kahlo. *My Nurse and I.* 1937.
Kahlo portrays herself as a baby with a grown-up face suckling at the breast of an impassive Indian nurse.

terpersonal intimacy. They do not look at each other at all. They stare out into the distance so as to suggest some cosmic drama in which each has a pre-ordained role. The nurse carries her charge in her arms like a sacrificial victim. The nursling wears on her face the knowledge that not even the drop of milk at her half-opened mouth can save her from martyrdom.

This tragic sense of life could be ascribed to Kahlo's Latino heritage, but it is equally, and more importantly, a product of her personal physical and psychological pain. This is all the more apparent in some of Kahlo's paintings from the mid-forties, when her deteriorating health required several surgical interventions and she began to depict herself more explicitly as a martyr.

In *The Broken Column* (1944), for example, Kahlo paints herself nude within the steel orthopedic corset she was obliged to wear for a period of five months. She presents her body, like that of a female Saint Sebastian, studded not with arrows but with nails. Even her breasts, squeezed between two steel bands, have their share of nails. But, however painful her martyrdom, Kahlo does not give in to self-pitying victimization. Her stance here, as in all her self-portraits, is stoic. Unlike the pictures of ecstatic female martyrs that pro-liferated during the Middle Ages and Renaissance, Kahlo stares out from her martyrdom with a defiant gaze. Men may very well want a victim, even (and sometimes especially) a mutilated one, but what are they to make of this un-flinching figure who stares us down with the impassiveness of an icon?

Whereas Kahlo in the forties was creating a graphic persona that became world-famous during her short life, her French American contemporary Louise Bourgeois (born 1911) was creating an oeuvre that would not be fully recognized until much later. The human body that dominates Bourgeois's world is often dismembered into its separate parts, into pairs of eyes, hands, arms, feet, and any number of breasts.

Her long-term fixation on breasts has found expression in works as varied as her 1940s drawings, her 1970s latex body casts, and the monumental sculp-tures of the 1980s and '90s. One of her favorites is the 1985 black marble statue titled *She Fox* (fig. 92). This is, in fact, a representation of the "good mother" as Bourgeois perceives her, with four powerful breasts emanating unlimited nurturance and unconditional love. Even mutilated, headless and armless, with her throat slit by the "mean child," the mother is "powerful enough to forgive."[35] Bourgeois does not represent herself as the mother (though she is indeed the mother of three sons). She portrays herself as the child, in the form of a female head at the mother's haunches.

Other variations on this theme similarly incarnate Bourgeois's fascina-tion with the archetypal mother. Her great bronze *Nature Study* (1984) rep-resents an enigmatic creature, halfway between the human and the animal, with three pairs of breasts hunched over clawed feet. Those who saw it at the Venice 1993 Biennale (where Bourgeois represented the United States) stood face to face with the irreducible quality of the female animal in all her strength and mystery. Though Bourgeois's depictions of body parts—espe-cially her breasts and phalluses—lend themselves to psychoanalytic interpre-

92. Louise Bourgeois. *She Fox.* 1985.
Bourgois portrays herself as a tiny head protected by the all-powerful, multibreasted mother.

tations of a Freudian and Kleinian ilk, her best works partake of a mythic dimension that transcends any particularist theory.

The Venice Biennale also contained a very different vision of multiple breasts. *Mamelles* (1991) is a frieze of pink rubber breasts that flow into each other like a stream of undulating flesh. These breasts, detached from any semblance of a female body, are on display like commodities thrown pell-mell into a container—turnips or eggs, purchasable and interchangeable. This meaning was surely primary when Bourgeois created *Mamelles* (the French word has the derogatory connotation of "teats" or "udders"), for she subsequently said that it "portrays a man who lives off the women he courts, making his way from one to the next. Feeding from them but returning nothing, he loves only in a consumptive and selfish manner."[36] Bourgeois attributes this point of view to the Don Juan–esque male, who treats women like disposable items he can never get enough of. It is no wonder that feminist artists have claimed Bourgeois, reading her art (like the psychoanalytic critics) as a paradigm of a particular school of thought. To her credit, Bourgeois's works interest viewers of vastly different ideological persuasions, and continue to haunt us long after we have stood before them.

Alongside their sister painters and sculptors, female photographers have also invented exciting new ways of representing women. In the thirties, Imogen Cunningham was already photographing headless torsos according to a vision of fragmented beauty that was to make her the most respected American woman photographer of her day. Breasts, like backs, arms, and legs, were susceptible to the harmonies of abstract composition, and, if not quite robbed of their erotic connotations, treated as something more than objects of male desire: high art demanded that lust be held in check.

Cunningham's younger West Coast contemporary Ruth Bernhard continued the tradition of the idealized nude with portraits of female bodies that were noteworthy for their sensuous elegance. In the 1960s, troubled by the commercialization that exploited and debased women's bodies, she produced a series of "images with rhythmic, fluid lines, evocative of music and poetry."[37] Her nudes, alone or in entwined pairs, speak of a world that still believed in harmony and beauty.

Bernhard and Cunningham were two of the most important female precursors of the very different photography produced by women in the seventies and eighties. Jo Spence in England and Cindy Sherman in America are both noteworthy for their shocking images of women. As Spence put it in her collaborative essay "Remodeling Photo History" (1982), she and her male collaborator, Terry Dennett, wanted to change the common practices of their trade through photographs that "do not merely parrot the dominant modes of visual representations," but call them into question. In trying to "break down some of the sacred cows of photography and bourgeois aesthetics," Spence and Dennett drew from theories of anthropology, theater, and film, as well as from their roots in the working class.[38] Their photos were, in fact, a form of "photo-theater" that entailed finding or staging a scene, adding and arranging different elements, and acting out a tableau for the camera.

In the photo titled *Colonization*, Spence stands in the back doorway of a tenement (fig. 93). With her broom in hand and two milk-filled bottles placed near her feet, with her heavy beads and pendulous bosom exposed for all the world to see, she looks like a working-class British housewife taking herself for an African native, who is proud to pose for the white man's camera. Certain carefully staged juxtapositions, such as the two milk bottles and the two juglike breasts, suggest humorous connections, and point to subtle links between the woman, her class, and consumerism.

In another photo, Spence is shown suckling a black-haired, black-bearded male. She cradles his head against her huge breast, looking down at him through her glasses with muted tenderness. The lower half of her hair is lit up with a halolike glow. Once again the picture within the frame clashes with our normal frame of reference. This pose is one we traditionally associate with a virginal Madonna and a fair-haired child. What are we to make of a hairy, bestial adult sucking contentedly at the breast of a contemporary woman, with her huge chest and mannish hands? At the least, we are made to understand that sucking breasts is not confined to babies.

Another Spence photo immortalizes a pair of fake breasts set on the kitchen table alongside a pile of groceries (fig. 94). The price of "65p" on the breasts reduces them to packaged meat, like the "Chicken with Giblets" with which they are placed. The picture of breasts as produce has the confrontational quality characteristic of Spence's best work, without becoming flatly didactic.[39]

In New York during the same period, Cindy Sherman was also staging scenarios aimed at deconstructing the common practices used to represent femininity. By photographing herself in stereotypical feminine roles, as in her 1977–80 series *Film Stills*, she parodied the glamorous bodies with vacant faces that are typically found on posters for B-movies. During the eighties, her increasingly sensational work set out to expose the exploitation of women's bodies found in the graphic arts as in society at large.

93. Jo Spence / Terry Dennett. *Colonization*. "Remodeling Photo History." 1982.
What are we to make of this working-class woman with her pendulous breasts uncovered,
holding a broom in the doorway?

94. (Right) Jo Spence / Terry Dennett. *Still Life*. "Remodeling Photo History." 1982.
This unconventional still life suggests that women's breasts are consumer products similar to
the chicken, fruit, and vegetables with which they have been grouped.

The series titled *History Portraits* (1988–90) pastiches the great masters, transforming them into bizarre parodies of themselves. In several of these works, Sherman highlights the traditional use of breasts by adding false breastplates. These patently unreal wax or rubberized objects produce grotesque effects. They clash with the real skin of Sherman's own body and the costumes she wears in imitation of the original paintings. There is no attempt to disguise her props. Instead, the false body parts strip away the illusion that the body has a "natural," invariable history. For Sherman, the body's history is the story of its social construction and manipulation.

Sherman's pastiches of the nursing Madonna inspire all sorts of irreverent feelings, among them laughter, bewilderment, fear, and revulsion. One work (*Untitled #223*) features a tiny false breast resembling the "stick-on" breasts of the earliest Madonna paintings. Another, based on *The Virgin of Melun* (*Untitled #216*), sports a phony globe where Agnès Sorel's "blasphemous" orb had been. A lactating mother (*Untitled #225*) wears a Rapunzel-like blond wig and squirts milk from an artificial breast strapped onto her torso (fig. 95). All of these "add-a-breast" photos bridge different media (painting, photography, and performance art), different modes (ironic, humorous, and macabre), different time frames, and, above all, different historical sensibilities.

Sherman's sensibility is quintessentially postmodern: she appropriates time-honored masterpieces so as to deflate their pretensions and expose the commodification of female body parts that was as prevalent in past high culture as it is in today's world of mass production. Yet it is not certain that Sherman herself has been able to remain outside the exploitation she purports to expose. All too often one has the impression that the acts of misogynistic violence in her photos carry with them a message of self-hatred. Though Sherman has become one of the most financially successful photographers of our age, with an audience of feminists, intellectuals, art critics, and serious collectors, that success may have carried a price beyond the market transaction. What is the social price we pay for parodic images of humiliated and dismembered women? Is this a form of liberation?[40]

Somewhere between art and pornography, ex-prostitute and porn star Annie Sprinkle is attempting to feminize photography in the sex market. From her work as a nude model, Sprinkle learned about photography on both sides of the camera. As a performing artist, she created her hilarious *Bosom Ballet*, which mimics the movements of classical dance—arabesques, glissades, and jetés—and debunks the traditional "ivory-orb" vision of breasts (fig. 96). Wearing long black gloves that contrast with her white skin and painted red nipples, Sprinkle pulled and twisted her breasts to the tune of "The Blue Danube" for a 1980 video and then for a series of performances in discothèques, art galleries, and theaters, which preceded the widely circulated *Bosom Ballet* poster and postcards.

In 1995, Sprinkle produced the series *Post-Modern Pin-Ups, Pleasure Activist Playing Cards* featuring her photos of nude and seminude women. As she puts it in the booklet that accompanies the cards: "These women . . . dare to pioneer the erotic frontiers, often playing with fire and sometimes getting burnt. There is a lot of resistance to what they do, especially when they receive money for it."[41] Some of the pin-ups were Sprinkle's close friends and some were lovers. Sprinkle says she encouraged them to use props and cos-

95. Cindy Sherman. *Untitled #225.* 1990.
Parodying Renaissance paintings of the nursing Madonna, Cindy Sherman straps a prosthesis
to her own body and poses her hand on a false breast exuding a drop of milk.

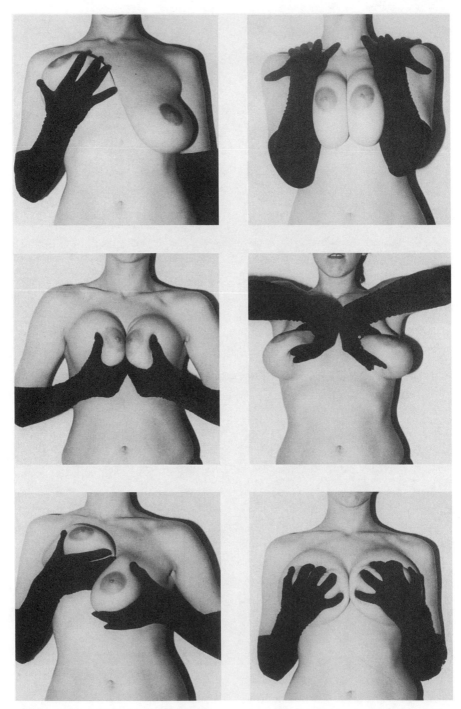

96. Annie Sprinkle's *Bosom Ballet*. 1991.

tumes in their own fantasy scenarios. From her point of view, it was a way of empowering women to express their own desires. Sprinkle's publisher and collaborator, Katharine Gates, adds that the women "are using a genre traditionally created by and for men, and transforming it through humor and irony into a female-positive statement." "Annie's pin-up photos are funny, hip, erotic and feminist." The cards are indeed often funny, as can be inferred merely from some of their titles: *Anarchist Porn Starlet, The Dyke from Hell, Dada Delight, Nude Celebrity Lookalike.* Whether they are "erotic" depends on the viewer. The men I've shown them to grab them excitedly, then seem puzzled, even mildly frightened.

As to their "feminist" content, several mock masculinist visions of women (e.g., the green-painted, pink-eared *Conceptual Bunny,* which takes off on the Playboy Bunny) or offer brazen images of women assuming power. Such is the image of Delores French, a *Prostitute Politician,* with her bare breasts propped up by an old-fashioned bodice studded with political buttons and dollar bills. She carries a sign that reads "Politically Correct Sluts Unite." French is, by the way, the founder of HIRE (Hooking Is Real Employment), a group dedicated to decriminalizing sex work. Though some people will undoubtedly be shocked by Sprinkle's pin-ups, they have a playful, nonviolent appeal, which removes them from my definition of pornography. In the new female-centered "sex biz," Sprinkle and her colleagues are dynamic forces to be reckoned with.

During the eighties and nineties, a new nude was introduced into the canon—the postmastectomy nude. *The Warrior* (1980), a portrait of writer Deena Metzger by photographer Hella Hammid, offered one of the first truly beautiful pictures of a one-breasted woman (fig. 97). A naked Metzger stretches out her arms to the sun, clearly exposing her asymmetrical chest with one intact breast and a tattoo over the scar where the other one had been. It is a stunning, life-affirming gesture.[42]

On the other hand, photographer Matuschka, who was diagnosed with breast cancer in 1991, expresses a deeply tragic vision in her postmastectomy works. It was her shocking self-portrait in a white dress cut away at the breast to reveal a mastectomy scar that appeared on the cover of *The New York Times Magazine* on August 15, 1993, and elicited such a tide of emotional responses. Though half the letters expressed outrage and shame, the other half praised Matuschka and the *Times* for their anguished truthfulness. Matuschka's postoperative self-portraits are indeed a way of saying what the *Times Magazine* announced on its cover: "You Can't Look Away Anymore."

97. Deena Metzger as photographed by Hella Hammid.
In the past fifteen years, this photo on posters and calendars has given heart to thousands of women.

Shortly after the controversial *Times* article, the Massachusetts Breast Cancer Coalition presented a large photographic exhibit entitled "Face to Face: Facing Breast Cancer Together." The organizers took the position that there is art that celebrates life and art that distances itself from life, and now the art of breast-cancer photography that tries to save life. Such photos are increasingly the staples of nationwide efforts to take the terror out of breast cancer and to convince women that the loss of a breast—however harrowing—is not the same as the loss of a life.

All these works constitute a new chapter in art history. Women painters and photographers, defying two thousand years of predominantly male-authored art, now vie with each other to present images they consider closer to the truths of female bodies and feminine sensibilities.

This same quest for "truer" images of women's bodies has found outlets in pictures that do not claim to be art—namely, those produced by computer technology. Several computer-imaging projects are attempting to represent a wide range of breast sizes and shapes. Plastic surgeon Dr. Loren Eskanazi of Stanford University, for example, is creating the first database of what "normal" breasts look like. She undertook her study because she wanted to dispel the myth of "the grapefruit breast" sported by Hollywood stars, comic-book heroines, and some fashion models. Since most breasts do not correspond to the commercially popular globe but are shaped like a teardrop, flatter on top and droopy below, many women suffer from an inaccurate portrayal of their bodies, and choose breast augmentation because they think "they don't look like every one else."[43]

Dr. Eskanazi uses scanning techniques similar to those used in science-fiction films. Each volunteer stands topless in a small room for about two minutes while a plane of laser light beamed from overhead passes across her body. A video camera peers down on the illuminated area at about a thirty-degree angle. Through simple triangulation, the exact coordinates of the contour mapped out by the moving plane of light can be calculated and stored.[44] The resulting data can then be rendered into a three-dimensional image on a computer screen, or used to produce an exact model of the breast. Eskanazi wants to use these data to help lingerie manufacturers create better-fitting bras and, eventually, to manufacture customized surgical implants for women desiring postmastectomy reconstructions.

Representations of breasts as nonidealized, noneroticized body parts have not yet found their way into the mass media. "Perfect" bodies still dominate films, videos, and popular magazines. Only occasionally is the "bigger-is-better" ideal called into question. In the 1992 film *Singles*, for example, a young woman contemplating breast augmentation sits with her prospective surgeon in front of a computer that shows her figure with a range of possible breast sizes. She keeps pressing the key that makes her breasts larger on the screen, because she knows this is what her lover wants. The good doctor keeps pressing the button that would make them smaller, because he is falling in love with her and sees no need for change. Predictably, the young woman's "liberation" begins with the realization that she does not have to enlarge her breasts to be attractive to men.

It has been barely twenty-five years since women began to wield their cameras and paintbrushes like arms in the gender war. Challenging male-authored conventions, they have portrayed bodies that are fat as well as thin, older as well as young, dark-skinned as well as white. The breasts they show are not all round, firm, and healthy. The implicit message of these works is that breasts cannot be "liberated" until the public has a better idea of what most breasts look like.

THE CONCEPT OF a liberated breast will bring different images to different women's minds. For some, it will mean walking down the street on a summer's day in a thin, revealing dress—without the fear of being hassled. For others, it will mean breast-feeding in a public place without the possibility of legal punishment or the insult of being told "that's disgusting" (fig. 98). Still others will be able to find an American beach close to home where they can swim topless. It will mean finding comfortable bras that really fit, or wearing no bra at all and not worrying about whether that is acceptable to others.

Claiming the body as a source of power and pleasure is high on the liberated woman's priority list. She often runs, swims, and exercises because it makes her feel good, and not just because it makes her look good. Some are willing to see their breasts virtually disappear into the muscular frame created by strenuous body-building. Others continue to be proud of their large breasts, to show them off and use them as sexual turn-ons.

Some will have breasts surgically reduced if their unusual size causes physical problems. Some will choose breast reconstruction in the aftermath of a mastectomy, and some will not. Others will seek out cosmetic breast surgery because they desire larger, firmer, younger-looking breasts. Some will wear nipple rings. Some will wear business suits and look forward to the day when the phrase "She's got breasts" is as common as "He's got balls."

Liberated breasts have infinite variety. They are brown, white, pink, yellow, and tea-colored. They resemble lemons, oranges, and grapefruits; apples, pears, and melons; turnips and eggplants. Some are sensitive to cold or to heat or the constraints of clothing. Some like to be touched in a certain way at certain times by certain people, and some do not like to be touched at all. Such breasts have only one thing in common: they belong to women who know what pleases them and refuse to be manipulated against their will.

As female flesh and blood, breasts deserve nothing more or less than the respect civilized people are expected to show toward all parts of the human body. Admittedly, some parts of the body have more popular appeal than others. Though breasts still carry an overload of cultural and sexual expectations, many women hope to see the day when their chests do not have to bear

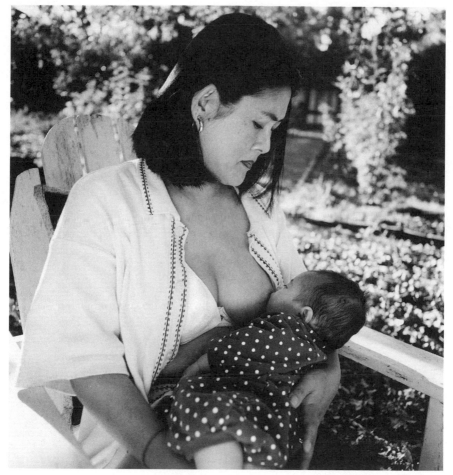

98. Reid S. Yalom. As of 1997, California women may nurse in public without fear of being hassled.

such a burden. Maybe the time will come when the affect surrounding the breast will be sensibly reduced to the level of excitement produced by an attractive knee or thigh. Perhaps our granddaughters will even be able to uncover their bosoms, if they choose, without the fear of moral censure, court action, or rape.

Not so very long ago, women risked such responses in baring their legs. In the mid-nineteenth century, some American and British middle-class families even covered up their piano legs with cloth and referred to them, prudishly, as "limbs." Although we tend to forget it, the emancipation of the female leg is a very recent phenomenon. We have only to look at family photos to recall how quickly, during and immediately after World War I, legs threw off the shackles of high boots and long, cumbersome skirts. Today, with leg nudity a given in the Western world, there are new zones to be uncovered. Will the liberated breast of the twenty-first century also demand and acquire the right of public nudity?

Nine

THE BREAST IN CRISIS

T HE MEANINGS ATTRIBUTED to the breast throughout history
have rarely expressed women's feelings about themselves. Only recently, in a medley of distinctive voices, have women begun to talk
openly about their breasts. They have spoken of the adolescent's embarrassed
pride, the adult woman's erotic pleasure, the nursing mother's joy, the
breast-cancer patient's anguish and the health activist's determination, the
brassiere designer's hype and the consumer's frustrations, the woman with big
breasts who wishes they were smaller and the woman with small breasts
who wishes they were bigger. How a woman regards her breasts is a good
indicator of her personal self-esteem, as well as the collective status of women
in general.

From the outside, the breast represents another reality, and one that
varies in the eyes of each beholder. Babies see food. Men see sex. Doctors see
disease. Businessmen see dollar signs. Religious authorities transform breasts
into spiritual symbols, whereas politicians appropriate them for nationalistic
ends. Psychoanalysts place them at the center of the unconscious, as if they
were unchanging monoliths. This multiplicity of meanings suggests the
breast's privileged place in the human imagination.

At any given moment in history, one of these possible meanings rises to
the fore and tends to dominate our view. In the late Middle Ages, the maternal breast became, for the first time, a widespread emblem of Christian nurturance. Two hundred years later, Renaissance painters and poets covered
over its religious significance with a shimmering veil of eroticism. Eighteenth-century European thinkers made of the breast a civic fount. Today, in
late-twentieth-century America, the word "breast" conjures up frankly sexual

scenarios for both men and women, as well as the reality of breast cancer for all too many women.

Just as the meaning of the breast changes according to the times, it takes on different accents according to the country. The cultural history of the breast is certainly not the same in England as in France. Both Northern and Southern Europe inherited a Greco-Roman tradition, but one might say that Aphrodite has reigned in Italy and France, whereas Athena has prevailed in England and Germany. Compare Marianne, with her seductive breasts, to Britannia, with her protective breastplate, or the heavily armored Valkyrie of Nordic mythology. Although one must always be wary of national generalizations, it is safe to say that the Catholic Mediterranean has historically been more indulgent toward public delight in the bosom than the Protestant countries of Northern Europe and America.

That the meaning of the breast varies according to time and place should come as no surprise. Historians and anthropologists have made a good case for the fundamental relativity of cultural values concerning every aspect of human existence, including the body. What has been less evident, until the last quarter-century, is the difference in attitudes held by women and by men. We know so little about what women really thought in premodern times, and virtually nothing of their thoughts about their bodies. What has come down to us in literature, art, and most public documents has been generally refracted through a lens fitted for male eyes. Did women themselves see their breasts as symbols of religious or political nurturance? Did they accept the notion that their breasts belonged in babies' mouths and in men's hands? Where was the woman in all this? What did she think and feel?

Today, it is the tragic reality of breast cancer that is bringing women into full possession of their breasts. They are learning, with the shock of life-threatening illness, that their breasts really are their own. Even husbands and lovers, family members and friends sometimes abandon them when their breasts become diseased. Many friends and relatives are simply unable to lend comfort when it is most needed.

Yet, paradoxically, breast cancer also has its inspirational side. The grassroots fight against the disease has taught us that it can be combatted, that it is not always fatal, that good medical care and support groups make a difference. Women have joined together with other women, men, and even children to create settings in which the breast-cancer patient can feel less alone.

A march of seven thousand people to raise money for breast cancer; an exhibition of breast images that includes those of mastectomy survivors; sympathetic poems and novels on breast cancer written by men as well as women—these are signs that American society is changing, that it is learning to embrace the woman with breast cancer in a new, empathic way.

What meanings we give our breasts will always be bound up with societal values and cultural norms. Few women and few men are unaffected by the mass media, which specialize in standardized breasts—large, firm, and thrusting upward. Those hemispheric orbs on boylike bodies represent an impossible ideal for almost all women. Confronted by such images, many women consider breast-augmentation surgery or succumb to bouts of bulimia, anorexia, and other forms of self-hatred. National polls, social science studies, and TV talk shows document the large-scale dissatisfaction American women feel toward their bodies. Other women fight back, refusing to internalize the advertising industry's vision of the breast. They are wresting their God-given bodies from the media and an overly commercialized society, so as to breathe into them a woman-centered spirit. Numerous activists, doctors, nurses, artists, and writers have made a conscious commitment to "liberate" the breast according to a female script.

We live in a historical moment when the breast has reappeared with renewed vigor. "Boobs are back," a heavyset society matron tells her astonished husband as she descends the stairway in a low-cut gown (The New Yorker, December 19, 1994). "Put On Your Best Chest—It's Time to Preen" announces a lengthy fashion article (New York Times, April 2, 1995). "Breast jokes will be found in abundance" is the headline of a seasonal television preview (USA Today, July 28, 1995). Mainstream women's magazines feature a continual flow of articles on breast cancer and breast cosmetics, whereas feminist magazines and calendars attempt to debunk the American breast obsession. From every indicator, the stock in breasts is on the rise.

No one can say for sure why the breast has, once again, become so prominent. In my reading of this phenomenon, I see both timeless and time-bound factors. As long as the breast has a nurturing capacity, it will hold, for both women and men, deeply etched associations with the earliest stage of life—a paradise forever lost as we meander into the responsibilities of adulthood and the various forms of alienation endemic to postindustrialized societies. The more daunting the world becomes with its awesome bureaucracies and endless inventions, the greater the nostalgia for intimacy and basic connections.

The breast we knew as infants, or we internalized through the vision of others at the breast, keeps getting further and further away.

We call it forth as a way of countering everything that menaces us, like some amulet that would restore us to the comfort and safety of the suckling babe. But such a return is inevitably denied us. Only in lovemaking do we sometimes find that sense of oneness with the (m)other's body. Then sucking and suckling can be, for both men and women, a form of primal bliss. (It is hard to get away from Freud, even when one has seen his shortcomings.)

But the breast as a timeless signifier of sex, life, and nurturance now has to fight against its opposite meaning: the vessel of disease and death. In this respect, it is hardly a comforting symbol, especially for women. We have come to fear our breasts, to see them as potential enemies, to fight against the fatal genes they sometimes harbor. For many people today, breast cancer is the catalyst that has transformed the way we conceptualize the breast, so that we see it, first and foremost, as a medical problem. Increasingly, the medicalization of the breast threatens to efface its erotic and maternal meanings.

Perhaps the return of the pronounced bosom to fashion and the media is a way of denying the fears we hold about the future of the breast. After all, nobody really knows why breast cancer is on the rise. Some of our best guesses are related to environmental toxins and the hazards of technology. Bring back the breast as it once was, before the ravages of breast cancer, before the world had run amok.

The breast has been, and will continue to be, a marker of society's values. Over time, it has assumed and shed various cloaks of religious, erotic, domestic, political, psychological, and commercial hues. Today it reflects a medical and global crisis. We are anxious about our breasts, just as we are anxious about the future of our world. What kind of breast will there be for the women and babies of tomorrow? Will women face an ever-growing incidence of breast cancer? Already we survivors feel lucky not to be the one-in-nine victim, and almost blessed if we die with our breasts on.

Or will we succeed in checking and even reversing the rise of breast cancer? If so, this would be a victory not only for women but for all of us—for life itself in the face of everything that threatens to annihilate us. "Save the breast" is a slogan the whole world can endorse.

The breast that may be saved will not be the breast that belonged to our ancestors, for women will have some say about its meaning and use. Just as we have found ways to go braless or topless, to promote more breast-cancer re-search, to fight for the right to breast-feed in public, to counter the glamorous images of the mass media with more realistic images, so too we shall find new ways of protecting and validating our breasts. For better or for worse, bigger or smaller, in sickness and in health, breasts are wedded to our bodies and, in the best of circumstances, can offer us both pleasure and power.

Notes

Select Bibliography

Index

Illustration Credits

Notes

CHAPTER ONE

1. Marija Gimbutas, *The Language of the Goddess*, p. 316. The vast, often contradictory literature on this subject has led one archeologist to conclude that the "Venus" figurines "have only gender in common" (Sarah Nelson, "Diversity of the Upper Paleolithic 'Venus' Figurines and Archeological Mythology," in *Gender in Cross-Cultural Perspective*, ed. Caroline Brettell and Carolyn Sargent, p. 51).

2. Buffie Johnson, *Lady of the Beasts: Ancient Images of the Goddess and Her Sacred Animals*, p. 44.

3. James Mellaart, *Çatal Hüyük*, figs. 25–28; Adele Getty, *Goddess: Mother of Living Nature*, pp. 11–12.

4. Juliet Clutton-Brock, "Representation of the Female Breast in Bone Carvings from a Neolithic Lake Village in Switzerland," *Antiquity*, vol. 65 (1991), pp. 908–10; V. C. C. Collum, *The Tressé Iron-Age Megalithic Monument: Its Quadruple Sculptured Breasts and Their Relation to the Mother-Goddess Cosmic Cult*, plate XXXV.

5. Tikva Frymer-Kensky, *In the Wake of the Goddesses: Women, Culture, and the Biblical Transformation of Pagan Myth*, pp. 159–60. See also Ruth Hestrin, " 'Astarte' figurines," in *Highlights of Archeology*, pp. 72–73.

6. Karen Armstrong, *A History of God: The 4000-Year Quest of Judaism, Christianity and Islam*, pp. 23–26, 49–50.

7. Anne Baring and Jules Cashford, *The Myth of the Goddess: Evolution of an Image*, p. 250.

8. Florence Maruéjol, "La Nourrice: Un Thème Iconographique," *Annales du Service des Antiquités de l'Égypte*, vol. 69 (1983), p. 311.

9. Gay Robins, *Women in Ancient Egypt*, p. 86.

10. Barbara G. Walker, *The Woman's Dictionary of Symbols and Sacred Objects*, p. 303.

11. Colin Renfrew, *The Cycladic Spirit: Masterpieces from the Nicholas P. Goulandris Collection*, p. 105. See also the more cautious speculations by J. Lesley Fitton, *Cycladic Art*, pp. 66–70.

12. Rodney Castleden, *Minoan Life in Bronze Age Crete*, p. 7; Elizabeth Wayland Barber, *Women's Work: The First 20,000 Years*, p. 110.

13. Reproduced in Baring and Cashford, p. 114.

14. Theodora Hadzisteliou Price, *Kourotrophos: Cults and Representations of the Greek Nursing Deities*.

15. Diana Darke, *Guide to Aegean and Mediterranean Turkey* (London: Michael Haag, 1989), p. 80; A. Frova, "La Statua de Artemide Efesia a Caesarea Maritima," *Bolletino d'Arte*, vol. XLVII, no. 4 (1962), pp. 305–13. Other multibreasted statues can be found in Rome at the Museum of the Vatican, the Palazzo dei Conservatori, and the Villa Albani; in Naples at the Museo Nazionale; in Paris at the Louvre; and in Jerusalem at the Israel Museum.

16. James Hall, *Dictionary of Subjects and Symbols in Art*, p. 52.

17. Eva C. Keuls, *The Reign of the Phallus: Sexual Politics in Ancient Athens*.

18. This wood carving is reproduced in Baring and Cashford, p. 314.

19. Anne Hollander, *Seeing Through Clothes*, p. 6.

20. K. J. Dover, "Classical Greek Attitudes to Sexual Behaviour," in *Women in the Ancient World: The Arethusa Papers*, ed. John Peradotto and J. P. Sullivan, p. 145.

21. Valerie A. Fildes, *Wet Nursing*, p. 10.

22. Athenaeus, *The Deipnosophists*, trans. Charles Burton Gulick [1937] (Cambridge, Mass.: Harvard University Press, 1959), vol. VI, pp. 185–87.

23. John J. Winkler, *The Constraints of Desire: The Anthropology of Sex and Gender in Ancient Greece*, p. 188.

24. Ibid., p. 190.

25. Mary R. Lefkowitz, *Women in Greek Myth*, p. 57.

26. Wm. Blake Tyrrell, *Amazons: A Study in Athenian Mythmaking*.

27. Keuls, pp. 4, 34.

28. Pliny the Elder, *Natural History*, trans. H. Rockham (Cambridge, Mass.: Harvard University Press, 1942), p. 587.

29. Jean Starobinski discusses this pictorial theme in *Largesse*, pp. 82–85.

30. *Tacitus' "Agricola," "Germany" and "Dialogue on Orators,"* trans. and ed. Herbert W. Benario [1967] (Norman and London: University of Oklahoma Press, 1991), p. 117.

31. David Biale, *Eros and the Jews: From Biblical Israel to Contemporary America*, p. 27.

32. Ibid., p. 26.

33. "Infant Feeding in the Bible," *Midwife, Health Visitor and Community Nurse*, vol. 23 (1987), p. 312.

34. Marcia Falk, *The Song of Songs, A New Translation*, p. xv. Citations from the *Song* come from nos. 25, 29, 15, 23.

35. Ariel Bloch and Chana Bloch, *The Song of Songs, A New Translation*, p. 31.

36. Josy Eisenberg, *La Femme au Temps de la Bible*, p. 85.

37. Jean Claude Bologne, *Histoire de la Pudeur*, p. 84.

38. Paul Valéry, *Écrits sur l'Art* (Paris: Club des Librairies de France, 1962), p. 138.

39. See E. Clive Rouse, *Medieval Wall Paintings*, p. 60.

40. Anglicus Bartholomaeus, *On the Properties of Things*, cited in Clarissa Atkinson, *The Oldest Vocation: Christian Motherhood in the Middle Ages*, p. 58.

41. Urban T. Holmes, *Medieval Man: His Understanding of Himself, His Society, and the World*, p. 90.

42. Doris Desclais Berkvam, *Enfance et Maternité dans la Littérature Française des XIIe et XIIIe Siècles*, p. 49.

43. Berkvam, ibid., p. 48, refers specifically to Philippe de Novare, *Les Quatre Âges de l'Homme* (Paris: F. Didot, 1888, p. 2).

44. This and the following citation from *Tristan de Nanteuil*, ed. K. V. Sinclair (Assen: Van Corcum, 1971), cited in Berkvam, ibid., p. 53.

45. Danièle Alexandre-Bidon, "La Lettre Volée: Apprendre à Lire à l'Enfant au Moyen-Âge," p. 988.

46. *Aucassin et Nicolette*, ed. Mario Roques (Paris: Champion, 1929), sec. 12.

47. Cited in Bologne, p. 54. English translation for quotes referenced in notes 47 and 48 suggested by Stanford Professor Brigitte Cazelles.

48. Cited in J. Houdoy, *La Beauté des Femmes dans la Littérature et dans l'Art du XIIe au XVIe Siècles*, pp. 60–61.

49. Adapted from *The Book of the Knight La Tour–Landry*, trans. from the original French into English in the reign of Henry VI, ed. Thomas Wright, p. 49.

50. Dante, *The Divine Comedy*, trans. Dorothy Sayers (Baltimore: Penguin Books, 1955), vol. 2, p. 250 (Purgatory, ch. 23, v. 102).

51. Marina Warner, *Alone of All Her Sex: The Myth and the Cult of the Virgin Mary*.

52. Margaret R. Miles, "The Virgin's One Bare Breast: Female Nudity and Religious Meaning in Tuscan Early Renaissance Culture," in *The Female Body in Western Culture*, ed. Susan Rubin Suleiman, pp. 193–208.

53. The following discussion derives heavily from James Bruce Ross, "The Middle-Class Child in Urban Italy, Fourteenth to Early Sixteenth Century," in *The History of Childhood*, ed. Lloyd deMause, pp. 183–96.

54. Ibid., p. 199.

55. Shari L. Thurer, *The Myths of Motherhood: How Culture Reinvents the Good Mother*, p. 83.

56. Carolyn Bynum, *Holy Feast and Holy Fast: The Religious Significance of Food to Medieval Women*, plate 17 and pp. 269–76.

57. Catherine of Siena, *The Dialogue*, trans. Suzanne Noffke, pp. 179–80.

58. Juliana, *A Book of Showings to the Anchoress Julian of Norwich*, pt. two, ed. Edmund Colledge and James Walsh, p. 592.

59. Saint Teresa, *The Complete Works*, trans. and ed. E. Allison Peers (London and New York: Sheed and Ward, 1946), vol. 2, pp. 130–31.

60. This discussion draws heavily from Atkinson, pp. 58–60, and her references to *The Golden Legend of Jacobus de Voragine*, ed. Grander Ryan and Helmut Rippeger (New York: Arno Press, 1969), p. 714. See also Donald Weinstein and Rudolph M. Bell, *Saints and Society*, pp. 24–25 for nursing stories from the lives of saints.

61. Nicholas Love, "The Myrrour of the Blessyd Life of Christ," in *The Oxford Book of Late Medieval Verse and Prose* (Oxford: Clarendon, 1985), p. 96.

62. Cited in Satia and Robert Bernen, *Myth and Religion in European Painting, 1270–1700*, p. 172. The original reads: "*L'enfant prend la mamelle / Et lacte pasci-*

tur. / C'est du lait de pucelle / Quod non corrumpitur. / La chose est bien nouvelle / Quod virgo mater est. / Et sans coulpe charnelle / Hic puer natus est."

63. John Calvin, *Tracts and Treatises on the Reformation of the Church*, ed. Henry Beveridge, vol. 1, p. 317.

64. Françoise Loux, *Le Corps dans la Société Traditionnelle*, p. 154.

65. A photo of this choir stall can be found in Isabel Mateo Gomez, *Temas Profanos en la Gótica Española—Las Sillerías de Coro* (Madrid: Consejo Superior de Investigaciones Científicas, Instituto Diego Velázquez, 1979), fig. 106.

CHAPTER TWO

1. Johan Huizinga, *The Waning of the Middle Ages*, p. 159.

2. Anne Hollander, *Seeing Through Clothes*, p. 187.

3. Romi, *La Mythologie du Sein*, p. 29.

4. Ibid., p. 30.

5. Dominique Gros, *Le Sein Dévoilé*, p. 27.

6. Pierre Champion, *La Dame de Beauté, Agnès Sorel*, p. 39.

7. Peter Fryer, *Mrs. Grundy: Studies in English Prudery*, pp. 172–73.

8. The original, from Villon's "Regrets de la Belle Heaumière," reads *"Ces gentes épaules menues, / Ces bras longs et ces mains traitisses, / Petits tetins, hanches charnues."*

9. The relevant lines from the fifteenth-century poet Gratien du Pont read: *"Tes tetins sont: blancz, rondz comme une pomme / Sy durs et fermes; que jamays en veit homme / Loing lung de laultre"* (cited by Alison Saunders, *The Sixteenth-Century Blason Poétique*, p. 63).

10. Ludovico Ariosto, *Orlando Furioso* (Bari: Laterza, 1928), p. 14. The original reads *"Vengon e van come onda al primo margo."*

11. Cited in Naomi Yavneh, "The Ambiguity of Beauty in Tasso and Petrarch," in *Sexuality and Gender in Early Modern Europe: Institutions, Texts, Images*, ed. James Grantham Turner, p. 141.

12. Agnolo Firenzuola, *Of the Beauty of Women*, trans. Clara Bell, p. 76.

13. J. Houdoy, *La Beauté des Femmes dans la Littérature et dans l'Art du XIIe au XVIe Siècles*, p. 96.

14. For a masterful account of Franco's life, see Margaret R. Rosenthal, *The Honest Courtesan: Veronica Franco, Citizen and Writer in Sixteenth-Century Venice.*

15. Mila Contini, *Fashion from Ancient Egypt to the Present Day*, p. 118.

16. I am grateful to historian Judith Brown for this communication from Guido Ruggiero. See also Guido Ruggiero, *Binding Passions: Tales of Magic, Marriage, and Power at the End of the Renaissance*, pp. 48–49.

17. Hollander, *Seeing Through Clothes*, pp. 188–98, 203–4.

18. Art historian Lynne Lawner calls attention to the many paintings of courtesans pointing to or cupping their breasts, which she sees as reminiscent of ancient goddess figures. Still, despite conceivable allusions to past religious sources, paintings like Paris Bordone's *Courtesan* (National Galleries of Scotland, Edinburgh), Palma Vecchio's *Portrait of a Woman* (Staatliche Museen Preussicher Kulturbesitz, Berlin), and

Giulio Romano's *La Fornarina* (Galleria Nationale, Rome) are nothing if not primarily erotic. (Lynne Lawner, *Lives of the Courtesans*, p. 96.)

19. Keith Thomas, *Religion and the Decline of Magic*, pp. 445–46.

20. Anne Llewellyn Barstow, *Witchcraze: A New History of the European Witch Hunts*, pp. 129–30.

21. Jim Sharpe, "Women, Witchcraft, and the Legal Process," in *Women, Crime, and the Courts in Early Modern England*, ed. Jenny Kermode and Garthine Walker, pp. 109–10.

22. Barstow, p. 144.

23. Margaret L. King, *Women of the Renaissance*, pp. 144, 146.

24. The original reads: "*Mais petite boulle d'Ivoire, / au milieu de qui est assise / Une Fraise ou une Serise . . . Quant on te voit, il vient à maintz / Une envie dedant les mains / De te taster, de te tenir: / Mais il se fault bien contenir / D'en approcher, bon gré ma vie, / Car il viendrait une autre envy. / . . . À bon droit heureux on dira / Celuy qui de laict l'emplira / Faisant d'ung tetin de pucelle / Tetin de femme entière et belle.*" (Pascal Laîné and Pascal Quignard, *Blasons Anatomiques du Corps Féminin*, pp. 51–52.)

25. The original reads: "*Tetin, qui n'as rien que la peau, / Tetin flat, Tetin de drappeau, . . . Tetin au grand villain bout noir / Comme celuy d'un entonnoir, / . . . Tetin propre pour en enfer / Nourri les enfans de lucifer. / . . . Va, grand vilain tetin puant, / Tu fournirois bien, en suant, / De civette & de parfuns, / Pour faire cent mille defunctz.*" (Ibid., pp. 118, 121.)

26. This discussion is indebted to Lawrence D. Kritzman, *The Rhetoric of Sexuality and the Literature of the French Renaissance*.

27. Labé's Sonnet 8 begins: "*Je vis, je meurs: je me brule et me noye*" (Louise Labé, *Oeuvres Complètes*, ed. Enzo Giudici, p. 148).

28. The original lines from Labé's Sonnet 4 are: "*Depuis qu'Amour cruel empoisonna / Premierement de son feu ma poitrine, / Tousjours brulay de sa fureur divine, / Qui un seul jour mon coeur n'abandonna.*" (Ibid., p. 144).

29. The original of Sonnet CXIV reads: "*. . . ma main, maugré moi, quelque fois / De l'amour chaste outrepasse les lois / Dans votre sein cherchant ce qui m'embraise*" (Pierre de Ronsard, *Les Amours*, ed. Henri et Catherine Weber, p. 72).

30. Sonnet XXXIX reads: "*Pleut il à Dieu n'avoir jamais tâté / Si follement le tetin de m'amie! / . . . Qui eût pensé, que le cruel destin / Eût enfermé sous un si beau tetin / Un si gran feu, pour m'en faire la proie?*" (Ibid., p. 26.)

31. Françoise Bardon, *Diane de Poitiers et le Mythe de Diane*.

32. Philippe Erlanger, *Diane de Poitiers: Déesse de la Renaissance*, p. 206.

33. Ibid., p. 193.

34. The Seigneur de Brantôme, *Lives of Fair and Gallant Ladies*, p. 150.

35. Ibid., p. 151.

36. Contini, p. 92.

37. Brantôme, p. 205; Paul Lacroix, *Les Secrets de Beauté de Diane de Poitiers*.

38. Cited in Anne de Marnhac, *Femmes au Bain: Les Métamorphoses de la Beauté*, p. 29.

39. Georges Vigarello, *Le Propre et le Sale: L'Hygiène du Corps Depuis le Moyen Âge*, p. 70.

40. Orest Ranum, "The Refuges of Intimacy," in *A History of Private Life: Passions of the Renaissance*, ed. Philippe Ariès and Georges Duby, vol. III, ed. Roger Chartier, trans. Arthur Goldhammer, p. 222.

41. King, p. 12.

42. Cited in Joseph Illick, "Anglo-American Child-Rearing," in *The History of Childhood*, ed. Lloyd deMause, p. 308.

43. Cited in Yvonne Knibiehler and Catherine Fouquet, *L'Histoire des Mères*, p. 86.

44. Philippe Erlanger, *Gabrielle d'Estrées: Femme Fatale*, p. 83.

45. Inès Murat, *Gabrielle d'Estrées*, pp. 425–26.

46. For a fuller discussion of this subject, see Eileen O'Neill, "(Re)Presentations of Eros: Exploring Female Sexual Agency," in *Gender/Body/Knowledge: Feminist Reconstructions of Being and Knowing*, ed. Alison Jaggar and Susan Bordo, pp. 69–70.

47. Cited in Judith Brown, *Immodest Acts: The Life of a Lesbian Nun in Renaissance Italy*, p. 167.

48. Guido Ruggiero, *The Boundaries of Eros: Sex Crime and Sexuality in Renaissance Venice*, pp. 189–90.

49. Brown, p. 6.

50. This section is indebted to Marina Warner, *Monuments and Maidens*, pp. 38–60; and Andrew Belsey and Catherine Belsey, "Icons of Divinity: Portraits of Elizabeth I," in *Renaissance Bodies: The Human Figure in English Culture c. 1540–1660*, ed. Lucy Gent and Nigel Llewellyn, pp. 11–35.

51. For Elizabethan women's apparel, see Elizabeth Ewing, *Fashion in Underwear*, pp. 20–27; Jane Ashelford, *Dress in the Age of Elizabeth*, pp. 11–42; Christopher Breward, *The Culture of Fashion*, pp. 44–48.

52. Valerie A. Fildes, *Breasts, Bottles, and Babies*, p. 102.

53. Christopher Hibbert, *The Virgin Queen: Elizabeth I, Genius of the Golden Age*, p. 10.

54. Nancy Vickers, " 'The blazon of sweet beauty's best': Shakespeare's *Lucrece*," in *Shakespeare and the Question of Theory*, ed. Patricia Parker and Geoffrey Hartman, pp. 95–115.

55. Kirkpatrick Sale, *The Conquest of Paradise: Christopher Columbus and the Columbian Legacy*, p. 176.

56. Catherine Keller, "The Breast, The Apocalypse, and the Colonial Journey," p. 64.

57. Louis B. Wright, *Middle-Class Culture in Elizabethan England*, p. 114.

58. Dorothy McLaren, "Marital Fertility and Lactation, 1570–1720," in *Women in English Society, 1500–1800*, ed. Mary Prior, pp. 26–28, and Rosalind K. Marshall, *Virgins and Viragos: A History of Women in Scotland from 1080–1980*, p. 117.

59. Mary Abbott, *Family Ties: English Families, 1540–1920*, p. 48.

60. Lawrence Stone, *The Family, Sex, and Marriage in England, 1500–1800*, p. 270, and Fildes, *Breasts*, p. 102.

61. Cited by Morwenna and John Rendle-Short, *The Father of Child Care: Life of William Cadogan (1711–1797)*, p. 26.

62. Germaine Greer, Susan Hastings, Jeslyn Medoff, Melinda Sansone, eds., *Kissing the Rod: An Anthology of Seventeenth-Century Women's Verse*, p. 243. The poems by "Eliza," Aphra Behn, and "Ephelia" are found on pp. 145–46, 243–46, and 274.

63. Fildes, *Breasts*, p. 101.

64. Based on illegitimacy statistics, Edward Shorter situates successive waves of increased extramarital sexual activity in the late sixteenth century, the early nineteenth century, and the late twentieth century. Edward Shorter, *The Making of the Modern Family*, p. 81.

65. Cited in William Manchester, *A World Lit Only by Fire*, p. 68.

66. Edward Lucie-Smith, *Sexuality in Western Art*, p. 75.

67. Linda Woodbridge, *Women and the English Renaissance: Literature and the Nature of Womankind, 1540–1620*, p. 218.

68. Joan Kelly Gadol, "Did Women Have a Renaissance?," in *Becoming Visible: Women in European History*, ed. Renate Bridenthal and Claudia Koonz, p. 160.

69. Alan Macfarlane, *Marriage and Love in England: Modes of Reproduction, 1300–1840*, p. 298.

CHAPTER THREE

1. This chapter is indebted to Simon Schama, *The Embarrassment of Riches: An Interpretation of Dutch Culture in the Golden Age*, especially pp. 536–44.

2. Wayne E. Franits, *Paragons of Virtue: Women and Domesticity in Seventeenth-Century Dutch Art*, pp. 111–19.

3. Cited by Mary Frances Durantini, *The Child in Seventeenth-Century Dutch Painting*, p. 18, with poetic changes added by Bram Dijkstra.

4. Teellinck, 1639, vol. 2, p. 85, cited by Franits, p. 227.

5. Jacob Cats, *Houwelijck* (Middleburg, 1625), chap. 5, p. 56, cited by Franits, p. 115.

6. Durantini, p. 19.

7. Cited in Schama, p. 538.

8. Zbigniew Herbert, *Still Life with a Bridle: Essays and Apocryphas*, trans. John and Bogdana Carpenter, p. 29.

9. Schama, p. 540.

10. Adriaen van de Venne, *Moeder*, in Jacob Cats, *Houwelijck* (Amsterdam, 1632), reproduced in Schama, p. 544, and Franits, p. 131.

11. Reproduced in Franits, p. 116.

12. "Woman Nursing a Child," 1474 engraving from the series *Nine Figures*, Amsterdam, Rijksmuseum-Stichting, reproduced in Franits, p. 114.

13. Durantini, pp. 6–21.

14. J. H. Huizinga, *Dutch Civilisation in the Seventeenth Century and Other Essays*, p. 114.

15. R. H. Fuchs, *Dutch Painting*, p. 42.

16. Schama, p. 459.

17. Anne Hollander, *Seeing Through Clothes*, pp. 110–11.

18. Schama, p. 402.

19. Schama, p. 403, referring to Diderot, "Voyage de Hollande" in *Oeuvres* (Paris, 1819), vol. 7, p. 41.

CHAPTER FOUR

1. Mervyn Levy, *The Moons of Paradise*, p. 87.
2. Linda Pollock, *Forgotten Children: Parent-Child Relations from 1500 to 1900*, p. 215.
3. *Hommage à Robert Debré (1882–1978): L'Épopée de la Médecine des Enfants* (Paris: Musée de l'Assistance Publique, 1988), p. 40.
4. Elisabeth Badinter, *Mother Love: Myth and Reality*, p. xix. See also George D. Sussman, *Selling Mothers' Milk: The Wet-Nursing Business in France, 1715–1914*, p. 22.
5. For nursing practices in Great Britain, see Valerie Fildes, *Breasts, Bottles, and Babies*, especially pp. 98–122 and pp. 152–63.
6. Lynn Hunt, "Introduction," in *Eroticism and the Body Politic*, ed. Lynn Hunt, p. 1.
7. Ruth Perry, "Colonizing the Breast: Sexuality and Maternity in Eighteenth-Century England," p. 216.
8. Cited in Morwenna and John Rendle-Short, *The Father of Child Care: Life of William Cadogan (1711–1797)*, p. 26.
9. William Cadogan, *An Essay upon Nursing, and the Management of Children, From their Birth to Three Years of Age*, reproduced in ibid. Cadogan citations from pp. 7, 24, 23, 24, 6, and 7.
10. Catherine M. Scholten, *Childbearing in American Society, 1650–1850*, p. 14.
11. Sylvia D. Hoffert, *Private Matters: American Attitudes Toward Childbearing and Infant Nurture in the Urban North, 1800–60*, p. 148.
12. Londa Schiebinger, *Nature's Body: Gender in the Making of Modern Science*, pp. 40–41.
13. Doris Desclais Berkvam, *Enfance et Maternité dans la Littérature Française des XIIe et XIIIe Siècles*, pp. 46–47.
14. Derrick B. Jelliffe and E. F. Patrice Jelliffe, *Human Milk in the Modern World*, p. 2.
15. Jean-Jacques Rousseau, *Émile: or On Education*, trans. Alan Bloom, pp. 254–64.
16. Jean-Jacques Rousseau, *The Confessions*, trans. J. M. Cohen, p. 301.
17. Madame Roland, *Mémoires* (Paris: Mercure de France, 1986), p. 333.
18. Marilyn Yalom, *Blood Sisters: The French Revolution in Women's Memory*, p. 125.
19. Reproduced in *Sklavin oder Bürgerin? Französische Revolution und Neue Weiblichkeit 1760–1830*, ed. Viktoria Schmidt-Linsenhoff, p. 515.
20. Marilyn Yalom, *Le Temps des Orages: Aristocrates, Bourgeoises, et Paysannes Racontent*, p. 105.
21. *Archives Parlementaires de 1787 à 1860*, 1st ser., vol. LXVII (1905), p. 614. See also Fanny Fay-Sallois, *Les Nourrices à Paris au XIXe Siècle*, p. 120.
22. Schiebinger, p. 69.
23. Mary Lindemann, "Love for Hire: The Regulation of the Wet-Nursing Business in Eighteenth-Century Hamburg," p. 390.
24. Madelyn Gutwirth, *The Twilight of the Goddesses: Women and Representation in the French Revolutionary Era*, p. 349.

25. Yalom, *Blood Sisters*, p. 166.

26. Mary Jacobus, "Incorruptible Milk: Breast-Feeding and the French Revolution," in *Rebel Daughters*, ed. Sara E. Melzer and Leslie W. Rabine, p. 54.

27. Cited by Gutwirth, p. 348.

28. *Égyptomanie* (Paris: Louvre, 1994), p. 160.

29. Hérault de Séchelles's speeches for the Festival of Regeneration were recorded in *Le Moniteur*, August 12, 1793.

30. Barbara Gelpi, "Significant Exposure: The Turn-of-the-Century Breast," *Nineteenth-Century Contexts*, forthcoming.

31. Willett and Phillis Cunnington, *The History of Underclothes*, p. 97.

32. Cited by Ewa Lajer-Burcharth, "La Rhétorique du Corps Féminin sous le Directoire," in *Les Femmes et la Révolution Française*, ed. Marie-France Brive, vol. 2, p. 221.

33. Cited by Julian Robinson, *The Fine Art of Fashion*, p. 44.

34. For an extensive commentary on Delacroix's "Liberty," see Marcia Pointon, *Naked Authority: The Body in Western Painting, 1830–1908*, pp. 59–82.

35. Michel Droit, "Quand Paris Applaudissait Sa Liberté," *Le Figaro*, August 11, 1994.

36. Thoughtful interpretations of the breasted images of republican France can be found in Paul Trouillas, *Le Complexe de Marianne*; Maurice Agulhon, *Marianne into Battle: Republican Imagery and Symbolism in France, 1789–1880*, trans. Janet Lloyd; and Gutwirth.

37. Sally G. McMillen, *Motherhood in the Old South: Pregnancy, Childbirth, and Infant Rearing*, p. 118.

38. *Victorian Women: A Documentary Account of Women's Lives in Nineteenth-Century England, France, and the United States*, ed. E. Hellerstein, L. Hume, K. Offen, E. Freedman, B. Gelpi, and M. Yalom, pp. 231–32.

39. Nell Painter, *Sojourner Truth: A Life, A Symbol*. I am grateful to Princeton Professor Painter for bringing the Sojourner Truth incident to my attention and for sharing her prepublication manuscript with me.

40. The Tennyson quotations were brought to my attention by Stanford English Professor Emeritus Wilfred Stone.

41. Peter Gay, *The Education of the Senses: The Bourgeois Experience, Victoria to Freud*, pp. 337–38.

42. Flora Thompson, *Lark Rise to Candleford* (London, New York, and Toronto: Oxford University Press, 1954), pp. 139–40.

43. Jane T. Costlow, "The Pastoral Source: Representations of the Maternal Breast in Nineteenth-Century Russia," in *Sexuality and the Body in Russian Culture*, ed. Jane T. Costlow, Stephanie Sandler, and Judith Vowles, p. 225.

44. Patrick P. Dunn, " 'That Enemy Is the Baby': Childhood in Imperial Russia," in *The History of Childhood*, ed. Lloyd deMause, p. 387.

45. Costlow, p. 228.

46. The following discussion is based largely on Paul Weindling, *Health, Race and German Politics Between National Unification and Nazism, 1870–1945*, pp. 192–205.

47. For French images, see Jean Garrigues, *Images de la Révolution: L'Imagerie Républicaine de 1789 à Nos Jours*, pp. 114–15, 118.

48. Dr. Magnus Hirschfeld, *Sittengeschichte des Weltkrieges*, vol. 1, plate opposite p. 64.

49. See Peter Paret, Beth Irwin Lewis, and Paul Paret, *Persuasive Images*; Libby Chenault, *Battlelines: World War I Posters from the Bowman Gray Collection*; and Walton Rawls, *Wake Up, America! World War I and the American Poster*.

50. Bernard Denscher, *Gold Gab Ich Für Eisen: Österreichische Kriegsplakate 1914–1918* (Vienna: Jugend & Volk, 1987), pp. 100, 106.

51. Hirschfeld, pp. 250–55.

52. *Varga: The Esquire Years, A Catalogue Raisonné*, ed. Robert Walker, p. 150.

53. Ralph Stein, *The Pin-Up from 1852 to Now*, p. 139.

54. Virginia Hewitt, *Beauty and the Banknote: Images of Women on Paper Money*, p. 18.

55. *New York Times*, April 5, 1994.

56. Barbara Sichtermann, *Femininity: The Politics of the Personal*, trans. John Whitlam, p. 61.

57. Françoise Thébaud, *Quand Nos Grand-Mères Donnaient la Vie: La Maternité en France dans l'Entre-Deux-Guerres*, p. 86.

58. I am grateful to Professor Robyn Owens of the University of Western Australia for information about the Tasmanian "Consent to Supplement Newborn Infants" and the politics of breast-feeding in Australia.

59. Datha C. Brack, "Social Forces, Feminism, and Breastfeeding," pp. 556–61.

60. Editorial, Boston *Globe*, May 31, 1994.

61. This section draws heavily on Linda M. Blum, "Mothers, Babies, and Breastfeeding in Late Capitalist America: The Shifting Contexts of Feminist Theory," pp. 1–21.

62. *New York Times*, April 7, 1988.

63. Zillah R. Eisenstein, *The Female Body and the Law*, p. 213.

64. Gabrielle Palmer, *The Politics of Breastfeeding*, p. 265.

65. San Francisco *Chronicle*, September 16, 1993.

66. *International Herald Tribune*, August 9, 1994.

67. Vanessa Maher, "Breast-Feeding in Cross-Cultural Perspective," in *The Anthropology of Breast-Feeding: Natural Law or Social Construct*, ed. Vanessa Maher, pp. 3–4.

CHAPTER FIVE

1. Sigmund Freud, *Complete Works of Sigmund Freud*, vol. VII, p. 181; vol. XVI, p. 314.

2. Ibid., vol. VII, p. 222.

3. Ibid., vol. XXIII, p. 188.

4. Ibid., vol. V, pp. 372–73.

5. Ibid., vol. IV, pp. 286–87.

6. Ibid., vol. VII, p. 51.

7. Ibid., p. 52.

8. Ibid., vol. IV, p. 204.

9. Ibid., vol. XXIII, p. 188.

10. Ibid., p. 189.

11. Ibid., vol. VII, p. 182.

12. Ibid., vol. XXIII, p. 193.

13. Ibid.

14. Ibid., p. 299.

15. This pastiche is modeled on Freud's essays "Some Psychic Consequences of the Anatomical Distinction Between the Sexes" (1925), "Female Sexuality" (1931), and "Femininity" (1933).

16. Freud, vol. XX, p. 122.

17. O. Isakower, "A Contribution to the Patho-Psychology of Phenomena Associated with Falling Asleep," pp. 331–45.

18. See, for example, O. Townsend Dann, "The Isakower Phenomenon Revisited: A Case Study," *International Journal of Psycho-Analysis*, vol. 73, no. 3 (Fall 1992): 481–91; and Charles A. Peterson, "Aloneness and the Isakower Phenomenon," *Journal of the American Academy of Psychoanalysis*, vol. 20, no. 1 (Spring 1992): 99–113.

19. This and the following citations are from Melanie Klein, "Some Theoretical Conclusions Regarding the Emotional Life of the Infant," in *Developments in Psychoanalysis*, ed. Melanie Klein et al., pp. 199–207.

20. Cited by permission of Minerva Neiditz.

21. John E. Beebe, M.D., personal communication. See also his introduction to Carl Jung, *Aspects of the Masculine*.

22. James Astor, "The Breast as Part of the Whole: Theoretical Considerations Concerning Whole and Part Objects," p. 118. The next citation is from p. 117.

23. Joellen Werne, ed., *Treating Eating Disorders*, p. xv.

24. Kim Chernin, *The Obsession: Reflections on the Tyranny of Slenderness*. See also Susan Bordo, *Unbearable Weight: Feminism, Western Culture, and the Body*, especially pp. 139–64.

25. Philip Roth, *The Breast*, pp. 66–67.

26. Freud, vol. XXII, p. 122.

27. Ibid., vol. I, pp. 117–28.

CHAPTER SIX

1. Interview with Dr. Dominique Gros, "Le Sein: Image du Paradis," *Le Nouvel Observateur*, April 20–26, 1995.

2. Anne Hollander, *Seeing Through Clothes*.

3. Susan Bordo, "The Body and Reproduction of Femininity," in *Gender/Body/Knowledge: Feminist Reconstructions of Being and Knowing*, ed. Alison Jaggar and Susan Bordo, p. 14. See also Duncan Kennedy, *Sexy Dressing*, p. 168.

4. This section has drawn upon Alison Carter, *Underwear: The Fashion History*; and Elizabeth Ewing, *Fashion in Underwear*.

5. David Kunzle, *Fashion and Fetishism: A Social History of the Corset, Tight-Lacing and Other Forms of Body-Sculpture in the West*, p. 111.

6. Montaigne, *The Complete Essays*, trans. Donald Frame (Stanford, Calif.: Stanford University Press, 1965), vol. I, pt. 14, p. 41.

7. For the French use of the busk and other underwear oddities, see Cécile Saint-Laurent, *Histoire Imprévue des Dessous Féminins*; and Béatrice Fontanel, *Corsets et Soutiens-Gorge: L'Épopée du Sein de l'Antiquité à Nos Jours*.

8. Citations from Peter Fryer, *Mrs. Grundy: Studies in English Prudery*, pp. 173–74.

9. Fontanel, pp. 31–32.

10. Both references are from Kunzle, pp. 81–82.

11. Two of the best-known French examples are *L'Essai du Corset* by A. F. Dennel *d'après* P. A. Wille, 1780, and *Tailleur Essayant un Corps* by Dupin *d'après* Le Clerc, 1778. For an English version of male opportunism vis-à-vis the breast, see Hogarth's *The Sleeping Congregation*, which shows a church clerk staring into the low-cut bodice of a woman who had fallen asleep during a boring sermon.

12. Jacques Bonnaud, *Dégradation de l'Espèce Humaine par l'Usage du Corps à Baleine: Ouvrage dans Lequel On Démontre Que C'est Aller Contre les Lois de la Nature, Augmenter la Dépopulation et Abâtardir pour Ainsi Dire l'Homme Que de Le Mettre à la Torture dès les Premiers Moments de Son Existence, sous Prétexte de Le Former*. For German examples, see Almut Junker and Eva Stille, *Geschichte des Unterwäsche 1700–1960*, pp. 39–40.

13. Philippe Perrot, *Le Travail des Apparences, ou les Transformations du Corps Féminin XVIIIe–XIXe Siècle*, pp. 235–36.

14. Cited in C. Willett and Phillis Cunnington, *The History of Underclothes*, p. 69. See also Norah Waugh, *Corsets and Crinolines*, p. 71.

15. See Claudia Brush Kidwell and Valerie Steele, *Men and Women: Dressing the Part*.

16. Rosemary Hawthorne, *Bras: A Private View*, p. 20.

17. Junker and Stille, pp. 152–53.

18. Cited in Cunnington, p. 126.

19. Cited in Gustave Joseph Witkowski, *Anecdotes Historiques et Religieuses sur les Seins et l'Allaitement Comprenant l'Histoire du Décolletage et du Corset*, p. 389.

20. See, for example, J. H. Kellogg, M.D., *The Influence of Dress in Producing the Physical Decadence of American Women*.

21. Abba Goold Woolson, *Women in America from Colonial Times to the 20th Century*. Citations are from pp. 11, 20, 54, 49, 75, 114–15, 134–35.

22. Lois W. Banner, *American Beauty*, p. 128.

23. Thorstein Veblen, *The Theory of the Leisure Class*, p. 172.

24. Dr. Magnus Hirschfeld, *Sittengeschichte des Weltkrieges*, vol. 1, p. 76.

25. Maidenform, Inc., pamphlet, 1992.

26. Clifford F. Dowkontt, M.D., *The Hygiene of the Breasts*, pp. 37–8.

27. Nora Ephron, "A Few Words About Breasts," *Esquire*, May 1972.

28. *Politique Hebdo*, August 28–September 3, 1975, pp. 19–20.

29. Sally Wadyka, "Bosom Buddies," *Vogue*, August 1994.

30. *Wall Street Journal*, December 2, 1988.

31. Jeremy Weir Alderson, "Breast Frenzy," *Self*, December 1988.

32. San Francisco *Chronicle*, August 11, 1994.

33. The Seigneur de Brantôme, *Lives of Fair and Gallant Ladies*, pp. 131, 143. Today, seeing one's partner undress ranks second only to the pleasure of sexual intercourse

NOTES

itself, with 93 percent of men and 81 percent of women considering the sight of the lover undressing either "very appealing" or "somewhat appealing" (Robert Michael et al., *Sex in America*, pp. 146–47).

4. Linda Nochlin, *Women, Art, and Power and Other Essays*, p. 138.

35. Eunice Lipton, *Alias Olympia: A Woman's Search for Manet's Notorious Model & Her Own Desire*, p. 151.

36. Cited in Michael Jubb, *Cocoa and Corsets*, n.p., opposite introduction.

37. Paul Hammond, *French Undressing: Naughty Postcards from 1900 to 1920*, p. 11.

38. Delia M. Rios, "Media and the Message: Sex," San Francisco *Examiner*, October 2, 1994.

39. This and Gail's following citations are from Daphna Ayalah and Isaac J. Weinstock, *Breasts: Women Speak About Their Breasts and Their Lives*, pp. 99–103.

40. Ellen Berscheid, Elaine Walster, and George Bohrnsted, "Body Image," *Psychology Today*, November 1973.

41. A. George Gitter, Jack Lomranz, Leonard Saxe, and Yoram Bar-Tal, "Perceptions of Female Physique Characteristics by American and Israeli Students," pp. 7–13; Lora Jacobi and Thomas Cash, "In Pursuit of the Perfect Appearance: Discrepancies Among Self-Ideal Percepts of Multiple Physical Attributes," pp. 379–96.

42. Cited in Robert Atwan, Donald McQuade, and John Wright, *Edsels, Luckies, & Frigidaires: Advertising the American Way*, p. 350.

43. Nicholas Drake, *The Fifties in Vogue*, p. 10.

44. John Steinbeck, *The Wayward Bus* (New York: The Viking Press, 1947), p. 5.

45. San Francisco *Examiner*, June 19, 1994.

46. Ayalah and Weinstock, pp. 72–77.

47. For one of the better books written about Madonna, see *The Madonna Connection: Representational Politics, Subcultural Identities, and Cultural Theory*, ed. Cathy Schwichtenberg.

48. Lori Parch, "The Quest for the Perfect Bra," *Self*, March 1995.

49. John d'Emilio and Estelle B. Freedman, *Intimate Matters: A History of Sexuality in America*, pp. xi, xii.

50. Nancy F. Cott, "The Modern Woman of the 1920's, American Style," in *A History of Women: Toward a Cultural Identity in the Twentieth Century*, ed. Françoise Thébaud, vol. V, *A History of Women in the West*, ed. Georges Duby and Michelle Perrot, p. 89.

51. *Die unveröffentlichten 271 SPIEGEL-Titel aus 1993* (Hamburg: SPIEGEL-Verlag Rudolf Augstein, 1994), p. 72.

52. *Rolling Stone*, October 20, 1994, pp. 75–76.

53. Diana Russell, *Against Pornography: The Evidence of Harm*, p. 3.

54. Susan Griffin, *Pornography and Silence: Culture's Revenge Against Nature*, p. 36.

55. This and similar references are from Russell, pp. 63, 64, 66, 82, 83. Ms. Russell had the courage to republish, without the consent of the original publishers, more than a hundred pornographic illustrations, accompanied by her probing comments.

56. Nadine Strossen, *Free Speech, Sex, and the Fight for Women's Rights*.

CHAPTER SEVEN

1. Valerie A. Fildes, *Breasts, Bottles, and Babies*, p. 5.

2. Gay Robins, *Women in Ancient Egypt*, pp. 90–91. Illustration of a vessel in the form of a lactating woman, plate 27, p. 81.

3. Frederick B. Wagner, "History of Breast Disease and Its Treatment," in *The Breast*, ed. Kirby I. Bland and Edward M. Copeland, vol. III, p. 1.

4. James V. Ricci, *The Genealogy of Gynaecology*, p. 20.

5. Lesley Dean-Jones, "The Cultural Construct of the Female Body in Classical Greek Science," in *Women's History and Ancient History*, ed. Sarah B. Pomeroy, p. 115.

6. Cited in Daniel de Moulin, *A Short History of Breast Cancer*, p. 2. I am heavily indebted to de Moulin for some of the material on breast cancer presented in this chapter.

7. Soranus, *Gynecology*, trans. Owsei Temkin, p. 90.

8. R. C. Hahn and D. B. Petitti, "Minnesota Multiphasic Personality Inventory–Rated Depression and the Incidence of Breast Cancer," pp. 845–48; A. B. Zonderman, P. T. Costa, and R. R. McCrae, "Depression as a Risk for Cancer Morbidity and Mortality in a Nationally Representative Sample," pp. 1191–95.

9. Cited by Moulin, pp. 5–6.

10. *Medieval Woman's Guide to Health: The First English Gynecological Handbook*, trans. Beryl Rowland, pp. 161–62.

11. Régine Pernoud, *La Femme au Temps des Cathédrales*, p. 119.

12. Salicet, *Chirurgie de Guillaume de Salicet*, ed. Paul Pifteau, pp. 108–9.

13. These two images are reproduced in Albert S. Lyons and R. Joseph Petrucelli, *Medicine: An Illustrated History*, figs. 490 and 498, pp. 326–27. Original source: Leiden University Library (Bibliothek des Rijksuniversitate), ms. Vossius lat. 3, fol. 90v.

14. Cited in Moulin, p. 15.

15. Thomas Laqueur, *Making Sex: Body and Gender from the Greeks to Freud*, pp. 104–5.

16. The drawing is reproduced in Kenneth Clark and Carlo Pedretti, *Leonardo da Vinci Drawings at Windsor Castle* [1935] (London: Phaidon, 1969), 19097 verso.

17. Andreas Vasalius, *The Epitome of Andreas Vesalius*, trans. L. R. Lind, pp. 86–87. *The Epitome* is a brief summary of Vesalius's *De Humani Corporis Fabrica Libri Septem* (Basel, 1543).

18. This and the following citations are from Ambroise Paré, *Oeuvres Complètes*, ed. J.-F. Malgaigne, vol. 2, pp. 687, 689.

19. Cited in Dorothy McLaren, "Marital Fertility and Lactation," in *Women in English Society 1500–1800*, ed. Mary Prior, p. 27.

20. Louise Bourgeois, Dite Boursier, Sage-Femme de la Reine, *Observations Diverses sur la Stérilité, Perte de Fruits, Fécondité, Accouchements et Maladies des Femmes et Enfants Nouveau-Nés, Suivi de Instructions à Ma Fille*, p. 90.

21. This and the following citation are in Leo M. Zimmerman and Ilza Veith, *Great Ideas in the History of Surgery*, pp. 245–46.

22. Ibid., pp. 252–53.

23. Moulin, p. 24.

24. On the breast cancer of Anne of Austria, see ibid., pp. 25–26; Ruth Kleinman, *Anne of Austria*, pp. 282–86; and Gui Patin, *Lettres de Gui Patin à Charles, Spon, Médecin à Lyon*, vol. 3, pp. 493–94.

25. Helvétius, "Lettre de Monsieur Helvétius D.E.M. à Monsieur Régis, sur la Nature et la Guérison du Cancer," appended to *Traité des Pertes de Sang*, pp. 139–48.

26. Barbara Duden, *The Woman Beneath the Skin: A Doctor's Patients in Eighteenth-Century Germany*, trans. Thomas Dunlap, p. 98.

27. Ibid., pp. 83–84.

28. Ruth Perry, *The Celebrated Mary Astell*, pp. 318–22.

29. George Ballard, *Memoirs of Several Ladies of Great Britain* (Oxford, 1752), p. 459.

30. Moulin, p. 43.

31. Lorenz Heister, *A General System of Surgery*, vol II, p. 14.

32. Fanny Burney, *Selected Letters and Journals*, ed. Joyce Hemlow. Citations are from pp. 129–39.

33. Edith Gelles, *Portia: The World of Abigail Adams*. The following citations are from pp. 161, 163, and 168.

34. Cited in Owen H. Wangensteen and Sarah D. Wangensteen, *The Rise of Surgery*, pp 155–56.

35. Moulin, pp. 58–61.

36. Geo. H. Napheys, A.M., M.D., *The Physical Life of Woman: Advice to the Maiden, Wife, and Mother*, 3rd Canadian ed. Quotations are taken from pp. 186 and 196.

37. I am grateful for this and other observations to the French oncologist Dr. Maurice Tubiana, *La Lumière dans l'Ombre: Le Cancer Hier et Demain*, pp. 33–34.

38. Dr. Cathy Read, *Preventing Breast Cancer: The Politics of an Epidemic*, p. 1.

39. *New York Times*, June 29, 1994.

40. Rose Kushner, *Breast Cancer: A Personal History and an Investigative Report*.

41. *Journal of the National Cancer Institute*, July 17, 1994, cited in *New York Times* of same date.

42. *New England Journal of Medicine*, December 1995, cited in *New York Times*, December 3, 1995.

43. Susan Love with Karen Lindsey, *Dr. Susan Love's Breast Book*, 2nd ed., pp. 325–26.

44. A. B. Miller and R. D. Bulbrook, "UICC Multidisciplinary Project on Breast Cancer: The Epidemiology, Aetiology and Prevention of Breast Cancer," pp. 173–77.

45. Read, p. 2.

46. "Your Breasts: The Latest Health, Beauty & Sexual Facts," *Glamour*, April 1994, p. 273.

47. The Long Island Breast Cancer Study Project, National Cancer Institute, project outline, 1993.

48. N. Krieger, M. S. Wolff, R. A. Hiatt, M. Rivera, J. Vogelman, and N. Orentreich, "Breast Cancer and Serum Organochlorines: A Prospective Study Among White, Black, and Asian Women," *Journal of the National Cancer Institute*, April 20, 1994 (86) 8:589–99.

49. Yumay Chen et al., "Aberrant Subcellular Localization of BRCA 1 in Breast Cancer," *Science*, November 3, 1995, pp. 789–91.

50. Irvin D. Yalom, M.D., and Carlos Greaves, M.D., "Group Therapy with the Terminally Ill," pp. 396–400.

51. David Spiegel, *Living Beyond Limits: New Hope and Help for Facing Threatening Illness*, p. xiii.

52. *Le Monde*, September 2, 1988.

53. Solveig Beale et al., "Augmentation Mammoplasty: The Surgical and Psychological Effects of the Operation and Prediction of the Result," pp. 279–97.

54. Kathy Davis, *Reshaping the Female Body*.

55. S. E. Gabriel et al., "Risk of Connective-Tissue Diseases and Other Disorders After Breast Implantation," *New England Journal of Medicine*, June 16, 1994, 330 (24): 1697–702.

56. Gail S. Lebovic, Donald R. Laub, Jr., Kenneth Hadler, Diana Guthaner, Frederick M. Durbas, and Donald Laub, manuscript in preparation (Stanford, Calif., 1996).

57. *New York Times*, June 29, 1994.

58. *Larger Firmer Breasts Through Self-Hypnosis* (San Juan, P.R.: Piedras Press, 1991).

59. San Francisco *Chronicle*, June 1, 1994.

CHAPTER EIGHT

1. Boston Women's Health Collective, *Our Bodies, Ourselves* [1969] (New York: Simon & Schuster, 1976).

2. *Time*, September 13, 1968.

3. Deborah L. Rhode, "Media Images, Feminist Issues," p. 693.

4. Sandy Polishuk, "Breasts," p. 78.

5. Germaine Greer, *The Female Eunuch*, p. 24.

6. For an early analysis of the antibra movement, see Denton E. Morrison and Carlin Paige Holden, "The Burning Bra: The American Breast Fetish and Women's Liberation," in *Deviance and Change*, ed. Peter K. Manning.

7. D. Ayalah and I. J. Weinstock, *Breasts: Women Speak About Their Breasts and Their Lives*, p. 125.

8. Ibid.

9. Santa Cruz *Sentinel*, October 7, 1984.

10. Jean-Claude Kaufmann, *Corps de Femmes, Regards d'Hommes: Sociologie des Seins Nus*.

11. René König, *À la Mode: The Social Psychology of Fashion*, trans. F. Bradley, p. 193.

12. Photo and quotation from *Le Matin*, May 29, 1987.

13. *Libération*, October 26, 1987.

14. *New York Times Magazine*, August 15, 1993.

15. *Time*, November 1, 1993.

16. *Chronicle of Higher Education*, November 18, 1992.

17. These attributes, rather than size, are what men desire in women's breasts, according to Harvard neuropsychologist Nancy Etcoff, as cited by Elizabeth Weil in "What Men Love," *Mademoiselle*, January 1995.

18. Alicia Suskin Ostriker, "Years of Girlhood (For My Students)," in "The Mastectomy Poems," from *The Crack in Everything*, © 1996. Reprinted by permission of the University of Pittsburgh Press.

19. Sharon Olds, "New Mother," in Olds, *The Dead and the Living* (New York: Alfred A. Knopf, 1984). Copyright © 1983 by Sharon Olds. Reprinted by permission of Alfred A. Knopf, Inc. Reprinted in *Touching Fire: Erotic Writings by Women*, ed. Louise Thorton, Jan Sturtevant, and Amber Sumrall, p. 62.

20. Alicia Suskin Ostriker, *The Mother/Child Papers*, pp. 18, 33. Reprinted by permission of the author.

21. *Media Watch*, vol. 6, no. 1 (Spring–Summer 1992), p. 7.

22. Rosanne Wasserman, "Moon-Milk Sestina," in *The Breast: An Anthology*, ed. Susan Thames and Marin Gazzaniga, p. 84.

23. Deborah Abbott, "This Body I Love," in *Touching Fire*, ed. Thorton et al., p. 98. Copyright © 1985, *With the Power of Each Breath: A Disabled Women's Anthology*, ed. Susan Browne, Debra Connors, and Nanci Stern. Pittsburgh: Cleis Press.

24. Linda Pastan, "Routine Mammogram," in Pastan, *A Fraction of Darkness*, p. 46. Copyright © 1985 by Linda Pastan. Reprinted by permission of W. W. Norton & Company, Inc.

25. Joan Halperin, "Diagnosis," in *Her Soul Beneath the Bone: Women's Poetry on Breast Cancer*, ed. Leatrice Lifshitz, p. 7. Copyright © 1988 by the University of Illinois Press.

26. Patricia Goedicke, "Now Only One of Us Remains," in *Her Soul*, ed. Lifshitz, p. 33.

27. Alice Davis, "Mastectomy," in *Her Soul*, ed. Lifshitz, p. 41.

28. Sally Allen McNall, "Poem for the Woman Who Filled a Prosthesis with Birdseed, and Others," in *Her Soul*, ed. Lifshitz, p. 67.

29. Audre Lorde, *The Cancer Journals*, p. 44.

30. Naomi Wolf, *The Beauty Myth: How Images of Beauty Are Used Against Women*.

31. Adrienne Rich, "A Woman Dead in Her Forties." Copyright © 1984 by Adrienne Rich, from *The Fact of a Doorframe: Poems Selected and New, 1950–1984*. Reprinted by permission of the author and W. W. Norton & Company, Inc.

32. Helena Michie, *The Flesh Made Word: Female Figures and Women's Bodies*, p. 127.

33. Therese Diamond Rosinsky, *Suzanne Valadon* (New York: Universe Publishing, 1994), p. 81.

34. Hayden Herrera, *Frida Kahlo: The Paintings*, p. 12.

35. Louise Bourgeois, personal interview, March 8, 1996.

36. *Louise Bourgeois: Recent Work/Opere Recenti* (Brooklyn Museum, printed by the United States Information Agency for the 45th Venice Biennale, 1993), n.p. For more complete studies of Bourgeois's work, see Christiane Meyer-Thoss, *Louise Bourgeois* and Marie-Laure Bernadac, *Louise Bourgeois*.

37. William Ewing, *The Body: Photographs of the Human Form*, p. 68.

38. The citations are from Terry Dennett and Jo Spence, "Remodeling Photo History: A Collaboration Between Two Photographers," *Screen*, vol. 23, no. 1 (1982), republished in Jo Spence, *Putting Myself in the Picture: A Political, Personal and Photographic Autobiography*, pp. 118–21.

39. I wish to thank Terry Dennett for generous commentary on his work with Jo Spence. Spence died of breast cancer in 1992.

40. The most in-depth interpretation of Sherman's work is found in Rosalind Krauss, *Cindy Sherman, 1979–1993*.

41. Annie Sprinkle with Katharine Gates, *Annie Sprinkle's Post-Modern Pin-Ups Booklet* (Richmond, Va.: Gates of Heck, 1995). Quotations are from pp. 7, 6, and 5.

42. Copies of the poster with the image of Deena Metzger as photographed by Hella Hammid, as well as information about Deena Metzger's books, tapes, and workshops, may be obtained from TREE, P.O. Box 186, Topanga, California 90290.

43. Stanford *Daily*, February 1, 1995.

44. *Economist*, December 25, 1993–January 7, 1994.

Select Bibliography

Abbott, Mary. *Family Ties: English Families, 1540–1920*. London and New York: Routledge, 1993.

Agulhon, Maurice. *Marianne into Battle: Republican Imagery and Symbolism in France, 1789–1880*. Janet Lloyd, trans. Cambridge: Cambridge University Press, 1981.

Alexandre-Bidon, Danièle. "La Lettre Volée: Apprendre à Lire à l'Enfant au Moyen-Âge." *Annales ESC*, no. 4, July–August 1989.

Ariès, Philippe, and Duby, Georges, eds. *A History of Private Life: Passions of the Renaissance*. Vol. III. Roger Chartier, ed. Arthur Goldhammer, trans. Cambridge, Mass.: Harvard University Press, 1989.

Armstrong, Karen. *A History of God: The 4000-Year Quest of Judaism, Christianity and Islam*. New York: Ballantine Books, 1993.

Ashelford, Jane. *Dress in the Age of Elizabeth*. London: B. T. Batsford, 1988.

Astor, James. "The Breast as Part of the Whole: Theoretical Considerations Concerning Whole and Part Objects." *Journal of Analytic Psychology*, vol. 34 (1989).

Atkinson, Clarissa. *The Oldest Vocation: Christian Motherhood in the Middle Ages*. Ithaca, N.Y.: Cornell University Press, 1991.

Atwan, Robert; McQuade, Donald; and Wright, John. *Edsels, Luckies, & Frigidaires: Advertising the American Way*. New York: Dell, 1979.

Ayalah, Daphna, and Weinstock, Isaac J. *Breasts: Women Speak About Their Breasts and Their Lives*. New York: Summit Books, 1979.

Badinter, Elisabeth. *Mother Love: Myth and Reality*. New York: Macmillan, 1981.

Banner, Lois W. *American Beauty*. New York: Alfred A. Knopf, 1983.

————. *In Full Flower: Aging Women, Power, and Sexuality*. New York: Vintage Books, 1993.

Barber, Elizabeth Wayland. *Women's Work: The First 20,000 Years*. New York and London: W. W. Norton, 1994.

Bardon, Françoise. *Diane de Poitiers et le Mythe de Diane*. Paris: Presses Universitaires de France, 1963.

Baring, Anne, and Cashford, Jules. *The Myth of the Goddess: Evolution of an Image*. London: Viking Arkana, 1991.

Barstow, Anne Llewellyn. *Witchcraze: A New History of the European Witch Hunts.* San Francisco: Pandora/HarperCollins, 1994.

Beale, Solveig, et al. "Augmentation Mammoplasty: The Surgical and Psychological Effects of the Operation and Prediction of the Result." *Annals of Plastic Surgery,* vol. 13, no. 4 (October 1984).

Bell, Susan Groag, and Offen, Karen M. *Women, the Family, and Freedom: The Debate in Documents.* Stanford, Calif.: Stanford University Press, 1983. Vols. I and II.

Berkvam, Doris Desclais. *Enfance et Maternité dans la Littérature Française des XIIe et XIIIe Siècles.* Paris: Honoré Champion, 1981.

Bernadac, Marie-Laure. *Louise Bourgeois.* Paris: Flammarion, 1995.

Bernen, Satia and Robert. *Myth and Religion in European Painting, 1270–1700.* London: Constable, 1973.

Biale, David. *Eros and the Jews: From Biblical Israel to Contemporary America.* New York: Basic Books, 1992.

Bland, Kirby I., and Copeland, Edward M. III. *The Breast: Comprehensive Management of Benign and Malignant Diseases.* Philadelphia: W. B. Saunders, 1991.

Bloch, Ariel, and Bloch, Chana. *The Song of Songs, A New Translation.* New York: Random House, 1995.

Blum, Linda M. "Mothers, Babies, and Breastfeeding in Late Capitalist America: The Shifting Contexts of Feminist Theory." *Feminist Studies,* vol. 19, no. 2 (Summer 1993).

Bologne, Jean Claude. *Histoire de la Pudeur.* Paris: Olivier Orban, 1986.

Bonnaud, Jacques. *Dégradation de l'Espèce Humaine par l'Usage du Corps à Baleine: Ouvrage dans Lequel On Démontre Que C'est Aller Contre les Lois de la Nature, Augmenter la Dépopulation et Abâtardir pour Ainsi Dire l'Homme Que de Le Mettre à la Torture dès les Premiers Moments de Son Existence, sous Prétexte de Le Former.* Paris: Chez Hérissant, le fils, 1770.

Bordo, Susan. *Unbearable Weight: Feminism, Western Culture, and the Body.* Berkeley, Los Angeles, and London: University of California Press, 1993.

Boston Women's Health Collective. *Our Bodies, Ourselves.* [1969.] New York: Simon & Schuster, 1976.

Bourgeois, Louise, Dite Boursier, Sage-Femme de la Reine. *Observations Diverses sur la Stérilité, Perte de Fruits, Fécondité, Accouchements et Maladies des Femmes et Enfants Nouveau-Nés, Suivi de Instructions à Ma Fille.* [1609.] Paris: Côté-Femmes Éditions, 1992.

Brack, Datha C. "Social Forces, Feminism, and Breastfeeding." *Nursing Outlook,* vol. 23 (September 1975).

Brantôme, The Seigneur de. *Lives of Fair and Gallant Ladies.* London: Fortune Press, 1934.

Breward, Christopher. *The Culture of Fashion.* Manchester and New York: Manchester University Press, 1995.

Bridenthal, Renate, and Koonz, Claudia, eds. *Becoming Visible: Women in European History.* Boston: Houghton Mifflin, 1977.

Brown, Judith. *Immodest Acts: The Life of a Lesbian Nun in Renaissance Italy.* New York: Oxford University Press, 1986.

Burney, Fanny. *Selected Letters and Journals.* Joyce Hemlow, ed. Oxford: Oxford University Press, 1986.

Bynum, Carolyn. *Holy Feast and Holy Fast: The Religious Significance of Food to Medieval Women.* Berkeley: University of California Press, 1987.

Cadogan, William. *An Essay upon Nursing, and the Management of Children, From Their Birth to Three Years of Age.* London: J. Roberts, 1748.

Calvin, John. *Tracts and Treatises on the Reformation of the Church.* Henry Beveridge, ed. Grand Rapids, Mich.: Wm. B. Eerdmans, 1958. Vol. 1.

Carter, Alison. *Underwear: The Fashion History.* London: B. T. Batsford, 1992.

Castleden, Rodney. *Minoan Life in Bronze Age Crete.* London and New York: Routledge, 1990.

Catherine of Siena. *The Dialogue.* Suzanne Noffke, trans. New York and Ramsey, Toronto: Paulist Press, 1980.

Champion, Pierre. *La Dame de Beauté, Agnès Sorel.* Paris: Librairie Ancienne Honoré Champion, 1931.

Chenault, Libby. *Battlelines: World War I Posters from the Bowman Gray Collection.* Chapel Hill: University of North Carolina Press, 1988.

Chernin, Kim. *The Obsession: Reflections on the Tyranny of Slenderness.* New York: Harper and Row, 1981.

Clark, Kenneth. *The Nude: A Study in Ideal Form.* Princeton, N.J.: Princeton University Press, 1972.

Collum, V. C. C. *The Tressé Iron-Age Megalithic Monument: Its Quadruple Sculptured Breasts and Their Relation to the Mother-Goddess Cosmic Cult.* London: Oxford University Press, 1935.

Contini, Mila. *Fashion from Ancient Egypt to the Present Day.* London: Paul Hamlyn, 1965.

Costlow, Jane T.; Sandler, Stephanie; and Vowles, Judith, eds. *Sexuality and the Body in Russian Culture.* Stanford, Calif.: Stanford University Press, 1993.

Craik, Jennifer. *The Face of Fashion: Cultural Studies in Fashion.* London and New York: Routledge, 1994.

Cunnington, C. Willett and Phillis. *The History of Underclothes.* London and Boston: Faber and Faber, 1981 [1951].

Davis, Kathy. *Reshaping the Female Body: The Dilemma of Cosmetic Surgery.* New York and London: Routledge, 1995.

Delporte, Henri. *L'Image de la Femme dans l'Art Préhistorique.* Paris: Picard, 1993.

deMause, Lloyd, ed. *The History of Childhood.* New York: Psychohistory Press, 1974.

d'Emilio, John, and Freedman, Estelle B. *Intimate Matters: A History of Sexuality in America.* New York: Harper and Row, 1988.

Dijkstra, Bram. *Idols of Perversity: Fantasies of Feminine Evil in Fin-de-Siècle Culture.* Oxford and New York: Oxford University Press, 1986.

Dowkontt, Clifford F., M.D. *The Hygiene of the Breasts.* New York: Emerson Books, 1948.

Drake, Nicholas. *The Fifties in Vogue*. New York: Henry Holt, 1987.

Duden, Barbara. *The Woman Beneath the Skin: A Doctor's Patients in Eighteenth-Century Germany*. Thomas Dunlap, trans. Cambridge, Mass., and London: Harvard University Press, 1991.

Durantini, Mary Frances. *The Child in Seventeenth-Century Dutch Painting*. [1979.] Ann Arbor, Mich.: UMI Research Press, 1983.

Eisenberg, Josy. *La Femme au Temps de la Bible*. Paris: Stock/L. Pernoud, 1993.

Eisenstein, Zillah R. *The Female Body and the Law*. Berkeley, Los Angeles, and London: University of California Press, 1988.

Erlanger, Philippe. *Diane de Poitiers: Déesse de la Renaissance*. Paris: Librairie Académique Perrin, 1976.

———. *Gabrielle d'Estrées: Femme Fatale*. Paris: Jean Dullis Éditeur, 1975.

Ewing, Elizabeth. *Fashion in Underwear*. London: B. T. Batsford, 1971.

Ewing, William. *The Body: Photographs of the Human Form*. San Francisco: Chronicle Books, 1994.

Falk, Marcia. *The Song of Songs, A New Translation*. San Francisco: HarperSanFrancisco, 1993.

Fay-Sallois, Fanny. *Les Nourrices à Paris au XIXe Siècle*. Paris: Payot, 1980.

Ferry, Alain. *La Mer des Mamelles: Roman d'Amour ès Lettres*. Paris: Seuil, 1995.

Fierens, E. "L'iconographie artistique du sein des origines à la modernité." *La Sein Normal et Pathologique à travers les Âges*. Brussels: Réunion Société Belge Sénologie, June, 1988.

Fildes, Valerie A. *Breasts, Bottles, and Babies*. Edinburgh: Edinburgh University Press, 1986.

———. *Wet Nursing*. Oxford: Basil Blackwell, 1988.

Firenzuola, Agnolo. *Of the Beauty of Women*. Clara Bell, trans. London: James R. Osgood, 1892.

Fitton, J. Lesley. *Cycladic Art*. London: British Museum Publications, 1989.

Flinders, Carol Lee. *Enduring Grace: Living Portraits of Seven Women Mystics*. San Francisco: HarperSanFrancisco, 1993.

Fontanel, Béatrice. *Corsets et Soutiens-Gorge: L'Épopée du Sein de l'Antiquité à Nos Jours*. Paris: Éditions de La Martinière, 1992.

Franits, Wayne E. *Paragons of Virtue: Women and Domesticity in Seventeenth-Century Dutch Art*. Cambridge: Cambridge University Press, 1993.

Freud, Sigmund. *Complete Works of Sigmund Freud*. London: Hogarth Press, 1955.

Fryer, Peter. *Mrs. Grundy: Studies in English Prudery*. New York: London House and Maxwell, 1964.

Frymer-Kensky, Tikva. *In the Wake of the Goddesses: Women, Culture, and the Biblical Transformation of Pagan Myth*. New York: Free Press, 1992.

Fuchs, R. H. *Dutch Painting* [1978]. New York: Thames and Hudson, 1989.

Garrigues, Jean. *Images de la Révolution: L'Imagerie Républicaine de 1789 à Nos Jours*. Paris: Éditions du May, 1988.

Gay, Peter. *The Education of the Senses: The Bourgeois Experience, Victoria to Freud*. Oxford, New York, and Toronto: Oxford University Press, 1984.

Gelles, Edith. *Portia: The World of Abigail Adams*. Bloomington: Indiana University Press, 1992.

Gent, Lucy, and Llewellyn, Nigel, eds. *Renaissance Bodies: The Human Figure in English Culture c. 1540–1660*. [1990.] London: Reaktion Books, 1995.

Getty, Adele. *Goddess: Mother of Living Nature*. London: Thames and Hudson, 1990.

Gimbutas, Marija. *The Language of the Goddess*. San Francisco: Harper and Row, 1989.

Gitter, George; Lomranz, Jack; Saxe, Leonard; and Bar-Tal, Yoram. "Perceptions of Female Physique Characteristics by American and Israeli Students." *Journal of Social Psychology*, vol. 121, no. 1 (October 1983).

Greer, Germaine. *The Female Eunuch*. [1970.] New York: McGraw-Hill, 1981.

Greer, Germaine; Hastings, Susan; Medoff, Jeslyn; and Sansone, Melinda, eds. *Kissing the Rod: An Anthology of Seventeenth-Century Women's Verse*. New York: Farrar Straus Giroux, 1988.

Griffin, Susan. *Pornography and Silence: Culture's Revenge Against Nature*. New York: Harper and Row, 1981.

Gros, Dominique. *Le Sein Dévoilé*. Paris: Stock/Laurence Pernoud, 1987.

Gutwirth, Madelyn. *The Twilight of the Goddesses: Women and Representation in the French Revolutionary Era*. New Brunswick, N.J.: Rutgers University Press, 1992.

Hahn, R. C., and Petitti, D. B. "Minnesota Multiphasic Personality Inventory–Rated Depression and the Incidence of Breast Cancer." *Cancer*, vol. 61 (1988).

Hall, James. *Dictionary of Subjects and Symbols in Art*. [1974.] London: J. Murray, 1979.

Hall, Nor. *The Moon and the Virgin: Reflections on the Archetypal Feminine*. New York: Harper & Row, 1980.

Hammond, Paul. *French Undressing: Naughty Postcards from 1900 to 1920*. [1976.] London: Bloomsbury Books, 1988.

Hawthorne, Rosemary. *Bras: A Private View*. London: Souvenir Press, 1992.

Heister, Lorenz. *A General System of Surgery*. Trans. from the Latin. London: Printed for W. Innys, 1748. Vol. II.

Hellerstein, E.; Hume, L.; Offen, K.; Freedman, E.; Gelpi, B.; and Yalom, M., eds. *Victorian Women: A Documentary Account of Women's Lives in Nineteenth-Century England, France, and the United States*. Stanford, Calif.: Stanford University Press, 1981.

Helvétius. "Lettre de Monsieur Helvétius D.E.M. à Monsieur Régis, sur la Nature et la Guérison du Cancer," appended to *Traité des pertes de sang*. Paris: L. d'Houry, 1697.

Herbert, Zbigniew. *Still Life with a Bridle: Essays and Apocryphas*. John and Bogdana Carpenter, trans. Hopewell, N.J.: Ecco Press, 1991.

Herrera, Hayden. *Frida Kahlo: The Paintings*. New York: HarperCollins, 1991.

Hestrin, Ruth. " 'Astarte' figurines," in *Highlights of Archeology*. Jerusalem: Israel Museum, 1984.

Hewitt, Virginia. *Beauty and the Banknote: Images of Women on Paper Money*. London: British Museum Press, 1994.

Hibbert, Christopher. *The Virgin Queen: Elizabeth I, Genius of the Golden Age*. Reading, Mass.; Menlo Park, Calif.; and New York: Addison-Wesley, 1991.

Hirschfeld, Dr. Magnus. *Sittengeschichte des Weltkrieges.* Leipzig and Vienna: Verlag für Sexualwissenschaft Schneider, 1930. 2 vols.

Hoffert, Sylvia D. *Private Matters: American Attitudes Toward Childbearing and Infant Nurture in the Urban North, 1800–60.* Urbana and Chicago: University of Illinois Press, 1989.

Hollander, Anne. *Seeing Through Clothes.* New York: Viking Press, 1978.

———. *Sex and Suits: The Evolution of Modern Dress.* New York: Alfred A. Knopf, 1994.

Holmes, Urban T. *Medieval Man: His Understanding of Himself, His Society, and the World.* Chapel Hill: North Carolina Studies in the Romance Languages and Literatures, 1980.

Houdoy, J. *La Beauté des Femmes dans la Littérature et dans l'Art du XIIe au XVIe Siècles.* Paris: A. Aubry; A. Détaille, 1876.

Huizinga, Johan. *Dutch Civilisation in the Seventeenth Century and Other Essays.* New York: Frederick Ungar, 1968.

———. *The Waning of the Middle Ages.* Garden City, N.Y.: Doubleday Anchor, 1954.

Hunt, Lynn, ed. *Eroticism and the Body Politic.* Baltimore and London: Johns Hopkins University Press, 1991.

Isakower, O. "A Contribution to the Patho-Psychology of Phenomena Associated with Falling Asleep." *International Journal of Psychoanalysis,* vol. 19 (1938).

Jacobi, Lora, and Cash, Thomas. "In Pursuit of the Perfect Appearance: Discrepancies Among Self-Ideal Percepts of Multiple Physical Attributes." *Journal of Applied Social Psychology,* vol. 24, no. 5 (March 1994).

Jacobus, Mary. "Incorruptible Milk: Breast-Feeding and the French Revolution." *Rebel Daughters.* Sara E. Melzer and Leslie W. Rabine, eds. New York: Oxford University Press, 1992.

Jaggar, Alison, and Bordo, Susan, eds. *Gender/Body/Knowledge: Feminist Reconstructions of Being and Knowing.* New Brunswick and London: Rutgers University Press, 1989.

Jelliffe, Derrick B. and Jelliffe, E. F. Patrice. *Human Milk in the Modern World.* Oxford, New York, and Toronto: Oxford University Press, 1978.

Johns, Catherine. *Sex or Symbol? Erotic Images of Greece and Rome.* London: British Museum Press, 1982.

Johnson, Buffie. *Lady of the Beasts: Ancient Images of the Goddess and Her Sacred Animals.* San Francisco: Harper and Row, 1988.

Jubb, Michael. *Cocoa and Corsets.* London: Her Majesty's Stationery Office, 1984.

Juliana. *A Book of Showings to the Anchoress Julian of Norwich.* Pt. two. Edmund Colledge and James Walsh, eds. Toronto: Pontifical Institute of Mediaeval Studies, 1978.

Jung, Carl. *Aspects of the Masculine.* Princeton: Princeton University Press, 1989.

Junker, Almut, and Stille, Eva. *Geschichte des Unterwäsche 1700–1960.* Frankfurt am Main: Historisches Museums Frankfurt, 1988.

Kaufmann, Jean-Claude. *Corps de Femmes, Regards d'Hommes: Sociologie des Seins Nus.* Paris: Nathan, 1995.

Keller, Catherine. "The Breast, the Apocalypse, and the Colonial Journey," *Journal of Feminist Studies in Religion*, vol. 10, no. 1 (1994).

Kellogg, J. H., M.D. *The Influence of Dress in Producing the Physical Decadence of American Women.* Battle Creek, Mich.: Michigan State Medical Society, 1891.

Kennedy, Duncan. *Sexy Dressing.* Cambridge, Mass.: Harvard University Press, 1993.

Kermode, Jenny, and Walker, Garthine, eds. *Women, Crime, and the Courts in Early Modern England.* London: UCL Press, 1994.

Keuls, Eva C. *The Reign of the Phallus: Sexual Politics in Ancient Athens.* Berkeley: University of California Press, 1985.

Kidwell, Claudia Brush, and Steele, Valerie. *Men and Women: Dressing the Part.* Washington, D.C.: Smithsonian Institution Press, 1989.

King, Margaret L. *Women of the Renaissance.* Chicago and London: University of Chicago Press, 1991.

Klein, Melanie, et al., eds. *Developments in Psychoanalysis.* London: Karnac Books, 1989.

Kleinman, Ruth. *Anne of Austria, Queen of France.* Columbus: Ohio State University Press, 1985.

Knibiehler, Yvonne, and Fouquet, Catherine. *La Femme et les Médecins: Analyse Historique.* Paris: Hachette, 1983.

———. *L'Histoire des Mères.* Paris: Montalba, 1980.

König, René. *À la Mode: The Social Psychology of Fashion.* F. Bradley, trans. New York: Seabury Press, 1973.

Krauss, Rosalind. *Cindy Sherman, 1979–1993.* New York: Rizzoli, 1993.

Kritzman, Lawrence D. *The Rhetoric of Sexuality and the Literature of the French Renaissance.* Cambridge, New York, Port Chester, Melbourne, and Sydney: Cambridge University Press, 1991.

Kunzle, David. *Fashion and Fetishism: A Social History of the Corset, Tight-Lacing and Other Forms of Body-Sculpture in the West.* Totowa, N.J.: Rowman and Littlefield, 1982.

Kushner, Rose. *Breast Cancer: A Personal History and an Investigative Report.* New York and London: Harcourt Brace Jovanovich, 1975.

Labé, Louise. *Oeuvres Complètes.* Enzo Giudici, ed. Geneva: Droz, 1981.

Lacroix, Paul. *Les Secrets de Beauté de Diane de Poitiers.* Paris: Adolphe Delahays, 1838.

Laîné, Pascal, and Quignard, Pascal. *Blasons Anatomiques du Corps Féminin.* Paris: Gallimard, 1982.

Lajer-Burcharth, Ewa. "La Rhétorique du Corps Féminin sous le Directoire." *Les Femmes et la Révolution Française.* Marie-France Brive, ed. Toulouse: Presses Universitaires du Mirail, 1990. Vol. 2.

Laqueur, Thomas. *Making Sex: Body and Gender from the Greeks to Freud.* Cambridge, Mass., and London: Harvard University Press, 1990.

La Tour-Landry, The Book of the Knight. Trans. from the original French into English in the Reign of Henry VI. Ed. Thomas Wright. London: Early English Text Society, 1868.

Lawner, Lynne. *Lives of the Courtesans.* New York: Rizzoli, 1986.

Lefkowitz, Mary R. *Women in Greek Myth*. London: Duckworth, 1986.

Levy, Mervyn. *The Moons of Paradise*. New York: Citadel Press, 1965.

Lifshitz, Leatrice, ed. *Her Soul Beneath the Bone: Women's Poetry on Breast Cancer*. Urbana and Chicago: University of Illinois Press, 1988.

Lindemann, Mary. "Love for Hire: The Regulation of the Wet-Nursing Business in Eighteenth-Century Hamburg," *Journal of Family History*, Winter 1981.

Lipton, Eunice. *Alias Olympia: A Woman's Search for Manet's Notorious Model & Her Own Desire*. New York: Charles Scribner's Sons, 1992.

Lorde, Audre. *The Cancer Journals*. Argyle, N.Y.: Spinsters, Ink, 1980.

Loux, Françoise. *Le Corps dans la Société Traditionnelle*. Paris: Berger-Levrault, 1979.

Love, Susan, with Lindsey, Karen. *Dr. Susan Love's Breast Book*. Reading, Mass.; Menlo Park, Calif.; and New York: Addison Wesley, 1995 (2nd ed.).

Lucie-Smith, Edward. *Sexuality in Western Art*. [1972.] London: Thames and Hudson, 1991.

Lyons, Albert S., and Petrucelli, R. Joseph. *Medicine: An Illustrated History*. New York: Harry N. Abrams, 1978.

Macdonald, Sharon; Holden, Pat; and Ardener, Shirley. *Images of Women in Peace & War: Cross-Cultural & Historical Perspectives*. Houndmills, Basingstoke, Hampshire, and London: Macmillan Education, 1987.

Macfarlane, Alan. *Marriage and Love in England: Modes of Reproduction, 1300–1840*. Oxford: Basil Blackwell, 1986.

Maher, Vanessa, ed. *The Anthropology of Breast-Feeding: Natural Law or Social Construct*. Oxford and Providence, R.I.: Berg, 1992.

Manchester, William. *A World Lit Only by Fire*. Boston, Toronto, and London: Little, Brown, 1992.

Marnhac, Anne de. *Femmes au Bain: Les Métamorphoses de la Beauté*. Paris: Berger-Levrault, 1986.

Marshall, Rosalind K. *Virgins and Viragos: A History of Women in Scotland from 1080–1980*. Chicago: Academy Chicago, 1983.

Mazza, Samuele. *Brahaus*. Joe Clinton, trans. San Francisco: Chronicle Books, 1994.

McLaren, Dorothy. "Marital Fertility and Lactation, 1570–1720." *Women in English Society, 1500–1800*. Mary Prior, ed. London and New York: Methuen, 1985.

McMillen, Sally G. *Motherhood in the Old South: Pregnancy, Childbirth, and Infant Rearing*. Baton Rouge and London: Louisiana State University Press, 1990.

Medieval Woman's Guide to Health: The First English Gynecological Handbook. Beryl Rowland, trans. Kent, Ohio: Kent State University Press, 1981.

Mellaart, James. *Çatal Hüyük*. New York: McGraw-Hill, 1967.

Meyer-Thoss, Christiane. *Louise Bourgeois*. Zurich: Ammann Verlag, 1992.

Michael, Robert, et al. *Sex in America*. Boston, New York, Toronto, and London: Little, Brown, 1994.

Michie, Helena. *The Flesh Made Word: Female Figures and Women's Bodies*. New York and Oxford: Oxford University Press, 1987.

Miller, A. B., and Bulbrook, R. D. "UICC Multidisciplinary Project on Breast Cancer: The Epidemiology, Aetiology and Prevention of Breast Cancer." *International Journal of Cancer*, vol. 37 (1986).

Morrison, Denton E., and Holden, Carlin Paige. "The Burning Bra: The American Breast Fetish and Women's Liberation." *Deviance and Change*. Peter K. Manning, ed. Englewood Cliffs, N.J.: Prentice-Hall, 1971.

Moser, Charles; Lees, Joann; and Christensen, Poul. "Nipple Piercing: An Exploratory-Descriptive Study." *Journal of Psychology & Human Sexuality*, vol. 6, no. 2 (1993).

Moulin, Daniel de. *A Short History of Breast Cancer*. Boston, the Hague, Dordrecht, and Lancaster: Martinus Nijhoff Publishers, 1983.

Murat, Inès. *Gabrielle d'Estrées*. Paris: Fayard, 1987.

Napheys, Geo. H., A.M., M.D. *The Physical Life of Woman: Advice to the Maiden, Wife, and Mother*. [1869.] Toronto: Rose Publishing Co., 1880 (3rd Canadian ed.).

Nelson, Sarah. "Diversity of the Upper Paleolithic 'Venus' Figurines and Archeological Mythology." *Gender in Cross-Cultural Perspective*. Caroline Brettell and Carolyn Sargent, eds. Englewood Cliffs, N.J.: Prentice Hall, 1993.

Neumann, Erich. *The Great Mother: An Analysis of the Archetype*. Ralph Mannheim, trans. Princeton: Princeton University Press, Bollingen Series, Vol. 47., 1964.

Nochlin, Linda. *Women, Art, and Power and Other Essays*. New York: Harper and Row, 1988.

Ostriker, Alicia. *The Crack in Everything*. Pittsburgh: University of Pittsburgh Press, 1996.

———. *The Mother/Child Papers*. Boston: Beacon Press, 1986.

Painter, Nell. *Sojourner Truth: A Life, A Symbol*. New York: W. W. Norton, 1996.

Palmer, Gabrielle. *The Politics of Breastfeeding*. London: Pandora Books, 1988.

Paré, Ambroise. *Oeuvres Complètes*. J.-F. Malgaigne, ed. Paris: Chez J. B. Baillière, 1840–41. Vol. 2.

Paret, Peter; Lewis, Beth Irwin; and Paret, Paul. *Persuasive Images*. Princeton: Princeton University Press, 1992.

Pastan, Linda. *A Fraction of Darkness*. New York: W. W. Norton, 1985.

Paster, Gail. *The Body Embarrassed*. Ithaca, N.Y.: Cornell University Press, 1990.

Peradotto, John, and Sullivan, J. P., eds. *Women in the Ancient World: The Arethusa Papers*. Albany: State University of New York Press, 1984.

Pernoud, Régine. *La Femme au Temps des Cathédrales*. Paris: Stock, 1980.

Perrot, Philippe. *Le Travail des Apparences, ou les Transformations du Corps Féminin XVIIIe–XIXe Siècle*. Paris: Éditions du Seuil, 1984.

Perry, Ruth. *The Celebrated Mary Astell*. Chicago and London: University of Chicago Press, 1986.

———. "Colonizing the Breast: Sexuality and Maternity in Eighteenth-Century England." *Journal of the History of Sexuality*, vol. 5, no. 2 (October 1991), special issue, pt. I.

Pluchinotta, Alfonso. *Storia Illustrata della Senologia: Tra Scienza e Mito*. Saranno: Cita-Geigy, 1989.

Pointon, Marcia. *Naked Authority: The Body in Western Painting, 1830–1908*. Cambridge: Cambridge University Press, 1991.

Polishuk, Sandy. "Breasts." *Bridges*, vol. 2, no. 2 (Fall 1991).

Pollock, Linda. *Forgotten Children: Parent-Child Relations from 1500 to 1900*. Cambridge: Cambridge University Press, 1983.

Pomeroy, Sarah B., ed. *Women's History and Ancient History*. Chapel Hill and London: University of North Carolina Press, 1991.

Price, Theodora Hadzisteliou. *Kourotrophos: Cults and Representations of the Greek Nursing Deities*. Leiden: E. J. Brill, 1978.

Prior, Mary, ed. *Women in English Society, 1500–1800*. London and New York: Methuen.

Rawls, Walton. *Wake Up, America! World War I and the American Poster*. New York: Abbeville Press, 1988.

Read, Dr. Cathy. *Preventing Breast Cancer: The Politics of an Epidemic*. London: Pandora/HarperCollins, 1995.

Rendle-Short, Morwenna and John. *The Father of Child Care: Life of William Cadogan (1711–1797)*. Bristol: John Wright & Sons, 1966.

Renfrew, Colin. *The Cycladic Spirit: Masterpieces from the Nicholas P. Goulandris Collection*. New York: Harry N. Abrams, 1991.

Rhode, Deborah L. "Media Images, Feminist Issues." *Signs: Journal of Women in Culture and Society*, vol. 10, no. 3 (Spring 1995).

Ricci, James V. *The Genealogy of Gynaecology*. Philadelphia: The Blakiston, 1943.

Rich, Adrienne. *The Fact of a Doorframe: Poems Selected and New, 1950–1984*. New York: W. W. Norton, 1984.

Robins, Gay. *Women in Ancient Egypt*. London: British Museum Press, 1993.

Robinson, Julian. *The Fine Art of Fashion*. New York and London: Bartley and Jensen, 1989.

Romi. *La Mythologie du Sein*. Paris: Pauvert, 1965.

Ronsard, Pierre de. *Les Amours*. Henri et Catherine Weber, eds. Paris: Garnier Frères, 1963.

Rosenthal, Margaret R. *The Honest Courtesan: Veronica Franco, Citizen and Writer in Sixteenth-Century Venice*. Chicago and London: University of Chicago Press, 1992.

Roth, Philip. *The Breast*. New York: Vintage Books, 1972.

Rouse, E. Clive. *Medieval Wall Paintings*. Buckinghamshire: Shire Publications, 1991.

Rousseau, Jean-Jacques. *The Confessions*. J. M. Cohen, trans. Harmondsworth, Middlesex: Penguin Books, 1953.

———. *Emile: or On Education*. Alan Bloom, trans. New York: Basic Books, 1979.

Ruggiero, Guido. *Binding Passions: Tales of Magic, Marriage, and Power at the End of the Renaissance*. New York and Oxford: Oxford University Press, 1993.

———. *The Boundaries of Eros: Sex Crime and Sexuality in Renaissance Venice*. New York and Oxford: Oxford University Press, 1985.

Russell, Diana. *Against Pornography: The Evidence of Harm.* Berkeley, Calif.: Russell Publications, 1993.

Rycroft, Charles. *A Critical Dictionary of Psychoanalysis.* London: Penguin, 1972 (1995).

Saint-Laurent, Cécile. *Histoire Imprévue des Dessous Féminins.* Paris: Éditions Herscher, 1986.

Sale, Kirkpatrick. *The Conquest of Paradise: Christopher Columbus and the Columbian Legacy.* New York: Plume/Penguin, 1991.

Salicet. *Chirurgie de Guillaume de Salicet.* Paul Pifteau, ed. Toulouse: Imprimerie Saint-Cyprien, 1898.

Saunders, Alison. *The Sixteenth-Century Blason Poétique.* Bern, Frankfurt am Main, and Las Vegas: Peter Lang, 1981.

Schama, Simon. *The Embarrassment of Riches: An Interpretation of Dutch Culture in the Golden Age.* Berkeley and Los Angeles: University of California Press, 1988.

Schiebinger, Londa. *Nature's Body: Gender in the Making of Modern Science.* Boston: Beacon Press, 1993.

Schmidt-Linsenhoff, Viktoria, ed. *Sklavin oder Bürgerin? Französische Revolution und Neue Weiblichkeit 1760–1830.* Frankfurt: Jonas Verlag, Historisches Museum Frankfurt, 1989.

Scholten, Catherine M. *Childbearing in American Society, 1650–1850.* New York and London: New York University Press, 1985.

Schwichtenberg, Cathy, ed. *The Madonna Connection: Representational Politics, Subcultural Identities, and Cultural Theory.* Boulder, San Francisco, and Oxford: Westview Press, 1993.

Serna, Ramón Gómez de la. *Seins.* Benito Pelegrin, trans. Marseilles: André Dimanche Éditeur, 1992.

Shorter, Edward. *The Making of the Modern Family.* New York: Basic Books, 1975.

Sichtermann, Barbara. *Femininity: The Politics of the Personal.* John Whitlam, trans. Cambridge and Oxford: Polity Press, 1986.

Soranus. *Gynecology.* Owsei Temkin, trans. Baltimore: Johns Hopkins Press, 1956.

Spence, Jo. *Putting Myself in the Picture: A Political, Personal and Photographic Autobiography.* London: Camden Press, 1986.

Spiegel, David. *Living Beyond Limits: New Hope and Help for Facing Threatening Illness.* New York: Times Books, 1993.

Sprinkle, Annie, with Gates, Katharine. *Annie Sprinkle's Post-Modern Pin-Ups Booklet.* Richmond, Va.: Gates of Heck, 1995.

Starobinski, Jean. *Largesse.* Paris: Réunion des Musées Nationaux, 1994.

Stein, Ralph. *The Pin Up from 1852 to Now.* Secaucus, N.J.: Ridge Press/Chartwell Books, 1974.

Stone, Lawrence. *The Family, Sex, and Marriage in England, 1500–1800.* London: Weidenfeld and Nicolson, 1977.

Strossen, Nadine. *Free Speech, Sex, and the Fight for Women's Rights.* New York: Charles Scribner's Sons, 1995.

Suleiman, Susan Rubin, ed. *The Female Body in Western Culture*. Cambridge, Mass.: Harvard University Press, 1986.

Sussman, George D. *Selling Mothers' Milk: The Wet-Nursing Business in France, 1715–1914*. Urbana: University of Illinois Press, 1982.

Thames, Susan, and Gazzaniga, Marin, eds. *The Breast: An Anthology*. New York: Global City, 1995.

Thébaud, Françoise, ed. *A History of Women: Toward a Cultural Identity in the Twentieth Century*. vol. V, *A History of Women in the West*. Georges Duby and Michelle Perrot, eds. Cambridge, Mass.: Harvard University Press, 1994.

———. *Quand Nos Grand-Mères Donnaient la Vie: La Maternité en France dans l'Entre-Deux-Guerres*. Lyon: Presses Universitaires de Lyon, 1986.

Thomas, Keith. *Religion and the Decline of Magic*. New York: Charles Scribner's Sons, 1971.

Thorton, Louise; Sturtevant, Jan; and Sumrall, Amber, eds. *Touching Fire: Erotic Writings by Women*. New York: Carroll & Graf Publishers, 1989.

Thurer, Shari L. *The Myths of Motherhood: How Culture Reinvents the Good Mother*. Boston: Houghton Mifflin, 1994.

Trouillas, Paul. *Le Complexe de Marianne*. Paris: Seuil, 1988.

Tubiana, Maurice, Dr. *La Lumière dans l'Ombre: Le Cancer Hier et Demain*. Paris: Éditions Odile Jacob, 1991.

Turner, James Grantham, ed. *Sexuality and Gender in Early Modern Europe: Institutions, Texts, Images*. Cambridge: Cambridge University Press, 1993.

Tyrrell, Wm. Blake. *Amazons: A Study in Athenian Mythmaking*. Baltimore and London: Johns Hopkins University Press, 1984.

Vasey, Frank B., M.D., and Feldstein, Josh. *The Silicone Breast Implant Controversy*. Freedom, Calif.: Crossing Press, 1993.

Veblen, Thorstein. *The Theory of the Leisure Class*. [1899.] New York: Random House, Modern Library, 1931.

Vesalius, Andreas. *The Epitome of Andreas Vesalius*. L. R. Lind, trans. New York: Macmillan Company/Yale Medical Library, no. 21, 1969.

Vickers, Nancy. " 'The blazon of sweet beauty's best': Shakespeare's *Lucrece*." *Shakespeare and the Question of Theory*. Patricia Parker and Geoffrey Hartman, eds. New York and London: Methuen, 1985.

Vigarello, Georges. *Le Propre et le Sale: L'Hygiène du Corps Depuis le Moyen Âge*. Paris: Éditions du Seuil, 1985.

Virgoe, Roger, ed. *Private Life in the Fifteenth Century*. New York: Weidenfeld and Nicolson, 1989.

Walker, Barbara G. *The Woman's Dictionary of Symbols and Sacred Objects*. San Francisco: HarperCollins, 1988.

Walker, Robert, ed. *Varga: The Esquire Years, A Catalogue Raisonné*. New York: Alfred Van Der Marck Editions, 1987.

Wangensteen, Owen H., and Wangensteen, Sarah D. *The Rise of Surgery*. Folkestone, Kent: Wm Dawson and Sons, 1978.

Warner, Marina. *Alone of All Her Sex: The Myth and the Cult of the Virgin Mary.* New York: Alfred A. Knopf, 1976.

———. *Monuments and Maidens.* London: Weidenfeld and Nicolson, 1985.

Waugh, Norah. *Corsets and Crinolines.* [1954.] New York: Routledge/Theatre Arts Books, 1995.

Weindling, Paul. *Health, Race and German Politics Between National Unification and Nazism, 1870–1945.* Cambridge: Cambridge University Press, 1989.

Weinstein, Donald, and Bell, Rudolf M. *Saints and Society.* Chicago: University of Chicago Press, 1982.

Werne, Joellen, ed. *Treating Eating Disorders.* San Francisco: Jossey-Bass Publishers, 1995.

Winkler, John J. *The Constraints of Desire: The Anthropology of Sex and Gender in Ancient Greece.* New York and London: Routledge, 1990.

Witkowski, Gustave Joseph. *Anecdotes Historiques et Religieuses sur les Seins et l'Allaitement Comprenant l'Histoire du Décolletage et du Corset.* Paris: A. Maloine, 1898.

Wolf, Naomi. *The Beauty Myth: How Images of Beauty Are Used Against Women.* New York: William Morrow, 1991.

Woodbridge, Linda. *Women and the English Renaissance: Literature and the Nature of Womankind, 1540–1620.* Urbana and Chicago: University of Illinois Press, 1984.

Woolson, Abba Goold. *Women in America from Colonial Times to the 20th Century.* [1874.] New York: Arno Press, 1974.

Wright, Louis B. *Middle-Class Culture in Elizabethan England.* [1935.] Ithaca, N.Y.: Cornell University Press, 1958.

Yalom, Irvin D., M.D., and Greaves, Carlos, M.D. "Group Therapy with the Terminally Ill." *American Journal of Psychiatry,* vol. 134, no. 4 (April 1977).

Yalom, Marilyn. *Blood Sisters: The French Revolution in Women's Memory.* New York: Basic Books, 1993.

———. *Le Temps des Orages: Aristocrates, Bourgeoises, et Paysannes Racontent.* Paris: Maren Sell, 1989.

Zimmerman, Leo M., and Veith, Ilza. *Great Ideas in the History of Surgery.* Baltimore: Williams and Wilkins, 1961.

Zonderman, A. B., Costa, P. T., and McCrae, R. R. "Depression as a Risk for Cancer Morbidity and Mortality in a Nationally Representative Sample." *Journal of the American Medical Association,* vol. 262 (1989).

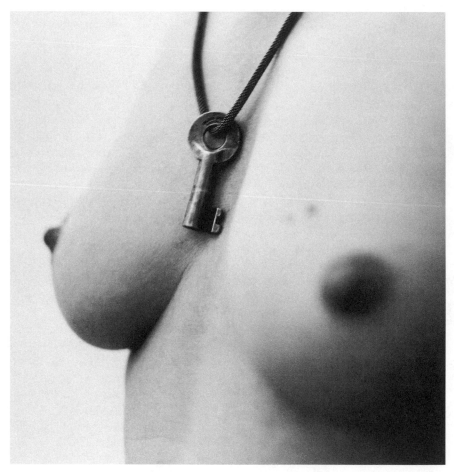

99. Reid S. Yalom. Key to the Breast. 1996.

Index

Illustration Credits

Frontispiece/title page. Painting: Attributed to Raphael. *La Fornarina*. Galleria Nazionale d'Arte Antica, Rome, Italy. Courtesy of Art Resource, New York. Illustration: Detail from *Le Petit Courrier des Dames*, 1837.

Fig. 1. Musée des Antiquités Nationales, Saint Germain. Photo R.M.N.

Fig. 2. Copyright British Museum, London.

Fig. 3. Gift of Mrs. Horace L. Mayer. Courtesy of the Museum of Fine Arts, Boston.

Fig. 4. Gift of Edward W. Forbes. Courtesy of the Museum of Fine Arts, Boston.

Fig. 5. Copyright British Museum, London.

Fig. 6. Gift of Mrs. W. Scott Fitz. Courtesy of the Museum of Fine Arts, Boston.

Fig. 7. Photo Jean Mazenod. *L'Art grec*, Éditions Citadelles & Mazenod, Paris.

Fig. 8. Museum of Ephesus (Selçuk), Turkey. Photo Erich Lessing/Art Resource.

Fig. 9. Louvre, Paris. Photo R.M.N.

Fig. 10. The National Gallery, London.

Fig. 11. Louvre, Paris. Photo Marilyn Yalom.

Fig. 12. Louvre, Paris. Photo R.M.N.

Fig. 13. Photo Michel Magat.

Fig. 14. Église St. Léonard, Léau. Photo Bulloz.

Fig. 15. Montpellier. Photo Bulloz.

Fig. 16. Musée Condée, Chantilly. Photo Giraudon.

Fig. 17. Church of S. Francesco, Siena. Photo Alinari/Art Resource.

Fig. 18. Liège. Photo Bulloz.

Fig. 19. Photo Bulloz.

Fig. 20. Anvers. Photo Bulloz.

Fig. 21. Wellcome Institute Library, London.

Fig. 22. Bibliothèque Nationale, Paris. Photo Roger Viollet.

Fig. 23. Beinecke Rare Book and Manuscript Library, Yale University.

Figs. 24 and 25. By courtesy of the Board of Trustees of the Victoria and Albert Museum, London.

Fig. 26. Beinecke Rare Book and Manuscript Library, Yale University.

Fig. 27. Louvre, Paris. Photo Bulloz.

Fig. 28. Bibliothèque Nationale, Paris. Photo Bulloz.

Fig. 29. Senlis. Photo Bulloz.

Fig. 30. Musée Condée, Chantilly. Photo Giraudon.

Fig. 31. Louvre, Paris. Photo Bulloz.

Fig. 32. National Portrait Gallery, London.

Fig. 33. Albertina, Vienna.

Fig. 34. M. H. de Young Memorial Museum, San Francisco.

Fig. 35. Louvre, Paris. Photo Bulloz.

Fig. 36. Paleis Het Loo, National Museum, Apeldoorn, The Netherlands. Photo A. A. Meine Jansen.

Fig. 37. Amsterdam. Photo Bulloz.

Fig. 38. Staatliche Gemäldegalerie, Dresden.

Fig. 39. Samuel H. Kress Collection, 1961.60; Allentown Art Museum, Allentown Pennsylvania.

Fig. 40. Copyright The Cleveland Museum of Art, 1996, John L. Severance Fund, 66. 239.

Fig. 41. Copyright Bibliothèque Nationale, Paris.

Fig. 42. Private Collection.

Fig. 43. Photo R.M.N.

Fig. 44. Wellcome Institute Library, London.

Fig. 45. Musée Carnavalet, Paris. Photo Bulloz.

Fig. 46. Musée Carnavalet, Paris.

Fig. 47. Photo Bulloz.

Fig. 48. Musée Fragonard, Grasse. Photo Bulloz.

Fig. 49. Louvre, Paris. Photo Bulloz.

Fig. 50. Peabody Museum, Harvard University.

Fig. 51. Bibliothèque de Documentation Internationale Contemporaine, Nanterre.

Fig. 52. From a 1917 issue of *La Vie Parisienne*.

Fig. 53. GE264, Poster Collection, Hoover Institution Archives.

Fig. 54. US2003A, Poster Collection, Hoover Institution Archives.

Fig. 55. US1021, Poster Collection, Hoover Institution Archives.

Fig. 56. US5718, Poster Collection, Hoover Institution Archives.

Fig. 57. US1237, Poster Collection, Hoover Institution Archives.

Fig. 58. Archivio Storico Ricordi, Milan.

Fig. 59. Reproduced in Hirschfeld, *Sittengeschichte des Welteskrieges* (Leipzig and Vienna, 1930).

Fig. 60. GE982, Poster Collection, Hoover Institution Archives.

Fig. 61. National Air and Space Museum, Washington, D.C.

Fig. 62. Portuguese colonial banknote.

Fig. 63. Penguin paperback, 1972 [1968, 1995].

Figs. 64 and 65. Wellcome Institute Library, London.

Figs. 66, 67, and 68. Sears, Roebuck & Co. Catalogue, 1897.

Fig. 69. Bibliothèque des Arts Décoratifs, Paris.

Fig. 70. Photo Jean-Loup Charmet.

Fig. 71. Private Collection.

Fig. 72. Courtesy of the Maidenform Museum, New York City.

Fig. 73. Archivio Storico Ricordi, Milan.

Fig. 74. S. Barita Co., Tucson, Arizona, and Fresno, California.

Fig. 75. Out of the West Publishing, Sacramento, California.

Fig. 76. Photography: Theda and Emerson Hall.

Fig. 77. Courtesy of the artist.

Fig. 78. Courtesy of The Kobal Collection.

Fig. 79. Snap A Shot, Inc., New York City.

Fig. 80. By permission of *Der Spiegel*.

Fig. 81. Courtesy of the artist.

Fig. 82. Versailles. Photo R.M.N.

Fig. 83. National Gallery, Prague. Photo Giraudon.

Fig. 84. Wellcome Institute Library, London.

Fig. 85. Courtesy of the University of Pennsylvania School of Medicine.

Fig. 86. Musée de l'Assistance Publique–Hôpitaux de Paris.

Fig. 87. Photo Shmuel Thaler.

Fig. 88. Photo *Le Matin*, May 29, 1987.

Fig. 89. Courtesy of the artist.

Fig 90. Courtesy of the artist.

Fig. 91. Museo Dolores Olmedo Patiño, Mexico City.

Fig. 92. Private Collection. Photo Peter Bellamy.

Figs. 93 and 94. The Jo Spence Archive, London.

Fig. 95. Courtesy of the artist and Metro Pictures, New York.

Fig. 96. Copyright L. Barany & A. Sprinkle, 1991. Photos by Leslie Barany.

Fig. 97. Courtesy of TREE, P.O. Box 186, Topanga, California 90290.

Fig. 98. Courtesy of the artist.

Fig. 99. Courtesy of the artist.

A NOTE ON THE TYPE

The text of this book was set in Electra, a typeface
designed by W. A. Dwiggins (1880–1956). This face
cannot be classified as either modern or old style. It
is not based on any historical model, nor does it
echo any particular period or style. It avoids the
extreme contrasts between thick and thin elements
that mark most modern faces, and it attempts to give
a feeling of fluidity, power, and speed.

Composed by North Market Street Graphics,
Lancaster, Pennsylvania

Printed and bound by Quebecor Printing,
Martinsburg, West Virginia

Designed by Iris Weinstein